HUMAN GEOGRAPHY

HUMAN GEOGRAPHY

T.N. Sachdeva

SUMIT ENTERPRISES
New Delhi-110 002 (India)

First Published 2011

ISBN 978-81-8420-277-9

Published by:

SUMIT ENTERPRISES
4649B/21, Ansari Road, Darya Ganj
New Delhi-110 002
Phone: 011-23279353, 9810217567
E-mail: sumit_enterprises2007@yahoo.co.in

PRINTED IN INDIA

Published by Sri Lokesh Kumar for Sumit Enterprises, New Delhi-110002, Typeset by Abhijeet Typesetters, Printed at Nev Prabhat Printing Press, Tronicacity (UP)

Contents

Preface

In primitive time population was limited and needs were limited, so resources were not so developed. But with development of time a number of changes has come in our civilization. It is called, 'necessity is the mother of invention'. It is a human nature who wants to spend more happy life and for the fulfilment of desires he projects his energy to do something. A number of raw materials are available in nature but it is human efforts who make it useful. As man development his skills, different types of mechanical devices were developed and today has touched the climax.

Human geography is one of the two major subfields of geography. Human geography is the study of human use and understanding of the Earth and the process which have affected this. It is linked to both social science and the humanities. Human geography broadly differs from physical geography in that it has a greater focus on studying intangible or abstract patterns surrounding human activity and is more receptive to qualitative research methodologies. It encompasses human, political, cultural, social and economic aspects of the social sciences. While the major focus of human geography is not the physical landscape of the Earth, it is not possible to discuss human geography without going into the physical landscape with which human activities are being played out and environmental geography which is an important link between the two. Human geography is both methodologically and theoretically diverse, including feminist, marxist, post-structural approaches, among others, and using both qualitative methods and quantitative methods.

Human geography (sometimes called Cultural geography) considers all human aspects (immigration, demographics, culture, farming, health, industry, etc). In other words, human geography focuses on how we make places, how we organise space and society, how we interact with each other in places and across space, and how we make sense of others and ourselves in our locality, region, and world. Physical geography considers natural phenomena (distribution of water, natural resources, soil properties, biodiversity, etc.)

Historical migration of human populations begins with the movement of *Homo erectus* out of Africa across Eurasia about a million years ago. *Homo sapiens* appear to have occupied all of Africa about 150,000 years ago, moved out of Africa 70,000 years ago, and had spread across Australia, Asia and Europe by 40,000 years BCE. Migration to the Americas took place 20,000 to 15,000 years ago, and by 2,000 years ago, most of the Pacific Islands were colonized. Later population movements notably include the Neolithic Revolution, Indo-European expansion, and the Early Medieval Great Migrations including Turkic expansion. Early humans migrated due to many factors such as changing climate and landscape and inadequate food supply. The evidence indicates that the ancestors of the Austronesian peoples spread from the South Chinese mainland to Taiwan at some time around 8,000 years ago. Evidence from historical linguistics suggests that it is from this island that seafaring peoples migrated, perhaps in distinct waves separated by millennia, to the entire region encompassed by the Austronesian languages. It is believed that this migration began around 6,000 years ago. Indo-Aryan migration to and within Northern India is presumed to have taken place in the Middle to Late Bronze Age, contemporary to the Late Harappan phase in India (ca. 1700 to 1300 BC). From 180 BC, a series of invasions from Central Asia followed, including those led by the Indo-Greeks, Indo-Scythians, Indo-Parthians and Kushans in the north-western Indian subcontinent.

The book simplifies the essential ingredients of an explicitly scientific human geography to the point at which they can be readily understood by the beginning student.

—*Editor*

1

Introduction

Human geography is one of the two major subfields of geography. Human geography is the study of human use and understanding of the Earth and the process which have affected this. It is linked to both social science and the humanities. Human geography broadly differs from physical geography in that it has a greater focus on studying intangible or abstract patterns surrounding human activity and is more receptive to qualitative research methodologies. It encompasses human, political, cultural, social and economic aspects of the social sciences. While the major focus of human geography is not the physical landscape of the Earth, it is not possible to discuss human geography without going into the physical landscape with which human activities are being played out and environmental geography which is an important link between the two. Human geography is both methodologically and theoretically diverse, including feminist, marxist, post-structural approaches, among others, and using both qualitative methods (such as ethnographies and interviews) and quantitative methods (such as survey research, statistical analysis and model building).

FIELDS OF HUMAN GEOGRAPHY

The main fields of study in human geography focus around the core fields of:

Culture: Cultural geography is the study of cultural products and norms and their variation across and relations to spaces and places. It focuses on describing and analysing the ways language, religion, economy, government, and other cultural phenomena vary or remain constant from one place to another and on explaining how humans function spatially.

Development: Development Geography is the study of the Earth's geography with reference to the Standard of living and the Quality of life of its human inhabitants, study of the location, distribution and spatial organization of economic activities across the Earth. The subject matter investigated is strongly influenced by the researcher's methodological approach.

Economic: Economic geography examines relationships between human economic systems, states, and other actors, and the biophysical environment.

Health: Health geography is the application of geographical information, perspectives, and methods to the study of health, disease, and health care.

Historical: Historical Geography is the study of the human, physical, fictional, theoretical, and "real" geographies of the past. Historical geography studies a wide variety of issues and topics. A common theme is the study of the geographies of the past and how a place or region changes through time. Many historical geographers study geographical patterns through time, including how people have interacted with their environment, and created the cultural landscape.

Political: Political geography is concerned with the study of both the spatially uneven outcomes of political processes and the ways in which political processes are themselves affected by spatial structures.

Population: Population geography is the study of the ways in which spatial variations in the distribution, composition, migration, and growth of populations are related to the nature of places.

Tourism: Tourism geography is the study of travel and tourism as an industry, as a human activity, and especially as a place-based experience.

Urban: Urban geography is the study of urban areas with specific regards to spatial and relational aspects and theories. That is the study of areas which have a high concentration of buildings and infrastructure. These are areas where the majority of economic activities are in the secondary sector and tertiary sectors. They probably have a high population density.

HUMAN MIGRATION

Human migration is physical movement by humans from one area to another, sometimes over long distances or in large groups. The movement of populations in modern times has continued under the form of both voluntary migration within one's region, country, or beyond, and involuntary migration (which includes the slave trade, Human traffic in human beings and ethnic cleansing).

People who migrate are called migrants or more specifically, emigrants, immigrants, or settlers, depending on historical setting, circumstances and perspective. The pressures of human migrations, whether as outright conquest or by slow cultural infiltration and resettlement, have affected the grand epochs in history and in land (for example, the Decline of the Roman Empire); under the form of colonization, migration has transformed the world (such as the prehistoric and historic settlements of Australia and the Americas).

Population genetics studied in traditionally settled modern populations have opened a window into the historical patterns of migrations, a technique pioneered by Luigi Luca Cavalli-Sforza.

Forced migration has been a means of social control under authoritarian regimes yet free initiative migration is a powerful factor in social adjustment and the growth of urban populations. In December 2003, The Global Commission on International Migration (GCIM) was launched with the support of Secretary-General of the United Nations Kofi Annan and several countries, with an independent 19-member Commission, a threefold mandate and a finite life span ending December 2005. Its report, based on regional consultation meetings with stakeholders and scientific reports from leading international migration experts, was published and presented to Kofi Annan on 5 October 2005.

Different types of migration include:

- Seasonal human migration mainly related to agriculture
- Rural to Urban, more common in developing countries as industrialization takes effect (urbanization)

- Urban to Rural, more common in developed countries due to a higher cost of urban living (suburbanization)
- International migration.

Pre-modern Migrations

Historical migration of human populations begins with the movement of *Homo erectus* out of Africa across Eurasia about a million years ago. *Homo sapiens* appear to have occupied all of Africa about 150,000 years ago, moved out of Africa 70,000 years ago, and had spread across Australia, Asia and Europe by 40,000 years BCE. Migration to the Americas took place 20,000 to 15,000 years ago, and by 2,000 years ago, most of the Pacific Islands were colonized. Later population movements notably include the Neolithic Revolution, Indo-European expansion, and the Early Medieval Great Migrations including Turkic expansion. Early humans migrated due to many factors such as changing climate and landscape and inadequate food supply. The evidence indicates that the ancestors of the Austronesian peoples spread from the South Chinese mainland to Taiwan at some time around 8,000 years ago. Evidence from historical linguistics suggests that it is from this island that seafaring peoples migrated, perhaps in distinct waves separated by millennia, to the entire region encompassed by the Austronesian languages. It is believed that this migration began around 6,000 years ago. Indo-Aryan migration to and within Northern India is presumed to have taken place in the Middle to Late Bronze Age, contemporary to the Late Harappan phase in India (ca. 1700 to 1300 BC). From 180 BC, a series of invasions from Central Asia followed, including those led by the Indo-Greeks, Indo-Scythians, Indo-Parthians and Kushans in the north-western Indian subcontinent.

From about 750 BC, the Greeks began 250 years of expansion, settling colonies in all directions. In Europe two waves of migrations dominate demographic distributions, that of the Celtic people, and the later Migration Period from the east. Other examples are small movements like ancient Scots moving from Hibernia to Caledonia and Magyars into Pannonia (modern-day Hungary). Turkic peoples spread across most of Central Asia into Europe and the Middle East between the 6th and 11th centuries. Recent research suggests that Madagascar was uninhabited until Austronesian seafarers from Indonesia arrived during the 5th and 6th centuries AD. Subsequent migrations from both the Pacific and Africa further consolidated this original mixture, and Malagasy people emerged.

Before the expansion of the Bantu languages and their speakers, the southern half of Africa is believed to have been populated by Pygmies and Khoisan speaking people, today occupying the arid regions around the Kalahari Desert and the forest of Central Africa. By about 1000 AD Bantu migration had reached modern day Zimbabwe and South Africa. The Banu Hilal and Banu Maqil were a collection of Arab Bedouin tribes from the Arabian Peninsula who migrated westwards via Egypt between the 11th and 13th centuries.

Their migration strongly contributed to the arabization and islamization of the western Maghreb, which was until then dominated by Berber tribes. Ostsiedlung was the medieval eastward migration and settlement of Germans. The 13th century was the time of the great Mongol and Turkic migrations across Eurasia.

Between the 11th and 18th centuries, the Vietnamese expanded southward in a process known as nam tien (southward expansion). Manchuria was separated from China proper by the Inner Willow Palisade, which restricted the movement of the Han Chinese into Manchuria during the Qing Dynasty, as the area was off-limits to the Han until the Qing started colonizing the area with them later on in the dynasty's rule.

The Age of Exploration and European Colonialism led to an accelerated pace of migration since Early Modern times. In the 16th century perhaps 240,000 Europeans entered American ports. In the 19th century over 50 million people left Europe for the Americas. The local populations or tribes, such as the Aboriginal people in Canada, Brazil, Argentina, Australia, Japan and the United States, were usually far overwhelmed numerically by the settlers. More recent examples are the movement of ethnic Chinese into Tibet and Xinjiang, ethnic Javanese into Western New Guinea and Kalimantan, Brazilians into Amazonia, Israelis into the West Bank and Gaza, ethnic Arabs into Iraqi Kurdistan, and ethnic Russians into Siberia and Central Asia.

MODERN MIGRATIONS

While the pace of migration had accelerated since the 18th century already (including the involuntary slave trade), it would increase further in the 19th century. Manning distinguishes three major types of migration: labour migration, refugee migrations, and urbanization. Millions of agricultural workers left the countryside and moved to the cities causing unprecedented levels of urbanization. This phenomenon began in Britain in the late 18th century and spread around the world and continues to this day in many areas. Industrialization encouraged migration wherever it appeared. The increasingly global economy globalized the labour market. The Atlantic slave trade diminished sharply after 1820, which gave rise to self-bound contract labour migration from Europe and Asia to plantations. Overpopulation, open agricultural frontiers, and rising industrial centres attracted voluntary migrants. Moreover, migration was significantly made easier by improved transportation techniques.

Transnational labour migration reached a peak of three million migrants per year in the early twentieth century. Italy, Norway, Ireland and the Quongdong region of China were regions with especially high emigration rates during these years. These large migration flows influenced the process of nation state formation in many ways. Immigration restrictions have been developed, as well as diaspora cultures and myths that reflect the importance of migration to the foundation of certain nations, like the American melting pot. The transnational labour migration fell to a lower level from 1930s to the 1960s and then rebounded. The United States experienced considerable internal migration related to industrialization, including its African American population. From 1910–1970, approximately 7 million African Americans migrated from the rural Southern United States, where blacks faced both poor economic opportunities and considerable political and social prejudice, to the industrial cities of the Northeast, Midwest and West where relatively well paid jobs were available. This phenomenon came to be known in the United States as its own Great Migration. With the demise of legalized segregation in the 1960s and greatly improved economic opportunities in the South in the subsequent decades, millions of blacks have returned to the South from other parts of the country since 1980 in what has been called the New Great Migration.

The twentieth century experienced also an increase in migratory flows caused by war and politics. Muslims moved from the Balkan to Turkey, while Christians moved the other way, during the collapse of the Ottoman Empire. 400,000 Jews moved to Palestine in the early twentieth century. The Russian Civil War caused some 3 million Russians, Poles and Germans to migrate out of the Soviet Union. World War II and decolonization also caused migrations.

World War II

The Jewish communities across Europe, the Mediterranean and the Middle East were formed from voluntary and involuntary migrants. After the Holocaust (1938 to 1945), there was increased migration to the British Mandate of Palestine, which became the modern state of Israel as a result of the United Nations Partition Plan for Palestine. Provisions of the Potsdam Agreement from 1945 signed by victorious Western Allies and the Soviet Union led to one of the largest European migrations, and the largest in the 20th century. It involved the migration and resettlement of close to or over 20 million people.

The largest affected group were 16.5 million Germans expelled from Eastern Europe westwards. The second largest group were Poles, millions of whom were expelled westwards from eastern Kresy region and resettled in the so-called Recovered Territories. Hundreds of thousands of Poles, Ukrainians (Operation Vistula), Lithuanians, Latvians, Estonians and some Belarusians, were expelled eastwards from Europe to the Soviet Union. Finally, many of the several hundred thousand Jews remaining in Eastern Europe after the Holocaust migrated outside Europe to Israel and the United States.

India

In 1947, upon the Partition of India, large populations moved from India to Pakistan and vice versa, depending on their religious beliefs. The partition was promulgated in the Indian Independence Act 1947 as a result of the dissolution of the British Indian Empire. The partition displaced up to 12.5 million people in the former British Indian Empire, with estimates of loss of life varying from several hundred thousand to a million. Muslim residents of the former British India migrated to Pakistan (including East Pakistan which is now Bangladesh), whilst Hindu and Sikh residents of Pakistan and Hindu residents of East Pakistan (now Bangladesh) moved in the opposite direction. In modern India, estimates based on industry sectors mainly employing migrants suggest that there are around 100 million circular migrants in India. Caste, social networks and historical precedents play a powerful role in shaping patterns of migration. Migration for the poor is mainly circular, as despite moving temporarily to urban areas, they lack the social security which might keep them there more permanently. They are also keen to maintain a foothold in home areas during the agricultural season. Research by the Overseas Development Institute identifies a rapid movement of labour from slower to faster growing parts of the economy. Migrants can often find themselves excluded by urban housing policies and migrant support initiatives are needed to give workers improved access to market information, certification of identity, housing and education.

THEORIES OF RAVENSTEIN

Certain laws of social science have been proposed to describe human migration. The following was a standard list after Ravenstein's proposals during the time frame of 1834 to 1913. The laws are as follows:

1. every migration flow generates a return or countermigration.
2. the majority of migrants move a short distance.
3. migrants who move longer distances tend to choose big-city destinations
4. urban residents are often less migratory than inhabitants of rural areas.
5. families are less likely to make international moves than young adults;
    - Migration stage by stage
    - Urban Rural difference
    - Migration and Technology
    - Economic condition.

Lee

Lee's Push-pull theory divides factors causing migrations into two groups of factors: Push and pull factors. Push factors are things that are bad about the country that one lives in and pull factors are things that attract one to another area.

Push Factors:

- Not enough jobs
- Few opportunities
- Primitive conditions
- Desertification
- Famine or drought
- Political fear or persecution
- Poor medical care
- Loss of wealth
- Natural disasters
- Death threats
- Lack of political or religious freedom
- Pollution
- Poor housing
- Landlord/tenant issues
- Bullying
- Discrimination
- Poor chances of marrying.

Pull Factors:

- Job opportunities
- Better living conditions
- Political and/or religious freedom
- Enjoyment
- Education
- Better medical care
- Attractive climates
- Security
- Family links
- Industry
- Better chances of marrying.

Climate Cycles

The modern field of climate history suggests that the successive waves of Eurasian nomadic movement throughout history have had their origins in climatic cycles, which have expanded or contracted pastureland in Central Asia, especially Mongolia and the Altai. People were displaced from their home ground by other tribes trying to find land that could be grazed by essential flocks, each group pushing the next further to the south and west, into the highlands of Anatolia, the plains of Hungary, into Mesopotamia or southwards, into the rich pastures of China.

Other Models

Migration occurs because individuals search for food, sex and security outside their usual habitation. (Idyorough, 2008) Idyorough is of the view that towns and cities are a creation of the human struggle to obtain food, sex and security. Migration occurs because individuals search for food, sex and security outside their usual habitation. To produce food, security and human reproduction of its species, human beings must, out of necessity, move out of their usual habitation and enter into indispensable social relationships that are cooperative or antagonistic.

Human beings also develop tools/equipment to enable them interact with nature to produce the desired food and security. The improved relationship (cooperative relationships) among human beings and improved technology further conditioned by the push and pull factors all interact together to cause or bring about migration and higher concentration of individuals into towns and cities. The higher the technology of production of food and security and the higher the cooperative relationship among human beings in the production of food and security and in the reproduction of the human species the higher would be the push and pull factors in the migration and concentration of human beings in towns and cities.

Countryside, towns and cities do not just exist but they do so to meet the human basic needs of food, security and the reproduction of the human species. Therefore, migration occurs because individuals search for food, sex and security outside their usual habitation. Social services in the towns and cities are provided to meet these basic needs for human survival and pleasure.

NATURE

Nature, in the broadest sense, is equivalent to the natural world, physical world, or material world. "Nature" refers to the phenomena of the physical world, and also to life in general. It ranges in scale from the subatomic to the cosmic.

The word *nature* is derived from the Latin word *natura*, or "essential qualities, innate disposition", and in ancient times, literally meant "birth". *Natura* was a Latin translation of the Greek word *physis*, which originally related to the intrinsic characteristics that plants, animals, and other features of the world develop of their own accord. The concept of nature as a whole, the physical universe, is one of several expansions of the original notion; it began with certain core applications of the word by pre-Socratic philosophers, and has steadily gained currency ever since. This usage was confirmed during the advent of modern scientific method in the last several centuries.

Within the various uses of the word today, "nature" may refer to the general realm of various types of living plants and animals, and in some cases to the processes associated with inanimate objects–the way that particular types of things exist and change of their own accord, such as the weather and geology of the Earth, and the matter and energy of which all these things are composed. It is often taken to mean the "natural environment" or wilderness–wild animals, rocks, forest, beaches, and in general those things that have not been substantially altered by human intervention, or which persist despite human intervention. For, example, manufactured objects and human interaction generally are not considered part of nature, unless qualified as, for example, "human nature" or "the whole of nature". This more traditional concept of natural things which can still be found today implies a distinction between the natural and the artificial, with the artificial being understood as that which has been brought into being by a human consciousness or a human mind. Depending on the particular context, the term "natural" might also be distinguished from the unnatural, the supernatural, and the artifactual.

Earth

Earth (or, "the earth") is the only planet presently known to support life, and its natural features are the subject of many fields of scientific research. Within the solar system, it is third nearest to the sun; it is the largest terrestrial planet and the fifth largest overall. Its most prominent climatic features are its two large polar regions, two relatively narrow temperate zones, and a wide equatorial tropical to subtropical region. Precipitation varies widely with location, from several metres of water per year to less than a millimetre. 71 percent of the Earth's surface is covered by salt-water oceans. The remainder consists of continents and islands, with most of the inhabited land in the Northern Hemisphere.

Earth has evolved through geological and biological processes that have left traces of the original conditions. The outer surface is divided into several gradually migrating tectonic plates, which have changed relatively quickly several times. The interior remains active, with a thick layer of molten mantle and an iron-filled core that generates a magnetic field.

The atmospheric conditions have been significantly altered from the original conditions by the presence of life-forms, which create an ecological balance that stabilizes the surface conditions. Despite the wide regional variations in climate by latitude and other geographic factors, the long-term average global climate is quite stable during interglacial periods, and variations of a degree or two of average global temperature have historically had major effects on the ecological balance, and on the actual geography of the Earth.

Geology

Geology is the science and study of the solid and liquid matter that constitutes the Earth. The field of geology encompasses the study of the composition, structure, physical properties, dynamics, and history of Earth materials, and the processes by which they are formed, moved, and changed. The field is a major academic discipline, and is also important for mineral and hydrocarbon extraction, knowledge about and mitigation of natural hazards, some engineering fields, and understanding past climates and environments.

GEOLOGICAL EVOLUTION

The geology of an area evolves through time as rock units are deposited and inserted and deformational processes change their shapes and locations. Rock units are first emplaced either by deposition onto the surface or intrude into the overlying rock. Deposition can occur when sediments settle onto the surface of the Earth and later lithify into sedimentary rock, or when as volcanic material such as volcanic ash or lava flows, blanket the surface. Igneous intrusions such as batholiths, laccoliths, dikes, and sills, push upwards into the overlying rock, and crystallize as they intrude.

After the initial sequence of rocks has been deposited, the rock units can be deformed and/or metamorphosed. Deformation typically occurs as a result of horizontal shortening, horizontal extension, or side-to-side (strike-slip) motion. These structural regimes broadly relate to convergent boundaries, divergent boundaries, and transform boundaries, respectively, between tectonic plates.

Historical Perspective

Earth is estimated to have formed 4.54 billion years ago from the solar nebula, along with the Sun and other planets. The moon formed roughly 20 million years later. Initially molten, the outer layer of the planet cooled, resulting in the solid crust. Outgassing and volcanic activity produced the primordial atmosphere. Condensing water vapour, most or all of which came from ice delivered by comets, produced the oceans and other water sources. The highly energetic chemistry is believed to have produced a self-replicating molecule around 4 billion years ago. Continents formed, then broke up and reformed as the surface of Earth reshaped over hundreds of millions of years, occasionally combining to make a supercontinent. Roughly 750 million years ago, the earliest known supercontinent Rodinia, began to break apart. The continents later recombined to form Pannotia which broke apart about 540 million years ago, then finally Pangaea, which broke apart about 180 million years ago.

There is significant evidence that a severe glacial action during the Neoproterozoic era covered much of the planet in a sheet of ice. This hypothesis has been termed the "Snowball

Earth", and it is of particular interest as it precedes the Cambrian explosion in which multicellular life forms began to proliferate about 530–540 million years ago.

Since the Cambrian explosion there have been five distinctly identifiable mass extinctions. The last mass extinction occurred some 65 million years ago, when a meteorite collision probably triggered the extinction of the non-avian dinosaurs and other large reptiles, but spared small animals such as mammals, which then resembled shrews. Over the past 65 million years, mammalian life diversified. Several million years ago, a species of small African ape gained the ability to stand upright. The subsequent advent of human life, and the development of agriculture and further civilization allowed humans to affect the Earth more rapidly than any previous life form, affecting both the nature and quantity of other organisms as well as global climate. By comparison, the oxygen catastrophe, produced by the proliferation of algae during the Siderian period, required about 300 million years to culminate.

The present era is classified as part of a mass extinction event, the Holocene extinction event, the fastest ever to have occurred. Some, such as E. O. Wilson of Harvard University, predict that human destruction of the biosphere could cause the extinction of one-half of all species in the next 100 years. The extent of the current extinction event is still being researched, debated and calculated by biologists.

ATMOSPHERE, CLIMATE, AND WEATHER

The atmosphere of the Earth serves as a key factor in sustaining the planetary ecosystem. The thin layer of gases that envelops the Earth is held in place by the planet's gravity. Dry air consists of 78% nitrogen, 21% oxygen, 1% argon and other inert gases, carbon dioxide, etc.; but air also contains a variable amount of water vapour. The atmospheric pressure declines steadily with altitude, and has a scale height of about 8 kilometres at the Earth's surface: the height at which the atmospheric pressure has declined by a factor of *e* (a mathematical constant equal to 2.71...). The ozone layer of the Earth's atmosphere plays an important role in depleting the amount of ultraviolet (UV) radiation that reaches the surface. As DNA is readily damaged by UV light, this serves to protect life at the surface. The atmosphere also retains heat during the night, thereby reducing the daily temperature extremes. Terrestrial weather occurs almost exclusively in the lower part of the atmosphere, and serves as a convective system for redistributing heat. Ocean currents are another important factor in determining climate, particularly the major underwater thermohaline circulation which distributes heat energy from the equatorial oceans to the polar regions. These currents help to moderate the differences in temperature between winter and summer in the temperate zones. Also, without the redistributions of heat energy by the ocean currents and atmosphere, the tropics would be much hotter, and the polar regions much colder.

Weather can have both beneficial and harmful effects. Extremes in weather, such as tornadoes or hurricanes and cyclones, can expend large amounts of energy along their paths, and produce devastation. Surface vegetation has evolved a dependence on the seasonal variation of the weather, and sudden changes lasting only a few years can have a dramatic effect, both on the vegetation and on the animals which depend on its growth for their food. The planetary climate is a measure of the long-term trends in the weather. Various factors are known to influence the climate, including ocean currents, surface albedo, greenhouse gases, variations in the solar luminosity, and changes to the planet's orbit. Based on historical records, the Earth is known to have undergone drastic climate changes in the past, including ice ages.

The climate of a region depends on a number of factors, especially latitude. A latitudinal band of the surface with similar climatic attributes forms a climate region. There are a number of such regions, ranging from the tropical climate at the equator to the polar climate in the northern and southern extremes. Weather is also influenced by the seasons, which result from the Earth's axis being tilted relative to its orbital plane. Thus, at any given time during the summer or winter, one part of the planet is more directly exposed to the rays of the sun. This exposure alternates as the Earth revolves in its orbit. At any given time, regardless of season, the northern and southern hemispheres experience opposite seasons. Weather is a chaotic system that is readily modified by small changes to the environment, so accurate weather forecasting is currently limited to only a few days. Overall, two things are currently happening worldwide: (1) temperature is increasing on the average; and (2) regional climates have been undergoing noticeable changes.

WATER ON EARTH

Water is a chemical substance that is composed of hydrogen and oxygen and is vital for all known forms of life. In typical usage, *water* refers only to its liquid form or state, but the substance also has a solid state, ice, and a gaseous state, water vapour or steam. Water covers 71% of the Earth's surface. On Earth, it is found mostly in oceans and other large water bodies, with 1.6% of water below ground in aquifers and 0.001% in the air as vapour, clouds (formed of solid and liquid water particles suspended in air), and precipitation. Oceans hold 97% of surface water, glaciers and polar ice caps 2.4%, and other land surface water such as rivers, lakes and ponds 0.6%. Additionally, a minute amount of the Earth's water is contained within biological bodies and manufactured products.

Oceans

An ocean is a major body of saline water, and a principal component of the hydrosphere. Approximately 71% of the Earth's surface (an area of some 361 million square kilometres) is covered by ocean, a continuous body of water that is customarily divided into several principal oceans and smaller seas. More than half of this area is over 3,000 meters (9,800 ft) deep. Average oceanic salinity is around 35 parts per thousand (ppt) (3.5%), and nearly all seawater has a salinity in the range of 30 to 38 ppt. Though generally recognized as several 'separate' oceans, these waters comprise one global, interconnected body of salt water often referred to as the World Ocean or global ocean. This concept of a global ocean as a continuous body of water with relatively free interchange among its parts is of fundamental importance to oceanography. The major oceanic divisions are defined in part by the continents, various archipelagos, and other criteria: these divisions are (in descending order of size) the Pacific Ocean, the Atlantic Ocean, the Indian Ocean, the Southern Ocean and the Arctic Ocean. Smaller regions of the oceans are called seas, gulfs, bays and other names. There are also salt lakes, which are smaller bodies of landlocked saltwater that are not interconnected with the World Ocean. Two notable examples of salt lakes are the Aral Sea and the Great Salt Lake.

Lakes

A lake (from Latin *lacus*) is a terrain feature (or physical feature), a body of liquid on the surface of a world that is localized to the bottom of basin (another type of landform or terrain feature; that is, it is not global) and moves slowly if it moves at all. On Earth, a body of water is considered a lake when it is inland, not part of the ocean, is larger and deeper than a pond, and is fed by a river. The only world other than Earth known to harbour lakes is Titan, Saturn's largest moon, which has lakes of ethane, most likely mixed with methane. It is not known if Titan's lakes are fed by rivers, though Titan's surface is carved by numerous river beds. Natural lakes on Earth are generally found in mountainous areas, rift zones, and areas with ongoing or recent glaciation. Other lakes are found in endorheic basins or along the courses of mature rivers. In some parts of the world, there are many lakes because of chaotic drainage patterns left over from the last Ice Age. All lakes are temporary over geologic time scales, as they will slowly fill in with sediments or spill out of the basin containing them.

Ponds

A pond is a body of standing water, either natural or man-made, that is usually smaller than a lake. A wide variety of man-made bodies of water are classified as ponds, including water gardens designed for aesthetic ornamentation, fish ponds designed for commercial fish breeding, and solar ponds designed to store thermal energy. Ponds and lakes are distinguished from streams via current speed. While currents in streams are easily observed, ponds and lakes possess thermally driven microcurrents and moderate wind driven currents. These features distinguish a pond from many other aquatic terrain features, such as stream pools and tide pools.

Rivers

A river is a natural watercourse, usually freshwater, flowing toward an ocean, a lake, a sea or another river. In a few cases, a river simply flows into the ground or dries up completely before reaching another body of water. Small rivers may also be called by several other names, including stream, creek, brook, rivulet, and rill; there is no general rule that defines what can be called a river. Many names for small rivers are specific to geographic location; one example is *Burn* in Scotland and North-east England. Sometimes a river is said to be larger than a creek, but this is not always the case, due to vagueness in the language. A river is part of the hydrological cycle. Water within a river is generally collected from precipitation through surface runoff, groundwater recharge, springs, and the release of stored water in natural ice and snowpacks (i.e., from glaciers).

Streams

A stream is a flowing body of water with a current, confined within a bed and stream banks. In the United States a stream is classified as a watercourse less than 60 feet (18 metres) wide. Streams are important as conduits in the water cycle, instruments in groundwater recharge, and they serve as corridors for fish and wildlife migration. The biological habitat in the immediate vicinity of a stream is called a riparian zone. Given the status of the ongoing Holocene extinction, streams play an important corridor role in connecting fragmented habitats and thus in conserving biodiversity. The study of streams and waterways in general is known as *surface hydrology* and is a core element of environmental geography.

Ecosystems

Ecosystems are composed of a variety of abiotic and biotic components that function in an interrelated way. The structure and composition is determined by various environmental factors that are interrelated. Variations of these factors will initiate dynamic modifications to the ecosystem. Some of the more important components are: soil, atmosphere, radiation from the sun, water, and living organisms. Central to the ecosystem concept is the idea that living organisms interact with every other element in their local environment. Eugene Odum, a founder of ecology, stated: "Any unit that includes all of the organisms (i.e.: the "community") in a given area interacting with the physical environment so that a flow of energy leads to clearly defined trophic structure, biotic diversity, and material cycles (i.e.: exchange of materials between living and nonliving parts) within the system is an ecosystem." Within the ecosystem, species are connected and dependent upon one another in the food chain, and exchange energy and matter between themselves as well as with their environment. The human ecosystem concept is grounded in the deconstruction of the human/nature dichotomy and the premise that all species are ecologically integrated with each other, as well as with the abiotic constituents of their biotope.

A smaller unit of size is called a microecosystem. For example, a microsystem can be a stone and all the life under it. A *macroecosystem* might involve a whole ecoregion, with its drainage basin.

Wilderness

Wilderness is generally defined as areas that have not been significantly modified by human activity. The WILD Foundation goes into more detail, defining wilderness as: "The most intact, undisturbed wild natural areas left on our planet-those last truly wild places that humans do not control and have not developed with roads, pipelines or other industrial infrastructure." Wilderness areas can be found in preserves, estates, farms, conservation preserves, ranches, National Forests, National Parks and even in urban areas along rivers, gulches or otherwise undeveloped areas. Wilderness areas and protected parks are considered important for the survival of certain species, ecological studies, conservation, solitude, and recreation. Some nature writers believe wilderness areas are vital for the human spirit and creativity, and some Ecologists consider wilderness areas to be an integral part of the planet's self-sustaining natural ecosystem (the biosphere). They may also preserve historic genetic traits and that they provide habitat for wild flora and fauna that may be difficult to recreate in zoos, arboretums or laboratories.

Life

Although there is no universal agreement on the definition of life, scientists generally accept that the biological manifestation of life is characterized by organization, metabolism, growth, adaptation, response to stimuli and reproduction. Life may also be said to be simply the characteristic state of organisms. Properties common to terrestrial organisms (plants, animals, fungi, protists, archaea and bacteria) are that they are cellular, carbon-and-water-based with complex organization, having a metabolism, a capacity to grow, respond to stimuli, and reproduce. An entity with these properties is generally considered life. However, not every definition of life considers all of these properties to be essential. Human-made analogs of life may also be considered to be life.

The biosphere is the part of Earth's outer shell – including land, surface rocks, water, air and the atmosphere – within which life occurs, and which biotic processes in turn alter or transform. From the broadest geophysiological point of view, the biosphere is the global ecological system integrating all living beings and their relationships, including their interaction with the elements of the lithosphere (rocks), hydrosphere (water), and atmosphere (air). Currently the entire Earth contains over 75 billion tons (150 *trillion* pounds or about 6.8 x 10 kilograms) of biomass (life), which lives within various environments within the biosphere.

Over nine-tenths of the total biomass on Earth is plant life, on which animal life depends very heavily for its existence. More than 2 million species of plant and animal life have been identified to date, and estimates of the actual number of existing species range from several million to well over 50 million. The number of individual species of life is constantly in some degree of flux, with new species appearing and others ceasing to exist on a continual basis. The total number of species is presently in rapid decline.

Evolution

Life is only known to exist on the planet Earth. The origin of life is still a poorly understood process, but it is thought to have occurred about 3.9 to 3.5 billion years ago during the hadean or archean eons on a primordial earth that had a substantially different environment than is found at present. These life forms possessed the basic traits of self-replication and inheritable traits. Once life had appeared, the process of evolution by natural selection resulted in the development of ever-more diverse life forms. Species that were unable to adapt to the changing environment and competition from other life forms became extinct. However, the fossil record retains evidence of many of these older species. Current fossil and DNA evidence shows that all existing species can trace a continual ancestry back to the first primitive life forms.

The advent of photosynthesis in very basic forms of plant life worldwide allowed the sun's energy to be harvested to create conditions allowing for more complex life. The resultant oxygen accumulated in the atmosphere and gave rise to the ozone layer. The incorporation of smaller cells within larger ones resulted in the development of yet more complex cells called eukaryotes. Cells within colonies became increasingly specialized, resulting in true multicellular organisms. With the ozone layer absorbing harmful ultraviolet radiation, life colonized the surface of Earth.

Microbes

The first form of life to develop on the Earth were microbes, and they remained the only form of life on the planet until about a billion years ago when multi-cellular organisms began to appear. Microorganisms are single-called organisms that are generally microscopic, and smaller than the human eye can see. They include Bacteria, Fungi, Archaea and Protista. These life forms are found in almost every location on the Earth where there is liquid water, including the interior of rocks within the planet. Their reproduction is both rapid and profuse. The combination of a high mutation rate and a horizontal gene transfer ability makes them highly adaptable, and able to survive in new environments, including outer space. They form an essential part of the planetary ecosystem. However some microorganisms are pathogenic and can post health risk to other organisms.

Plants and Animals

Originally Aristotle divided all living things between plants, which generally do not move, and animals. In Linnaeus' system, these became the kingdoms Vegetabilia (later Plantae) and Animalia. Since then, it has become clear that the Plantae as originally defined included several unrelated groups, and the fungi and several groups of algae were removed to new kingdoms. However, these are still often considered plants in many contexts. Bacterial life is sometimes included in flora, and some classifications use the term *bacterial flora* separately from *plant flora*. Among the many ways of classifying plants are by regional floras, which, depending on the purpose of study, can also include *fossil flora*, remnants of plant life from a previous era. People in many regions and countries take great pride in their individual arrays of characteristic flora, which can vary widely across the globe due to differences in climate and terrain.

Regional floras commonly are divided into categories such as *native flora* and *agricultural and garden flora*, the lastly mentioned of which are intentionally grown and cultivated. Some types of "native flora" actually have been introduced centuries ago by people migrating from one region or continent to another, and become an integral part of the native, or natural flora of the place to which they were introduced. This is an example of how human interaction with nature can blur the boundary of what is considered nature. Another category of plant has historically been carved out for *weeds*. Though the term has fallen into disfavour among botanists as a formal way to categorize "useless" plants, the informal use of the word "weeds" to describe those plants that are deemed worthy of elimination is illustrative of the general tendency of people and societies to seek to alter or shape the course of nature. Similarly, animals are often categorized in ways such as *domestic*, *farm animals*, *wild animals*, *pests*, etc., according to their relationship to human life.

Animals as a category have several characteristics that generally set them apart from other living things, though not traced by scientists to having legs or wings instead of roots and leaves. Animals are eukaryotic and usually multicellular, which separates them from bacteria, archaea and most protists. They are heterotrophic, generally digesting food in an internal chamber, which separates them from plants and algae. They are also distinguished from plants, algae, and fungi by lacking cell walls. With a few exceptions, most notably the sponges (Phylum Porifera), animals have bodies differentiated into separate tissues. These include muscles, which are able to contract and control locomotion, and a nervous system, which sends and processes signals. There is also typically an internal digestive chamber. The eukaryotic cells possessed by all animals are surrounded by a characteristic extracellular matrix composed of collagen and elastic glycoproteins. This may be calcified to form structures like shells, bones, and spicules, a framework upon which cells can move about and be reorganized during development and maturation, and which supports the complex anatomy required for mobility.

HUMAN INTERRELATIONSHIP

Although humans currently comprise only a minuscule proportion of the total living biomass on Earth, the human effect on nature is disproportionately large. Because of the extent of human influence, the boundaries between what humans regard as nature and "made environments" is not clear cut except at the extremes. Even at the extremes, the amount of natural environment that is free of discernible human influence is presently diminishing at an increasingly rapid pace. The development of technology by the human race has allowed the greater exploitation of natural resources and has helped to alleviate some of the risk from natural hazards. In spite of this progress, however, the fate of human civilization remains closely linked to changes in the environment. There exists a highly complex feedback loop between the use of advanced technology and changes to the environment that are only slowly becoming understood. Man-made threats to the Earth's natural environment include pollution, deforestation, and disasters such as oil spills. Humans have contributed to the extinction of many plants and animals.

Humans employ nature for both leisure and economic activities. The acquisition of natural resources for industrial use remains the primary component of the world's economic system. Some activities, such as hunting and fishing, are used for both sustenance and leisure, often by different people. Agriculture was first adopted around the 9th millennium BCE. Ranging from food production to energy, nature influences economic wealth. Although early humans gathered uncultivated plant materials for food and employed the medicinal properties of vegetation for healing, most modern human use of plants is through agriculture. The clearance of large tracts of land for crop growth has led to a significant reduction in the amount available of forestation and wetlands, resulting in the loss of habitat for many plant and animal species as well as increased erosion.

Aesthetics and Beauty

Beauty in nature has historically been a prevalent theme in art and books, filling large sections of libraries and bookstores. That nature has been depicted and celebrated by so much art, photography, poetry and other literature shows the strength with which many people associate nature and beauty. Reasons why this association exists, and what the association consists of, is studied by the branch of philosophy called aesthetics. Beyond certain basic characteristics that many philosophers agree about to explain what is seen as beautiful, the opinions are virtually endless. Nature and wildness have been important subjects in various epochs of world history. An early tradition of landscape art began in China during the Tang Dynasty (618-907). The tradition of representing nature *as it is* became one of the aims of Chinese painting and was a significant influence in Asian art. Wilderness portrayals in art became more prevalent in the 1800s, especially in the works of the Romantic movement. British artists John Constable and JMW Turner turned their attention to capturing the beauty of the natural world in their paintings. Before that, paintings had been primarily of religious scenes or of human beings. William Wordsworth's poetry described the wonder of the natural world, which had formerly been viewed as a threatening place. Increasingly the valuing of nature became an aspect of Western culture. This artistic movement also coincided with the Transcendentalist movement in the Western world. A common classical idea of beautiful art involves the word mimesis, the imitation of nature. Also in the realm of ideas about beauty in nature is that the perfect is implied through symmetry, equal division, and other perfect mathematical forms and notions.

Matter and Energy

Some fields of science see nature as matter in motion, obeying certain laws of nature which science seeks to understand. For this reason the most fundamental science is generally understood to be "physics" – the name for which is still recognizable as meaning that it is the study of nature. Matter is commonly defined as the substance of which physical objects are composed. It constitutes the observable universe. The visible components of the universe are now believed to compose only 4 percent of the total mass. The remainder is believed to consist of 23 percent cold dark matter and 73 percent dark energy. The exact nature of these components is still unknown and is currently under intensive investigation by physicists.

The behaviour of matter and energy throughout the observable universe appears to follow well-defined physical laws. These laws have been employed to produce cosmological models that successfully explain the structure and the evolution of the universe we can observe. The mathematical expressions of the laws of physics employ a set of twenty physical constants that appear to be static across the observable universe. The values of these constants have been carefully measured, but the reason for their specific values remains a mystery.

Beyond Earth

Outer space, also simply called *space*, refers to the relatively empty regions of the universe outside the atmospheres of celestial bodies. *Outer* space is used to distinguish it from airspace (and terrestrial locations). There is no discrete boundary between the Earth's atmosphere and space, as the atmosphere gradually attenuates with increasing altitude. Outer space within the solar system is called interplanetary space, which passes over into interstellar space at what is known as the heliopause. Outer space is certainly spacious, but it is far from empty. Outer space is sparsely filled with several dozen types of organic molecules discovered to date by microwave spectroscopy, blackbody radiation left over from the big bang and the origin of the universe, and cosmic rays, which include ionized atomic nuclei and various subatomic particles.

There is also some gas, plasma and dust, and small meteors. Additionally, there are signs of human life in outer space today, such as material left over from previous manned and unmanned launches which are a potential hazard to spacecraft. Some of this debris re-enters the atmosphere periodically. Although the planet Earth is currently the only known body within the solar system to support life, current evidence suggests that in the distant past the planet Mars possessed bodies of liquid water on the surface. For a brief period in Mars' history, it may have also been capable of forming life. At present though, most of the water remaining on Mars is frozen. If life exists at all on Mars, it is most likely to be located underground where liquid water can still exist.

Conditions on the other terrestrial planets, Mercury and Venus, appear to be too harsh to support life as we know it. But it has been conjectured that Europa, the fourth-largest moon of Jupiter, may possess a sub-surface ocean of liquid water and could potentially host life. Recently, the team of Stephane Udry have discovered a new planet named Gliese 581 d, which is an extrasolar planet orbiting the red dwarf star Gliese 581. Gliese 581 d appears to lie in the habitable zone of space surrounding the star, and therefore could possibly host life as we know it.

2

Indicators of Human Development

Development necessarily involves change. Over time, in the economic context, the term has evolved, and it has now come to mean much more than change on a purely material level. Traditionally, development and economic growth have been considered synonymous, indicating the capacity of a country's economy, which had remained static for some time, to generate and sustain an annual increase in its gross national product at rates of about 5 to 7 per cent or more. Alternatively, economic development has been measured in terms of the rates of growth of per capita GNP, thus taking into account the ability of a nation to increase its output at a rate faster than the growth rate of its population. The economic well-being of a population is generally measured by the levels and rates of growth of 'real' per capita GNP (i.e., monetary growth of per capita GNP adjusted for inflation). By 'economic well-being' would be meant how much the average citizen can consume and invest in terms of real goods and services.

Faster economic growth, i.e., more production of godds and services, would, it was believed, inevitably and ultimately eradicate poverty, through the 'trickle down' effect. The rapid gains in GNP would either create jobs and other economic opportunities or the necessary conditions for a wider distribution of economic and social benefits of growth. So it was more important to concentrate on the 'growth' of the economy.

Also a part of traditional thinking was the tendency to view economic development in terms of the planned alteration of the structure of production and employment so that the share of agriculture in both declines even as that of manufacturing and services sectors increases. Rapid industrialization thus became pivotal to development strategies at the coast of agricultural and rural development.

From the 1950s to the 1970s, development was seen, thus, as a purely economic phenomenon. What was actually experienced by a large number of Third World countries in 1950s and 1960s brought about a rethinking on the meaning of development? In this period it was seen that these countries achieved the growth targets set by the United Nations (UN) but there was no change in the standard of living of the masses. This could not surely signify 'development'. An increasing number of economists and policymakers started calling for the 'development of GNP' and the elevation of social indicators to measure development.

In other words, during the 1970s economic development came to be redefined in terms of reduction or elimination of poverty, inequality and unemployment within the context of a growing economy. Development should, it was felt, have the goal of redistributing the income from growth. Dudley Seers posed three of these have declined from high levels, then, beyond doubt, the country concerned had seen a period of development. If one or two or all three of these central problems have been growing worse, "it would be strange to call the result 'development' even if per capita income doubled". This assertion merely reflected the hard reality-a number of developing countries experienced high rates of growth of per capita income during the 1960s and 1970s but showed no improvement, rather an actual decline, in employment, equality and the real incomes of the bottom 40 percent of their populations. By the earlier definition of 'growth', these countries* were 'developing', but from the point of view of poverty, equality and employment, they were not.

In the 1980s GNP growth rates turned negative for many less developed countries and the governments, faced with the problem of mounting foreign debts, were forced with the problem of mounting foreign debts, were forced to cut back on their already limited social and economic programmes. Significantly enough, while during the 1980s, the World Bank championed "economic growth" as the goal of development, its World Development Report of 1991 said that improving the quality of life of the poor was the real challenge of development. And 'quality of life' for the poor countries meant much more than a higher income; it meant better education, better health and nutrition, cleaner environment, greater equality of opportunity, a richer cultural life. Thus income distribution was not enough; the goal of development was to see that all human beings were provided with the basic necessities of life as well as an opportunity for a 'rich and varied life'.

Michael Todaro thus redefines development as a multidimensional process involving the reorganization and reorientation of entire economic and social systems. In addition to improvements in incomes and output, it typically involves radical changes in institutional, social and administrative structures as well as in popular attitudes and, in many cases, even customs and beliefs. Finally, although development is usually defined in a national context, its widespread realization may necessitate fundamental changes of the international economic and social system as well.

Three Core Values of Development

According to Denis Goulet, at least three basic components or core values serve as a conceptual basis and practical guideline for understanding the 'inner' meaning of development. These core values are life sustenance, self-esteem and freedom representing common goals sought by all individuals and societies.

Life sustenance

The life-sustaining basic human needs include food shelter, health and protection. When any one of these is in critically short supply or absent, a condition of absolute 'underdevelopment' exists. Therefore, a major objective of development must be to raise people out of primary poverty and to provide basic needs simultaneously.

Self-esteem

Self-esteem is concerned with the feeling of self-respect and independence. No country can be regarded as fully developed if it is exploited by others and does not have the power and influence to conduct itself on equal terms in its relation with other countries. Developing countries seek development for self-esteem. They aid to eradicate the feeling of dominance and dependence that is associated with inferior economic status.

Freedom

Freedom refers to a fundamental sense of emancipation from alienating material conditions of life and from social servitude to nature, ignorance, other people, misery, institutions and dogmatic beliefs. W. Arthur lewis stressed the relationship between economic growth and freedom from servitude when he concluded that "the advantage of economic growth is not that wealth increases happiness, but that it increases the range of human choices". Wealth can enable people to gain greater control over nature and their physical environment (e.g., through the production of food, clothing and shelter) than they would have managed if they remained poor.

Towards a New Definition

Amartya Sen too has viewed development in terms of the expansion of 'entitlements' and 'capabilities', the former giving life sustenance and self-esteem; the latter, freedom. The focus and stress on expanding entitlements and capabilities for all people is a natural extension of the change in development, thinking away from maximization of growth towards concern with the structure of production and consumption and distribution of income. If we try to answer the question, 'development for what?', we may say that development has occurred when there has been an improvement in fulfillment of basic needs, when economic progress has contributed to a greater sense of self-esteem for the country and its inhabitants, and when material advancement has expanded people's entitlements and capabilities.

Extensively quoting Michael P. Todaro, we may say "that development is both a physical reality and a state of mind in which society has, through some combination of social, economic, and institutional processes, secured the means for obtaining a better life. Whatever the specific components of this better life, development in all societies must have at least the following three objectives: To increase the availability and widen the distribution of basic life-sustaining goods such as food, shelter, health and protection. To raise levels of living including, in addition to higher incomes, the provision of more jobs, better education and greater attention to cultural and humanistic values, all of which will serve not only to enhance material well-being but also to generate greater individual and national self-esteem. To expand the range of economic and social choices available to individuals and nations by feeling them from servitude and dependence not only in relation to other people and nation-states but also to the forces of ignorance and human misery.

We may therefore reformulate and broaden Professor Seers' questions about the meaning of development as follows: Have general levels of living within a nation risen to the point that there has been lessening of absolute poverty (i.c., deprivation of life-sustaining goods) and of inequality in income distribution, as well as improvements in the level of employment and the nature and quality of education, health and other social and cultural services? Has economic progress enhanced individual and group esteem both internally vis-à-vis one another and externally vis-à-vis other nation and regions? Finally, has economic progress expanded the range of human choice and freed people from external dependence and internal servitude to other people and institution, rather than merely substituting one from of dependence? If for a given nation the answer to each of the above three question is yes, then clearly that nation has undergone development. If the first question (which is equivalent to Seers' three questions) can be answered affirmatively but the other two remain negative, then the country may properly be designated a s" economically more developed" yet it remains underdeveloped in a more fundamental sense. In this context, it is more appropriate to refer to the rich nations of the world as economically developed and reserve judgment as to whether or not they are actually developed to more thoroughgoing social, political and cultural analysis. To paraphrase Seers, if the second and third of these central questions evoke negative responses (i.e., if people feel less self-esteem, respect, or dignity and/or if their freedom to choose has been constrained), then even if the provision of life-sustaining goods and improvements in levels of living are occurring, it would be misleading to call the result development".

MEASURES OF DEVELOPMENT

Measuring 'development' depends on what you understand by the term. If you take it in purely economic term, s as the traditional view did, and then the GNP per capita is the measure for assessing development. A major objection to its use is the failure to include non-marketed (and, therefore, nonpriced) subsistence production (for instance, wheat which farmers produce for their own consumption) and much of a housewife's world and other welfare and income distribution considerations. As a result, there have been numerous attempts to remedy these defects and to create a composite indicator of development.

Basically, indicators of development can be classified in tow groups those that measure development in terms of normal' pattern of interaction among social economic and political factors and those that measure development in terms of the 'quality of life'. In 1970, a study was conducted by the United Nations research Institute on Social Development (UNRISED). The study attempted to select the most appropriate indicators of development and conducted an analysis of the relationship between these indicators at different levels of development. The result of the study was the construction of *a* composite social development index. The new index consisted of 16 core indicators (9 social indicators and 7 economic indicators) and was found to correlate more highly with individual social and economic indicators than did per capita GNP. The rankings of some countries under the development index differed from their per capita GNP rankings. It was also found that the development index correlated more closely with per capita GNP in the case of developed countries than in the case of developing ones.

Another study was made by Adelman and Morris to seek a measure of development by analysing the pattern of interaction among social, economic and political factors. They classified 74 developing countries on the basis of 41 variables. The method of factor analysis was used to examine the interdependence between social and political variables and the level of economic development. They found numerous correlations between certain key variables and economic development.

A Major criticism of these studies was that they sought to measure development in terms of structural change in the country rather than human welfare. There is also the implicit assumption that developing countries must develop along the lines of the developed countries. Further, there is an undue emphasis on measuring inputs (such as number of doctors per 1000 population or enrolment of figures in school) rather than on outputs (such as life expectancy, literacy) which are the actual objectives of development. In response to these criticisms, further studies were conducted to develop composite indicators to measure development in terms of meeting the basic needs of the majority of the population of a country or in terms of "quality of life". This led to the development of a new index. It was in 1979 that Morris D. Morris developed a single composite index using three indicators-life expectancy at age one, infant mortality and literacy.

For each indicator, the performance of a country is rated on a scale of 1 to 100, where 1 represents the "worst" performance and 100 the "best" performance. In case of life expectancy, the upper limit of 100 was assigned to 77 years and the lower limit of 1 was assigned to 28 years. Similarly, for infant mortality, the upper limit was set at 9 per 1000 and the lower limit at 229 pr 1000. Literacy rates, measured as percentages 1 to 100, provided their own direct scale. Once a country's performance in life expectancy, infant mortality and literacy has been rated on a scale of 1 to 100, the composite index-the physical quality of life index (PQLI)-for the country is calculate by averaging the three ratings, giving equal weightage to each. A study conducted in early 1980s found that countries with low per capita GNP tended to have low PQLI s and countries with high per capita GNPs tended to have high pQLIs although the correlation between GNP and PQLI was not substantially close. There were also some countries with high per capita GNP but very low PQLIs.

On the surface, PQLI seems to be free of the basic problems associated with GNP as a measure of development. It aims at incorporating welfare considerations by measuring the ends of development in forms of quality of life. It also incorporates distributional characteristics since a country cannot achieve high national averages of life expectancy, infant mortality and literacy unless majorities of its population are receiving the benefits of progress in each of these areas. Moreover, like GNP, this simple measure can be used to make inter-country comparisons as data on these indicators is easily available.

A major criticism of the PQLI, however, is that it fails to include many other social and pshychological characteristics suggested by the term 'quality of life'-human rights, justice, and security and so on. The index has also been criticized on the grounds of lacking a rationale is giving equal weights to all the tree indicators and the possibility that measures such as life expectancy and infant mortality reflect practically the same phenomenon. To overcome the limitations of PQLI and other indicators, the Human development index (HDI) was developed. The index was pioneered by the Pakistani economist, the late Mahbub-ul-Haq, in partnership with the Indian economist. Prof. Amartya Sen, and is being annually worked out by the United Nations Development Programme (UNDP) since 1990. The UNDP has deformed human development as "a process of enlarging people's choices". This depends not only on income but also on other social indicators such as life expectancy, education, literacy and health provisions. The HDI is based on three variables:

Life Expectancy at Birth

Educational attainment measured by a combination of adult literacy (two-thirds weight) and combined primary, secondary and tertiary school enrolment ratios (one-third weight). Per capita income (ability to buy basic goods and services). The HDI, unlike other indices which measure absolute level, ranks countries in relation to each other. For example, for life expectancy the current minimum value is 37,2 years in Sierra Leone, and the maximum desirable value is 80 years in Japan (1997 figures). The index takes the progress made from the minimum towards the maximum. The distance traveled is expressed in percentage terms. A clear picture emerges of the wide disparities that exist in the levels of human development between the developing and the developed countries. The same exercise is repeated in respect of the other two components of the index. The distance traveled in each case is then used as the basis for combining the three devices, and this gives a common denominator to rank countries on a uniform

The weight assigned to income tapers off sharply beyond

the threshold income regarded as sufficient for human 'survival. In other words, as the income goes beyond the cut-off point, it becomes increasingly less important, the assumption being that the rise in income beyond a certain point is subject to diminishing returns. As a consequence, the other two indicators gain importance in determining the final index.

The human development indicators may be defined as some selected indices which throw light on inter-and intra-country variations in socio-economic and political well-being. Thus it is possible for geographers to study regional disparity with the help of these indices.

HDR 2000 the indicators used in the Human Development Report (HDR) 2000 which refer to the year, 1998, are discussed below. The recent data was obtained from the world Population Prospects (UN 1998) prepared by the United Nations Population Division or UNPD. The UNPD gets population estimates and projections on a biannual basis from population censuses. The census data is than supplemented with information from national survey data. The 1998 revision made by the UNPD has incorporated the demographic impact of deadly diseases like HIV/AIDS because of its widespread impact on the changes in the life expectancy in sub-Saharan Africa as well as other parts of the world. This has prompted the UNPD to consider migration factor in data collection. The estimates of life expectancy on the HDI published by the UNPD were derived from linear interpolation based on five-year averages.

Adult Literacy

The data presented in the HDR 2000 are fresh estimates and are derived from UNESCO's February 2000 assessment of literacy. The UNESCO estimates have incorporated the UNPD population estimates and literacy data gathered by national census agencies. Gross primary, secondary and tertary enrolment the 1998 data is derived from primary estimates from UNESCO. Gross enrolment ratios are derived from dividing the number of enrolled children in every level of schooling by the total number of children in the age group corresponding to that level. UNESCO estimates are unavailable for 13 countries listed in the main statistical tables. So estimates made by the Human Development Report Offices have been used. Gross enrolment ratios do not reveal the reality due to differences in the age range corresponding to the levels of education and differences that exist in different countries regarding the duration of schooling. There are genuine problems in relation to the use of net enrolment data (for which data exists for single years of age) because very few countries produce net enrolment data.

GDP per Capita (PPP US$)

The data used in the HDR 2000 are obtained from the World Bank and are based on the surveys conducted by the latest International Comparison Programme (ICP) covering 118 countries. The year 1996 has been taken as the base year was one by considering relative price movements over time between each country and the base country, the United States. In the case of those countries not covered by the World Bank, PPP estimates were calculated by Alan Heston and Robert Summers (1999) of the University of Pennsylvania.

Methodology and Presentation of the Human development Indicators In HDR 2000, countries have been classified in four ways, viz., in major world aggregates, by region, by human development level and by income. HDR 2000 has replaced the term "industrialized countries' by Organization for Economic Cooperation and Development (OECD). The other groups are all developing countries, Eastern Europe and the CIS. These global groups are held to be "mutually exclusive". A total of 174 countries are included in the classification of the world.

In regional classifications, developing countries are categorized into the following regions: Arab states, East Asia, Latin America and the Caribbean (Mexico included), South Asia, South East Asia and the Pacific, Southern Europe and Sub-Saharan Africa. The regional classifications are consistent with the classification done by the Regional Bureauz of UNDP. The United Nations has added one more classification, viz., least developed countries. On the basis of the levels of human developmental countries are divided into three cluster: high human development for which the HDI value is 0.800 or above, medium human development for which the HDI is 0.500 to 0.799 and low human development if the HDI is less than 0.500.

The World Bank has also classified all countries on the basis of income (valid through July 2000): high income countries having GNP per capita of $9,361 or more (in 1998), middle income if GNP per capita varies from $761 to $9,360 and low income if GNP per capita is less than $760.

Change in Indicators The indicators used in HDI in HDR 1999 were life expectancy at birth, adult literacy rate, combined first, second and third level gross enrolment ratio, real GDP per capita, life expectancy index and GDP index. HDR 2000 has made some changes in the indicators of HDI; for instance, the combined first, second and third level gross enrolment ratio ha been enlarged tocover combined primary, secondary and tgetiary groos enrolcmnt ratio, the term, real GDP per capita (PPP$), is replace by the term, GDP oer capita (PPP$).

In terms of HDI, 174 countries of the world have beeb divided into countries having high human development, medium human development and lowhuman development. According to HDR 2000, Canada occupies the first rank (HDI value 1998 is 0.935), followed by Norway (HDI value 1998 is 0.934) and the USA (DAI value 1998 is 0.929). Since 1990 the HDR has been evolving newer and better composite indices for measurement of the different facets of human development for 174 UN members-countries of the world.

The HDR has beeb using HDI since 1990. The purpose of construction of the HDI is to measure average achievement in basic human development with the help of a single composite index. The HDI is the basis of ranking 174 countries which easily signifies the position of a country in terms of human resources development. HDR 1995 introduced the gender-related development index (GDI) and the gender empowerment measure (GEM). These are compositc moasures, among which the former takco into account the same dimensions and variables a the HDI; however, the emphasis is placed on the existing inoquality between men and women. The later, i.e., GEM, shows gender inequality in economic as well as political opportunities.

The human poverty index (HPI) was introduced for the first time by HDR 1997. It measures deprivations in basic dimensions of human development. Human Development Trends 1975 to 1998 Study of the HDI from 1975 to 1998 is possible only for 101 countries because of unavailability of data.

Although almost all countries have improved in terms of providing the basic capabilities to their people between 1975 and 1998, some countries have made faster progress than others. The differences are the result of a combination of factors-both internal as well as external. Zambia of Sub-Saharan Africa is the only country in the world which has slipped from its 1975 position vis-a-vis HDI 1998 due to reduced life expectancy caused by HIV/AIDS. Similarly, six countries belonging to Sub-Saharan Africa, viz., Botswana, Burundi, Congo, the Democratic Republic of the Congo, Kenya and Zimbabwe have experienced a fall in the HDI rankings from 1985 to 1998 due to the attack of HIV/AIDS which has reduced the life expectancy of their people.

Countries like the Central African Republic, Namibia and South Africa experienced a decline in HDI rank between 1990 and 1998 due to the HIV/AIDS factor. Uganda is the only country in Africa to have improved its position after 1990. The HDI value of Uganda decline between 1985 and 1990 due to HIV/AIDS but a significant improvement was made between 1990 and 1998.

The HDI rank of six countries located in Eastern Europe and the CIS, viz., Armenia, Belarus, Lithuania, Kazakhstan, Tajikistan, Ukraine and Uzbekistan, have witnessed decline in the HDI rank between 1990 and 1998. The Phenomena is mainly due to economic stagnation/recession in these countries. The decline of Tajikistan may also be attributed to socio-political conflicts in the country.

HUMAN DEVELOPMENT INDICATORS REPORT

According to the Human Development Report (HDR) 2000, India moved up four notches from 132 ranks to 128; it had made the noteworthy transition from the low to the medium human development range in the last report itself (i.e. HDR 1999). The country's overall human development index (HDI) has been assessed at 0.563 as against a maximum possible figure of one, which means shortfall in human development of 43.7 percent. Significantly India's HDI value has gone up steadily over the years from 0.405 in 1975 to 0.431 in 1980 to

0.470 in 1985, 0.510 in 1990 and to 0.563 in 1998. This increase has been made possible by an increase in GDP per capita from $222 in 1975 to $331 in 1990, and $444 in 1998 (all inconstant 1995 purchasing power prices) as well as improvement in various other indicators. As far as the HDI rakings in the SAARC region is concerned, India is behind Sri Lanka (at 84 position) and the Maldives (89), but ahead of Bangladesh (146), Bhutan (142), Nepal (144) >and Pakistan (135). India's status as regards some of the indicators is as follow:

Life Expectancy

India's life expectancy at birth has increased from 50.3 years during 1970-75 to 62.6 years in 1995-2000.

Infant Mortality

The infant mortality rate (per 1000 live births) has come down from 130 in 1970 to 69 in 1998, accompanied by a corresponding reduction in the under-five mortality rate from 206 to 105.

Poverty

The report has rated India amongst the notable countries that have made spectacular progresses in reducing poverty levels. India has reduced poverty level from 54 percent in 1974 to 39 percent in 1994.

Literacy

India's adult literacy level in 1998 was 55.7% the figures for females and males being 43.5% and 67.1% respectively.

Health Profile

The health profile of the country is disturbing. A total 41, 00,000 people below the age of 50 are alleged to be susceptible to HIV/AIDS. In 1997, India had 275 cases of malaria per 1000 people as compared to 163 in Thailand. About 25% of the population is without access to proper healthcare.

Education

India has failed in its endeavour to provide universal primary education says the UNDP and quotes the findings of a survey that 30 percent of all children in 1992-in the 6 to 14 years age group-or about 59 million children were out of school.

The country's Constitution has failed to make mandatory primary education a right for all citizens. The report also says that resources are not a critical constraint since countries with similar constraints, such as China, have legal guarantees for his right. India's public expenditure on education is 3.2% of its GNP. This is low when compared to other Asian countries, such as Thailand which spends 4.8 percent. The country's Constitution has failed to make mandatory primary education a right for all citizens. The report also says that resources are not a critical constraint since countries with similar constraints, such as China, have legal guarantees for this right. India's public expenditure on education is 3.2% of its GNP. This is such as Thailand which spends 4.8 percent. Citing findings from a 1996 survey, the report concluded that most of the actors-parents, government, community and the media failed in their obligations leading to a collective social failure which could not just be corrected by new policies but also by local community solutions. The facilities provided by the government are dismal. Only 92 percent of the rural population had a primary school within 1 km distance. This figure tumbled drastically for middle and secondary schools as just 49 percent of rural population had access to these within 1km. the number of teachers too was woefully inadequate with 12 percent primary schools having only one teacher. The survey is critical of the media which failed to report on the neglect of basic education, as in a year the lion's share of articles expounded on foreign investment, trade and defence as compared to education.

Gender Development

India was ranked at 108 out of 143 countries on the Gender Development Index. The reservation of 33 percent seats for women in panchayats is cited as a plus point for India. As a result, more than one million women have been elected to the three-tier panchayats, indicating that women are now finding a space and voice in the hitherto male-dominated decision-making structures. Social norms and traditional attitudes, however, continue to impede their access to education. Surveys show how girls are discriminated against, and those living in rural areas and belonging to the scheduled castes and tribes are even more vulnerable.

3

Physical and Human Geography: Division or Integration

Recent discussions over the nature of geography often refer to the human/physical divide in the subject. Despite protests and pleading to the contrary, the divide is often seen as insurmountable, with some even claiming that geography has become effectively split into two specialisms (some even carry the subdivision amongst specialisms further). Massey (1999) tried to tease out the commonalities between the two parts of geography via a consideration of the role of entities. Raper and Livingstone (1995) confirm the potential for discussion, as did the ensuing printed debate. Despite these overtures across the divide, there seems to be little real movement of positions so far. This debate about the possibility of integrating physical and human geography is not a new one.

A special issue of the Transactions of the Institute of British Geographers in 1986 provided a series of short papers on different geographers' opinions on the likelihood of such common study. These concerns and hopes have also been expressed further back in the century, as in Man's Role in Changing the Face of the Earth (Thomas, 1956). Several geographers have explicitly been concerned with developing concepts that would provide this integration, such as Carl Sauer and the concept of landscape (1956). By the end of the twentieth century, the debate still continued without resolution.

Keeping the two sides apart are centrifugal forces that vary from place to place, but which collectively are likely to prevent the integration wished for by many. Academics, as noted above, are only human. Career paths and funding requirements mean that people will pursue courses of action profitable to them in their particular context. If funding councils do not recognize an integrative physical/human geography then why pursue it? There is no money in it; there are no rewards. This may sound cynical, but an academic life is short, the period available to make an impact even shorter, so why waste it in pursuit of an unattainable goal? There is also the feeling amongst key researchers on both sides that what they study is different from that being studied on the other side. The subject matter of human and physical geography is seen as fundamentally different. Hacking's (1999) distinction between indifferent and interactive kinds may be taken by some to be a good description of the differences between physical and human geography respectively. This may be simplifying the matter, but it does have an appeal in explaining the continued divide. If the subject matter is different at a fundamental level then the techniques employed to study one kind cannot necessarily be easily transferred to the study of the other kind. This means that a reductionist approach will not be of any use in a post-modern analysis of asylum seekers. Likewise, what could a post-modernist say that is meaningful to the study of gravel-bedded rivers? Acceptance of such a key divide will justify the lack of communication between the camps. With such entrenched and well-funded camps is there any point in pursuing the issue of integrating physical and human geography? Maybe, unsurprisingly, my reply is yes! Although some may regard any integration as superficial and part of a propaganda drive to maintain a university subject that has run its course, I still believe that there is room for an integrative approach. The methodologies of human geography can be applied to the study of the practice of physical geography. Collier and Inkpen (2002, 2003), somewhat simplistically, began to analyse how surveying at the RGS in the nineteenth century was influenced in its practice by the context of the period. Livingstone (1984, 1987) has analysed Shaler's work in both eugenics and geology in the context of the development of Darwinian concepts at the time. Such historic studies can help us to see how seemingly objective facts and concepts are actually constructed by individuals in societies and how the nature of 'objectivity' is affected by these contexts.

Likely to be of more significance to current physical geography is the increasing recognition (stating the obvious maybe) that it is difficult to separate human and physical environments. The interpenetration of the physical and human means that it is difficult to justify that processes of environmental change are purely physical or that social structures rely solely upon human processes. Maintaining that one realm does not influence the other would be to view each as meshing together at increasingly smaller scales, but never actually overlapping or merging. Gould (2001) provides a similar image of the relationship between science and religion, labelling it as 'fractal' as the two spheres mixed, but never merged no matter the scale of resolution they were observed at. For human geography I mean the more humanistic approaches that seem to address different questions and a different reality from the 'scientific' approaches.

The seemingly clear divide between the two becomes messy when closely examined in terms of, say, the purpose of study, the questions asked, the entities and processes identified. The two, however, never mix, their realities remain different but interwoven. The two never merged as each answered questions about a specific realm. science, what reality was like: religion, how we ought to live. One could not answer questions about the other. Keeping human and physical geography separate implies the same key distinction. Interestingly, however, this separatist view would not actually deny the importance of either branch of geography; it would merely accept that human and physical questions were distinct and separate, but equally as valid to ask in the first place. This view would enable an uneasy truce to prevail in conflict over the integration or division of the subject. An important consideration that has rarely been considered is that both human and physical geography are not homogeneous masses.

There are distinct approaches within both with differing methodologies and views of reality. Arguments for separation, and even some for integration, have usually focused upon the extreme members of both realms. The argument seems to run that if these end members cannot be integrated then none of physical and human geography can. It may be that these end members follow Gould's fractal description, but other parts of human and physical geography may be easier or rather more appropriate to integrate. The approaches and topics that ask the same questions about reality or can inform the questions that each subdiscipline asks may be more appropriate candidates for integration. As environmental degradation continues, this may be an area that of necessity becomes a concern for geography as a subject for both its relevance and survival.

FIELDS OF PHYSICAL GEOGRAPHY

Geomorphology is the science concerned with understanding the surface of the Earth and the processes by which it is shaped, both at the present as well as in the past. Geomorphology as a field has several sub-fields that deal with the specific landforms of various environments e.g. desert geomorphology and fluvial geomorphology, however, these sub-fields are united by the core processes which cause them; mainly tectonic or climatic processes. Geomorphology seeks to understand landform history and dynamics, and predict future changes through a combination of field observation, physical experiment, and numerical modelling. (Geomorphometry). Early studies in geomorphology are the foundation for pedology, one of two main branches of soil science:

- Hydrology is predominantly concerned with the amounts and quality of water moving and accumulating on the land surface and in the soils and rocks near the surface and is typified by the hydrological cycle. Thus the field encompasses water in rivers, lakes, aquifers and to an extent glaciers, in which the field examines the process and dynamics involved in these bodies of water.

Hydrology has historically had an important connection with engineering and has thus developed a largely quantitative method in its research; however, it does have an earth science side that embraces the systems approach. Similar to most fields of physical geography it has sub-fields that examine the specific bodies of water or their interaction with other spheres e.g. limnology and ecohydrology.

- Glaciology is the study of glaciers and ice sheets, or more commonly the cryosphere or ice and phenomena that involve ice. Glaciology groups the latter (ice sheets) as continental glaciers and the former (glaciers) as alpine glaciers. Although, research in the areas are similar with research undertaken into both the dynamics of ice sheets and glaciers the former tends to be concerned with the interaction of ice sheets with the present climate and the latter with the impact of glaciers on the landscape. Glaciology also has a vast array of sub-fields examining the factors and processes involved in ice sheets and glaciers e.g. snow hydrology and glacial geology.
- Biogeography is the science which deals with geographic patterns of species distribution and the processes that result in these patterns. Biogeography emerged as a field of study as a result of the work of Alfred Russel Wallace, although the field prior to the late twentieth century had largely been viewed as historic in its outlook and descriptive in its approach. The main stimulus for the field since its founding has been that of evolution, plate tectonics and the theory of island biogeography. The field can largely be divided into five sub-fields: island biogeography, paleobiogeography, phylogeography, zoogeography and phytogeography.
- Climatology is the study of the climate, scientifically defined as weather conditions averaged over a long period of time. It differs from meteorology, which studies atmospheric processes over a shorter duration, which are then examined by climatologists to find trends and frequencies in weather patterns/phenomena. Climatology examines both the nature of micro (local)

and macro (global) climates and the natural and anthropogenic influences on them. The field is also sub-divided largely into the climates of various regions and the study of specific phenomena or time periods e.g. tropical cyclone rainfall climatology and paleoclimatology.

- Pedology is the study of soils in their natural environment. It is one of two main branches of soil science, the other being edaphology. Pedology mainly deals with pedogenesis, soil morphology, soil classification. In physical geography pedology is largely studied due to the numerous interactions between climate (water, air, temperature), soil life (micro-organisms, plants, animals), the mineral materials within soils (biogeochemical cycles) and its position and effects on the landscape such as laterization.
- Palaeogeography is the study of the distribution of the continents through geologic time through examining the preserved material in the stratigraphic record. Palaeogeography is a cross-discipline, almost all the evidence for the positions of the continents comes from geology in the form of fossils or geophysics the use of this data has resulted in evidence for continental drift, plate tectonics and supercontinents this in turn has supported palaeogeographic theories such as the Wilson cycle.
- Coastal geography is the study of the dynamic interface between the ocean and the land, incorporating both the physical geography (i.e coastal geomorphology, geology and oceanography) and the human geography of the coast. It involves an understanding of coastal weathering processes, particularly wave action, sediment movement and weathering, and also the ways in which humans interact with the coast. Coastal geography although predominantly geomorphological in its research is not just concerned with coastal landforms, but also the causes and influences of sea level change.
- Oceanography is the branch of physical geography that studies the Earth's oceans and seas. It covers a wide range of topics, including marine organisms and

ecosystem dynamics (biological oceanography); ocean currents, waves, and geophysical fluid dynamics (physical oceanography); plate tectonics and the geology of the sea floor (geological oceanography); and fluxes of various chemical substances and physical properties within the ocean and across its boundaries (chemical oceanography). These diverse topics reflect multiple disciplines that oceanographers blend to further knowledge of the world ocean and understanding of processes within it.

- Quaternary science is an inter-disciplinary field of study focusing on the Quaternary period, which encompasses the last 2.6 million years. The field studies the last ice age and the recent interstadial the Holocene and uses proxy evidence to reconstruct the past environments during this period to infer the climatic and environmental changes that have occurred.
- Landscape ecology is a sub-discipline of ecology and geography that address how spatial variation in the landscape affects ecological processes such as the distribution and flow of energy, materials and individuals in the environment (which, in turn, may influence the distribution of landscape "elements" themselves such as hedgerows). The field was largely founded by the German geographer Carl Troll Landscape ecology typically deals with problems in an applied and holistic context. The main difference between biogeography and landscape ecology is that the latter is concerned with how flows or energy and material are changed and their impacts on the landscape whereas the former is concerned with the spatial patterns of species and chemical cycles.
- Geomatics is the field of gathering, storing, processing, and delivering of geographic information, or spatially referenced information. Geomatics includes geodesy (scientific discipline that deals with the measurement and representation of the earth, its gravitational field, and other geodynamic phenomena, such as crustal motion, oceanic tides, and polar motion) and G.I.S. (a

system for capturing, storing, analysing and managing data and associated attributes which are spatially referenced to the earth) and remote sensing (the short or large-scale acquisition of information of an object or phenomenon, by the use of either recording or real-time sensing devices that are not in physical or intimate contact with the object).

- Environmental geography is a branch of geography that analyzes the spatial aspects of interactions between humans and the natural world. The branch bridges the divide between human and physical geography and thus requires an understanding of the dynamics of geology, meteorology, hydrology, biogeography, and geomorphology, as well as the ways in which human societies conceptualize the environment. Although the branch was previously more visible in research than at present with theories such as environmental determinism linking society with the environment. It has largely become the domain of the study of environmental management or anthropogenic influences on the environment and vice a versa.

PHYSICAL GEOGRAPHY LITERATURE

Physical geography and Earth Science journals communicate and document the results of research carried out in universities and various other research institutions. Most journals cover a specific field and publish the research within that field, however unlike human geographers, physical geographers tend to publish in inter-disciplinary journals rather than predominantly geography journal; the research is normally expressed in the form of a scientific paper. Additionally, textbooks, books, and magazines on geography communicate research to laypeople, although these tend to focus on environmental issues or cultural dilemmas.

Historic Evolution of Physical Geography

From the birth of geography as a science during the Greek classical period and until the late nineteenth century with the birth of anthropography or Human Geography, Geography was almost exclusively a natural science: the study of location and descriptive gazetteer of all places of the known world. Several works among the best known during this long period could be cited as an example, from Strabo (Geography), Eratosthenes (Geography) or Dionisio Periegetes (Periegesis Oiceumene) in the Ancient Age to the Alexander von Humboldt (Cosmos) in the century XIX, in which geography is regarded as a physical and natural science, of course, through the work Summa de Geografia of Martin Fernandez de Enciso from the early sixteenth century, which is indicated for the first time the New World.

During the eighteenth and nineteenth centuries, a controversy exported from Geology, between supporters of James Hutton (uniformitarianism Thesis) and Georges Cuvier (catastrophism) strongly influenced the field of geography, because geography at this time was a natural science since Human Geography or Antropogeography had just developed as a discipline in the late nineteenth century.

Two historical events during the nineteenth century had a great effect in the further development of physical geography. The first was the European colonial expansion in Asia, Africa, Australia and even America in search of raw materials required by industries during the Industrial Revolution. This fostered the creation of geography departments in the universities of the colonial powers and the birth and development of national geographical societies, thus giving rise to the process identified by Horacio Capel as the institutionalization of geography.

One of the most prolific empires in this regard was the Russian. A mid-eighteenth century many geographers are sent by the Russian altamirazgo different opportunities to perform geographical surveys in the area of Arctic Siberia. Among these is who is considered the patriarch of Russian geography: Mikhail Lomonosov who in the mid-1750s began working in the Department of Geography, Academy of Sciences to conduct research in Siberia, their contributions are notable in this regard, shows the soil organic origin, develops a comprehensive law on the movement of the ice that still governs the basics, thereby founding a new branch of Geography: Glaciology. In 1755 his initiative was founded Moscow University where he promotes the study of geography and the training of geographers. In 1758 he was appointed director of the Department of Geography, Academy of Sciences, a post from which would develop a working methodology for geographical survey guided by the most important long expeditions and geographical studies in Russia.

Thus followed the line of Lomonosov and the contributions of the Russian school became more frequent through his disciples, and in the nineteenth century we have great geographers as Vasily Dokuchaev who performed works of great importance as a "principle of comprehensive analysis of the territory" and "Russian Chernozem" latter being the most important where introduces the geographical concept of soil, as distinct from a simple geological strata, and thus founding a new geographic area of study: the Pedology. Climatology also receive a strong boost from the Russian school by Wladimir Koppen whose main contribution, climate classification, is still valid today. However, this great geographer also contributed to the Paleogeography through his work "The climates of the geological past" which is considered the father of Paleoclimatology. Russian geographers who made great contributions to the discipline in this period were: NM Sibirtsev, Pyotr Semyonov, K. D. Glinka, Neustrayev, among others.

The second important process is the theory of evolution by Darwin in mid-century (which decisively influenced the work of Ratzel, who had academic training as a zoologist and was a follower of Darwin's ideas) which meant an important impetus in the development of Biogeography. Another major event in the late nineteenth and early twentieth century will give a major boost to development of geography and will take place in United States. It is the work of the famous geographer William Morris Davis who not only made important contributions to the establishment of discipline in his country, but revolutionized the field to develop geographical cycle theory which he proposed as a paradigm for Geography in general, although in actually served as a paradigm for Physical Geography. His theory explained that mountains and other landforms are shaped by the influence of a number of factors that are manifested in the geographical cycle.

He explained that the cycle begins with the lifting of the relief by geological processes (faults, volcanism, tectonic upheaval, etc.).. Geographical factors such as rivers and runoff begins to create the V-shaped valleys between the mountains (the stage called "youth"). During this first stage, the terrain is steeper and more irregular. Over time, the currents can carve wider valleys ("maturity") and then start to wind, towering hills only ("senescence"). Finally, everything comes to what is a plain flat plain at the lowest elevation possible (called "baseline") This plain was called by Davis' "peneplain" meaning "almost plain" Then the rejuvenation occurs and there is another mountain lift and the cycle continues. Although Davis's theory is not entirely accurate, it was absolutely revolutionary and unique in its time and helped to modernize and create Geography subfield of Geomorphology. Its implications prompted a myriad of research in various branches of Physical Geography. In the case of the Paleogeography this theory provided a model for understanding the evolution of the landscape.

For Hydrology, Glaciology and Climatology as a boost investigated as studying geographic factors shape the landscape and affect the cycle. The bulk of the work of William Morris Davis led to the development of a new branch of Physical Geography: Geomorphology whose contents until then did not differ from the rest of Geography. Shortly after this branch would present a major development. Some of his disciples made significant contributions to various branches of physical geography such as Curtis Marbut and his invaluable legacy for Pedology, Mark Jefferson, Isaiah Bowman, among others.

PHYSICAL CHARACTERISTICS

Landforms are categorised by characteristic physical attributes such as elevation, slope, orientation, stratification, rock exposure, and soil type. Gross *physical features or landforms* include intuitive elements such as berms, mounds, hills, ridges, cliffs, valleys, rivers, peninsulas and numerous other structural and size-scaled (i.e. ponds vs. Lakes, Hills vs. Mountains) elements including various kinds of inland and oceanic waterbodies and sub-surface features.

Hierarchy of Classes

Oceans and continents exemplify the highest-order landforms. Landform elements are parts of a high-order landforms that can be further identified and systematically given a cohesive definition such as hill-tops, shoulders, saddles, foreslopes and backslopes. Some generic landform elements including: pits, peaks, channels, ridges, passes, pools and plains, may be extracted from a digital elevation model using some automated techniques where the data has been gathered by modern satellites and stereoscopic aerial surveillance cameras. Until recently, compiling the data found in such data sets required time consuming and expensive techniques of many man-hours.

Terrain (or *relief*) is the third or vertical dimension of *land surface*. Topography is the study of terrain, although the word is often used as a synonym for relief itself. When relief is described underwater, the term bathymetry is used. In cartography, many different techniques are used to describe relief, including contour lines and TIN (Triangulated irregular network).

Elementary landforms (segments, facets, relief units) are the smallest homogeneous divisions of the land surface, at the given scale/resolution. These are areas with relatively homogenous morphometric properties, bounded by lines of discontinuity. A plateau or a hill can be observed at various scales ranging from few hundred meters to hundreds of kilometres. Hence, the spatial distribution of landforms is often scale-dependent as is the case for soils and geological strata.

A number of factors, ranging from plate tectonics to erosion and deposition, can generate and affect landforms. Biological factors can also influence landforms— for example, note the role of vegetation in the development of dune systems and salt marshes, and the work of corals and algae in the formation of coral reefs.

Landforms do not include man-made features, such as canals, ports and many harbours; and geographic features, such as deserts, forests, grasslands, and impact craters. Many of the terms are not restricted to refer to features of the planet Earth, and can be used to describe surface features of other planets and similar objects in the Universe. Examples are mountains, polar caps, and valleys, which are found on all of the terrestrial planets.

Terrain

Terrain, or land relief, is the vertical dimension of land surface. When relief is described underwater, the term bathymetry is used. Topography has recently become an additional synonym, though in many parts of the world it retains its original more general meaning of description of place. Terrain is used as a general term in physical geography, referring to the lie of the land. This is usually expressed in terms of the elevation, slope, and orientation of terrain features. Terrain affects surface water flow and distribution. Over a large area, it can affect weather and climate patterns.

Importance

The understanding of terrain is critical for many reasons:

- The terrain of a region largely determines its suitability for human settlement: flatter, alluvial plains tend to have better farming soils than steeper, rockier uplands.
- In terms of environmental quality, agriculture, and hydrology, understanding the terrain of an area enables the understanding of watershed boundaries, drainage characteristics, water movement, and impacts on water quality. Complex arrays of relief data are used as input parameters for hydrology transport models (such as the SWMM or DSSAM Models) to allow prediction of river water quality.
- Understanding terrain also supports on soil conservation, especially in agriculture. Contour plowing is an established practice enabling sustainable agriculture on sloping land; it is the practice of plowing along lines of equal elevation instead of up and down a slope.
- Terrain is militarily critical because it determines the ability of armed forces to take and hold areas, and move troops and material into and through areas. An understanding of terrain is basic to both defensive and offensive strategy.
- Terrain is important in determining weather patterns. Two areas geographically close to each other may differ radically in precipitation levels or timing because of elevation differences or a "rain shadow" effect.
- Since terrain comes in vast varieties, certain features can be specific according to one type terrain, but also

other features can be specific to multiple types of terrain. Basically, different terrains can both share the same features as well as have their own unique features.

PHYSICAL ENVIRONMENTS

Water

The rate of diffusion of carbon dioxide and oxygen is approximately 10,000 times slower in water than it is in air. When soils become flooded, they quickly lose oxygen from low-concentration (hypoxic) to an (anoxic) environment where anaerobic bacteria thrive among the roots.

Water also influences the spectral properties of light that becomes more diffuse as it is reflected off the water surface and submerged particles. Aquatic plants exhibit a wide variety of morphological and physiological adaptations that allow them to survive, compete and diversify these environments. For example, the roots and stems develop large cellular air spaces to allow for the efficient transportation gases (for example, CO_2 and O_2) used in respiration and photosynthesis.

In drained soil, microorganisms use oxygen during respiration. In aquatic environments, anaerobic soil microorganisms use nitrate, manganic ions, ferric ions, sulfate, carbon dioxide and some organic compounds. The activity of soil microorganisms and the chemistry of the water reduces the oxidation-reduction potentials of the water.

Carbon dioxide, for example, is reduced to methane (CH_4) by methanogenic bacteria. Salt water also requires special physiological adaptations to deal with water loss. Salt water plants (or halophytes) are able to osmo-regulate their internal salt (NaCl) concentrations or develop special organs for shedding salt away. The physiology of fish is also specially adapted to deal with high levels of salt through osmoregulation. Their gills form electrochemical gradients that mediate salt excrusion in salt water and uptake in fresh water.

Gravity

The shape and energy of the land is affected to a large degree by gravitational forces. On a larger scale, the distribution of gravitational forces on the earth are uneven and influence the shape and movement of tectonic plates as well as having an influence on geomorphic processes such as orogeny and erosion.

These forces govern many of the geophysical properties and distributions of ecological biomes across the Earth. On a organism scale, gravitational forces provide directional cues for plant and fungal growth (gravitropism), orientation cues for animal migrations, and influence the biomechanics and size of animals.

Ecological traits, such as allocation of biomass in trees during growth are subject to mechanical failure as gravitational forces influence the position and structure of branches and leaves. The cardiovascular systems of all animals are functionally adapted to overcome pressure and gravitational forces that change according to the features of organisms (e.g., height, size, shape), their behaviour (e.g., diving, running, flying), and the habitat occupied (e.g., water, hot deserts, cold tundra).

Pressure

Climatic and osmotic pressure places physiological constraints on organisms, such as flight and respiration at high altitudes, or diving to deep ocean depths. These constraints influence vertical limits of ecosystems in the biosphere as organisms are physiologically sensitive and adapted to atmospheric and osmotic water pressure differences.

Oxygen levels, for example, decrease with increasing pressure and are a limiting factor for life at higher altitudes. Water transportation through trees is another important ecophysiological parameter dependent upon pressure. Water pressure in the depths of oceans requires adaptations to deal with the different living conditions. Mammals, such as whales, dolphins and seals are adapted to deal with changes in sound due to water pressure differences.

Wind and Turbulence

Turbulent forces in air and water have significant effects on the environment and ecosystem distribution, form and dynamics. On a planetary scale, ecosystems are affected by circulation patterns in the global trade winds. Wind power and the turbulent forces it creates can influence heat, nutrient, and biochemical profiles of ecosystems.

For example, wind running over the surface of a lake creates turbulence, mixing the water column and influencing the environmental profile to create thermally layered zones, partially governing how fish, algae, and other parts of the aquatic ecology are structured. Wind speed and turbulence also exert influence on rates of evapotranspiration rates and energy budgets in plants and animals.

Wind speed, temperature and moisture content can vary as winds travel across different landfeatures and elevations. The westerlies, for example, come into contact with the coastal and interior mountains of western North America to produce a rain shadow on the leeward side of the mountain.

The air expands and moisture condenses as the winds move up in elevation which can cause precipitation; this is called orographic lift. This environmental process produces spatial divisions in biodiversity, as species adapted to wetter conditions are range-restricted to the coastal mountain valleys and unable to migrate across the xeric ecosystems of the Columbia Basin to intermix with sister lineages that are segregated to the interior mountain systems.

Fire

Plants convert carbon dioxide into biomass and emit oxygen into the atmosphere. Approximately 350 million years ago (near the Devonian period) the photosynthetic process brought the concentration of atmospheric oxygen above 17%, which allowed combustion to occur. Fire releases CO_2 and converts fuel into ash and tar.

Fire is a significant ecological parameter that raises many issues pertaining to its control and suppression in management. While the issue of fire in relation to ecology and plants has been recognized for a long time, Charles Cooper brought attention to the issue of forest fires in relation to the ecology of forest fire suppression and management in the 1960s.

Fire creates environmental mosaics and a patchiness to ecosystem age and canopy structure. Native North Americans were among the first to influence fire regimes by controlling their spread near their homes or by lighting fires to stimulate the production of herbaceous foods and basketry materials. The altered state of soil nutrient supply and cleared canopy structure also opens new ecological niches for seedling establishment.

Most ecosystem are adapted to natural fire cycles. Plants, for example, are equipped with a variety of adaptations to deal with forest fires. Some species (e.g., *Pinus halepensis*) cannot germinate until after their seeds have lived through a fire. This environmental trigger for seedlings is called serotiny. Some compounds from smoke also promote seed germination.

4

Thinking of Mapping, Modes, Methods and Moments

INTRODUCTION

By way of conclusion to *Rethinking Maps* we want to set out a manifesto for map studies for the coming decade. Its goal is to generate ideas and enthusiasm for scholarship that advance our understanding of the philosophical underpinnings of maps, and also enhances the practices of mapping. This is not a call for ever more introspective intellectual navel gazing about maps. Instead it traces routes and methods that might help people to *do* mapping differently and more *productively*, in ways that might be more efficient, democratic, sustainable, ethical or even more fun. This manifesto is, of course, preliminary and partial, coming as it does from a social scientific tradition and the authors' experiences as Anglophone human geographers. It also focuses on understanding *everyday* mapping practices and the various *socio-technological infrastructures* that are a necessary, but often unquestioned, support for contemporary mapping. The aim is to suggest and provoke. Our manifesto for map studies is structured into three 'levels': first, looking at *modes* ('what to study'); second, *methods* ('how to study'); and finally, *moments* ('when and where to study').

MODES OF MAPPING

For us, map studies needs to continue to develop alternative ways to think through cartographic history and contemporary practice that are not wedded to simplifying, modernist, narratives of 'advancement'. In this pursuit, we might build on the relational thinking of Matthew Edney. He forwards the notion of 'cartography without progress' (1993: 54), in which mapping is read as 'a complex amalgam of cartographic *modes* rather than a monolithic enterprise'. For Edney, a cartographic mode is not simply a linear chronological sequence, instead it is a unique set of cultural, social, economic and technical relations within which cartographers and the map production processes are situated. The mode is thus the milieu in which mapping practices occur. Each cartographic mode gives rise to its own kind of map artefacts, and critically this conceptualization does not assume that one is inherently better than another, or that one mode will inevitably evolve into a 'superior' mode. As Edney (1993: 58) elaborates: '[t]he mode is thus the combination of cartographic form and cartographic function, of the internal construction of the data, their representation on the one hand and the external *raison d'être* of the map on the other.'

Modes are unique to their time and place, and are transitory. Modes of mapping practice are coupled to the continual emergence of new knowledges, spatial problems, methods and institutions, and drive developments in the design of map representations and in the roles that maps play in society. There are usually multiple but distinct mapping modes operating at the same time in the same place. Modes can interact and may well overlap, merge and diverge. The boundaries between them are likely to be fuzzy and permeable. Cartographic history, according to Edney's theorization, is therefore best read as a plural and relational network of activities, rather than a single linear process. In contemporary cartographic epistemologies, a diverse range of mappings is seen to emerge from a shifting creative milieu, the end result of which is not a unidirectional evolutionary tree of maps, but rather a complex, many-branching, rhizomatic structure.

Part of the undoubted excitement at the moment about maps stems from the fact that contemporary mapping practices consist of multiple, overlapping modes. Mapping is emergent and variegated, drawing on many disparate ideas and data sources, produced by a diverse collection of practitioners and activists, utilizing many forms of visualization. Mapping is thoroughly situated in wider socio-technical changes (particularly the diffusion of the Internet throughout map production and the use of the Web as the main medium of dissemination). To begin to excavate the nature of contemporary mapping modes requires empirical analysis to unpack cultural, social and technological relations that determine these cartographic practices. It seems to us that it would be productive for researchers to focus attention on: (i) interfaces, (ii) algorithms, (iii) cultures, (iv) authorships and (v) infrastructures.

Interfaces: Mapping out Screen Spaces

More and more, everyday mapping is encountered as part of a digital interface, or the map is itself an interface that can be queried. These 'screen spaces' are becoming an important site for analysis in map studies. What are the cultural, social and economic relations that bring the interface into being? Interrogating the interfaces of mapping is an ontological project with political ramifications. There is an emerging body of work on the critical reading of computer interfaces that can be drawn upon and might inform map study. For example, Selfe and Selfe (1994: 485) argue that one can hermeneutically read what gets screened as if it is a cultural map that 'order(s) the virtual world according to a certain set of historical and social values that make up our culture'. Interfaces en-frame and exclude, working as mediating windows onto the world. The task of decoding the embedded cultural biases and distortions in processes of interface screening is challenging, even for supposedly 'open' Web mapping interfaces because, as Parks (2004: 39) notes, they 'tend to keep users naïve about the apparatus that organizes and facilitates online navigation and how its processes occur in time and extend across space'.

Beyond the cultural politics within spaces of display, there are also phenomenological considerations relating to interfaces (cf. Introna and Ilharco 2006). Mapping often dynamically updates to reflect embodied position and kinetics (Willim 2007), inviting interrogation of the differences digital interfaces make to individual identity and social behaviour that stem from 'being on the screen'. This interface between person, map and the world in motion would once have been reserved for specialized and particularly military applications, but is now the everyday experience for many when walking with a mobile phone, driving with a satnav, flying with the airshow maps on an in-flight entertainment system, and even playing with handheld GPS units in treasure hunting games of geocaching.

Algorithms of Mapping

As outlined above, the technological practices of map representation are increasingly rendered through computer interfaces on digital screens. What lies beneath these interfaces? They are all products of software, continuously brought into being by a complex amalgam of data and algorithms. These codes are highly technical but also deeply culturally contingent, yet from an investigative point of view they are very hard to read or critique.

Map studies needs to open the 'black boxes' of mapping software, to start to interrogate algorithms and databases, and in particular to investigate the production of ready-made maps that appear almost magically on the interfaces of gadgets and devices we carry and use everyday, often without much overt thought about how they work and whose map they project onto their interface. This agenda was aptly expressed by Laura Kurgan (1994: 17) in her imagina-tive work examining the inherent indeterminacy of the inner workings of GPS software from the external mappings its produces: [b]ut the space or the architecture of the information system that wants to locate and fix us in space has its own complexity, its own invisible relays and delays. The difficulty of charting the spaces that chart the spaces, of mapping the scaleless networks of the very system that promises to end our disorientation, demands redefining the points and lines and planes that build the map, and lingering in their strange spaces and times.

Opening the 'black box' of cartographic algorithms was a core element of the social science critique of GIS in the 1990s (Pickles 2004). The rapid popularization of digital mapping in the last five years makes this even more pertinent for map studies, as millions of people walk and drive around with what are effectively mini-GIS mapping gadgets in their pockets and on their vehicle dashboards.

It seems there are several productive routes to critique mapping codes. First, we can draw on emerging ideas in the field of 'software studies' that treat code as a form of material culture that can be examined from multiple points of reference to reveal how it comes into being, and works often automatically and autonomously in the world. These ideas seek an expanded understanding of software beyond the technical. They also critique how the world itself is captured within code in terms of algorithmic potential and formal data descriptions (cf. Dodge and Kitchin 2009). This research is trans-disciplinary, often driven by scholars and intellectual hackers in media theory and new media art. Fuller (2008: 2) argues that this kind of approach: 'proposes that software can be seen as an object of study and an area of practice for kinds of thinking and areas of work that have not historically "owned" software, or indeed often had much of use to say about it.' There is much, we believe, that needs to be said by people who have traditionally not 'owned' mapping codes.

Socially rich work investigating the spatiality of software algorithms and data structures has begun in human geography, notably with Thrift and French's (2002) theorization of the 'automatic production of space' and Graham's (2005) discussion of the socio-geographical effects of 'software sorting'. However, analysing algorithmic processing underlying new forms of online mapping has so far received little attention. A noteworthy exception is Zook and Graham's (2007) work on 'digiplace' as the mapped interface arising from the opaque complexity of search engine databases and spatial-relevance ranking algorithms. This research offers a significant opening and needs to followed-up and expanded upon.

A second route toward analysing mapping algorithms is to build explicit connections between cartography and the emerging conceptual agenda of 'surveillance studies' to reveal the social power frozen in code and the dangers of discriminatory effects emerging from automated sorting of people and code-based representations of place. There is a focus on power at the heart of 'surveillance studies' according to Lyon (2007: 1) with explicit attempts to explain surveillance practices in terms of 'rationalization, the application of science and technology, classification and the knowledgeability of subject'. Considering the computerized map as a surveillant technology was initially undertaken by Pickles (1991) who argued that nation states, trans-national corporations and the interests of capital and technology deploy the surveillant potential of mapping to restructure local, regional, national and global geographies. Notable examples of recent work in this vein includes Crampton (2004) who explored parallels between the nineteenth-century emergence of crime mapping and contemporary post-9/11 surveillance discourses as reflections of Foucauldian rational governance.

Mapping Visual Culture

In the 1990s, a research focus on the analytical functions of GIS led to a significant retreat from design issues that had hitherto formed a central concern for cartographic research. It has been argued that this retreat has almost led to the death of cartography as a discipline (Wood 2003). Everyday mapping however, grew apace from the end of the decade, and meanwhile a newly energized emphasis on the visual pervades much critical thought across cultural and media studies. We would argue that a new and critical engagement with visual studies could usefully inform research into mapping. Cartography may or may not be heading toward extinction as a technical discipline, but mapping is very much alive and technology alone is insufficient an explanation for the role that new kinds of mapping are playing in society.

Such research might usefully explore new ways of envisioning spatial data in interactive and animated systems, building on the innovative work carried out by researchers such as Dykes *et al.* (2005). Which new ways of symbolizing data work best? Which widgets offer the most appealing ways of performing screen navigation and selection and why? How might geovisualization best represent movement, change and dynamic data? What are the best ways of situating the observer on and in mapping displayed on different kinds of device?

Among areas that might usefully receive attention here are the interplay between screen design issues and display design issues: a much greater contextual awareness of the intertextuality of displays could inform critical approaches to the burgeoning literature around usability. Although a concern with designing better maps has led to a profusion of expert systems encouraging effective use of industry-standard software designs (e.g. Harrower and Brewer's (2003) innovative work on Colorbrewer tool), innovative design solutions for the representation of phenomena only rarely feed through to the mainstream consumption. Yet the immediate appeal of Google Earth stems in large part from the visual novelty of its interface. Mapping researchers could usefully learn from this approach. The difference that media make is also a rich research area: interesting work is already exploring the roles that sound and taste mapping might play in multimedia map design.

To realize this kind of research result, mapping needs to be situated in relation to other media. It is noticeable that the mainstream of visual culture and visual studies research almost completely elides mapping at present and that mainstream visualization research largely remains grounded in scientific representation. Critical insights from visual studies, with its emphasis upon innovative methodolo-gies could usefully be applied in the more narrowly defined worlds of geovisualization. Researchers might learn much here from the practical worlds of computer game design and some of the roles that maps play in these. Surely dialogue between visual studies and cartography would yield richer and more complex insights into the nature of mapping.

Authorship of Mapping

It is also important, we believe, to focus attention in map studies on authorship. Significant changes in notions of authorship are at the heart of many contemporary modes of mapping. In particular there is a fracturing of authorship with the emergence of a more 'writerly' kind of mapping (following Roland Barthes), which according to Pickles (2004: 161) can 'engage the reader as an "author" and insist upon the openness and intertextuality of the text'. Moreover, many aspects of mapmaking practices are undergoing a metamor-phosis towards a 'remix' cultural model of production that is apparent in many other media, in which new media constantly reinterpret existing media in a process facilitated by rapid and unconstrained access. Manovich (2005: no pagination) argues that '[r]emixability becomes practically a built-in feature of digital networked media universe.'

Research needs to consider the implications for mapping. How do new models of map authorship work in practice, for example: How are power structures altered by the rise of the amateur mappers? How do crowds generate wisdom in cartography? To what extent is the democratization of production really taking place? How might map 'hackers' fashion genuinely useful hybrid forms of cartography as opposed to merely creative experiments with little lasting value? Who are the new collaborative authors and why are they motivated to map? and What kinds of mapping do they do and is that mapping of quality and utility to others?

The rise of map mashups has been a significant marker of changing authorship and possibly a new mode of mapping that Crampton (2008) has termed 'Maps 2.0'. Mapping mashups are websites or Web applications combining content from more than one source to serve a new service, and usually depend upon a third party releasing an application programming interface. We might usefully investigate the pragmatic effects and wider political implications of the emergence of these new ways of mashing maps together. Are they a relatively transitory burst of creativity that will fade as most users return to a few maps produced by high-profile institutions, or do they herald the beginnings of a lasting 'prosumer' revolution? The deeper motivations for being a prosumer, and the degree to which these changes will create trusted and reliable mapping are still largely unknown.

The vanguard of prosumer authorship however, lies beyond mashing together existing data. Instead it offers newly made and often collaborative geospatial data under the guise of FOSS ('free and open source software') doctrines. The authorship of so-called 'open-source' mapping has a strongly counter-cultural ethos, itself a mixing of libertarian freedom of access to information, the socially progressive benefits of non-profit production and opposition to corporate capitalism. Of course it is ironic that much of this work is currently heavily reliant on the GPS system, designed, funded and maintained by the US military. Prosumer mapping has emerged outside of mainstream cartography, driven by enthusiastic and loosely coordinated collectives of activists, artists and programmers. Most have no formal cartographic training or professional GIS credentials, just an interest in the geography in its common-sense meaning, a liking for maps, a deep affinity with technology and, above all, passion for hacking their own elegant solutions; indeed, one of the first books to formalize the field is called *Mapping Hacks.*

Open-source authorship changes who can make maps and how they are made and open-source mapping seeks to harness the tremendous productive potential of mass-participation (the so-called 'crowd-sourcing' methodology). Such 'bottom-up' volunteer knowledge creation exploits the collaborative capacity of the Web and seeks to remake mapmaking as a social activity. Open-source mapping potentially becomes a way of thinking critically about the *practices* of cartography and not the end *products*. The map is not revered and reified as a special-knowledge product (akin to the 'Master Map' as Ordnance Survey markets its main digital topographic product) created by an elite organization and then used by a select few. Instead it becomes something that can be creatively made by many hands and enjoyed by anyone and everyone, without onerous and restrictive licencing. In the particular context of British mapping infrastructure for example, this ethos is mixed with a distinctly anti-establishment streak focused on the longstanding critique of Ordnance Survey's monopolistic pricing/licencing model, which has effectively excluded many individuals, non-profit groups, small businesses and local communities (Dodson 2005). This restrictive local context has certainly been a spur to citizen cartographers aiming 'to build a set of people's maps: charted and owned by those who create them, which are as free to share as the open road'. Open-source mapping alternatives increasingly represent a direct challenge to the closed-world of cartographic officialdom, with its unaccountable state authorship, its emphasis upon owned and protected products as capital assets, and its claims to provide an exclusive topographic text that spatially prescribes so many aspects of daily life.

Within the domain of authorship map studies might also explore so-called 'counter-mappings', to pin down the scope of genuinely alternative, subversive and emancipatory mapmaking and the degree to which this mapping has effect. For example, one could argue that much open-source mapping is actually not radical at all – it simply recreates a mirror copy of existing topographic mapping, albeit distributed under a more egalitarian licencing regime. Is it possible to author counter-mappings that really challenge established power relations and effect political change? Pickles (2004: 185), for example, invokes the work of William Bunge, which he typifies as a nomadic counter-cartography, with its '[s]imple maps of hazardous materials along streets, incidences of rat-bites, or unlit alleyways'. But did Bunge's map really help 'take-back' the streets by empowering communities?

Infrastructures of Mapping

The fifth and final domain through which map studies can investigate contemporary modes of mapping is to engage with infrastructure. Despite the fact that '[i]nfrastructure can be dullest of all topics', Norman (1998: 55) notes '[i]t can also be the most important. Infrastructure defines the basis of society; it is the underlying foundation of the facilities, services and standards upon which everything else builds'. Critical interrogation of the infrastructures of everyday living has been widely overlooked by the social sciences because of the ways they tend to slip beneath the surface. Infrastructure is often materially unseen and hidden from view; most users are unaware of it and have no experience of its significance in their everyday lives; technical systems are largely ignored as banal and 'taken-for-granted'; and infrastructure is hard to analyse because complex corporate ownership structures and fragmented regimes of regulation in the wider neo-liberal political economy tend to mask its existence. From a political perspective, critical studies of infrastructures are made more difficult because of the ways in which institutions deliberately structure them as 'black-boxed' systems to keep people from easily observing (and questioning) their design and operational logic. The invisibility of the infrastructure provides an effective cloak under which market manipulation and socially iniquitous practices can be safely carried out by institutions owning and operating them without undue negative public attention.

The lack of critical studies of mapping infrastructures tends to reify biases in the ongoing production of common cartographic data (such as topographic, routing, statistical maps) and to deny alternative ways to build and operate infrastructures. However, these infrastructures have the tendency to widen social difference and inequalities across space. As Pickles (2004: 146) argues:

[a]s the new digital mappings wash across our world, perhaps we should ask about the worlds that are being produced in the digital transition of the third industrial revolution, the conceptions of history with which they work, and the forms of socio-political life to which they contribute.

Researching mapping as an infrastructure needs to foreground the materiality of production, render transparent usage, and denaturalize the everyday appearance of maps by highlighting corporate structures that are underlying mapping. Working through infrastructures can be approached in two ways: first, one can consider the infrastructures that make a mapping mode possible. For example, the pivotal role of military infrastructures in everyday mapping has long been appreciated in historical studies (e.g. Harley 1988). But it important to realize that the current paths of technical development in mapping are still dependent, in large part, on military infrastructures in various guises and their significance munificence of capital and other resources. In particular the underlying geospatial capture infrastructures, such as earth imaging and GPS, are strongly influenced by military funding and imperatives of state security and secrecy. A recent example reported in the press amply illustrates this, with the launch in September 2008 of a new high-resolution commercial imaging satellite, called Geoeye, which is part supported by Google (who gain exclusive commercial access), but over half of the $502 million cost was financed by the US military. Furthermore, the Geoeye system operates under licence from the US government, who ensures their continued primary access to imagery ('shutter control') and denies highest potential resolution to anyone without explicit government authorization (cf. Chen 2008).

Second, it is important to analyse the ways in which mapping modes contribute to infrastructures themselves. The mundane disciplining role of mapping infrastructures in systems of computerized governmentality continues to grow, for example, in consumer marketing and crime mapping (Crampton 2003); this needs to be actively questioned by map studies. Rather than contributing to a more democratic society, one could argue that the powerful gaze of cartographic visualization at the heart of surveillance infrastructure means mapping is active in deepening the social power of corporations and the state over the citizen, particularly after 9/11. This is evident from the prominence of mapping in the fetishization of geospatial capabilities to 'target terrorism' (Beck 2003). A critical approach is needed here – one research possibility is to follow the money directly from military and intelligence sources towards the mapping research that they fund. Such surveillance requirements are also a driver in the development of new mapping techniques for cyberspace, particularly for visualizing online social networks.

MAPPING METHODOLOGIES FOR MAP STUDIES

How can contemporary mapping practices and socio-technological infrastructures of cartography be studied empirically? What are the new methodological routes in the study of map modes? Do approaches from science and technology studies (STS), Actor-Network Theory, ethno-methodology and non-progressive genealogy that are now *de rigueur* in many areas of social science work for mapping? Can they help scholars to reconstruct the real conditions under which mapping is brought into being, or offer novel insights into how a map might make a difference in the world? It seems clear to us that there are many valid and potentially valuable routes into the study of contemporary mapping practice. Some of these have been touched upon, in varying degrees, by the contributions to this volume. It is, we would argue, a stimulating time for mapping scholarship with many challenges and opportunities opening up: no single epistemological position now dominates interpretation. We suggest here a range of methodological routes that might be worth pursuing, focused upon (i) materiality, (ii) political economy, (iii) affect and (iv) ethnography.

Materiality of Mapping

In many other areas of the social sciences there has been a marked turn towards the materiality of objects in social processes, with a concern for the tactile experience of things, the ways this facilitates action and a focus on how the physicality of their production affords particular solutions to problems. The materiality of mapping has been largely overlooked in cartographic scholarship, and in particular in contemporary research on digital products and the virtualization of interaction and experience online. In practice, paper maps are still used and many times digital maps are printed out for immediate, convenient use and annotation. Meanwhile, digital map interfaces need to be interacted with in very material ways. Consequently, there is a need for work that moves beyond the narrow examination of the effectiveness of 'special' tactile map products, to interrogate *everyday* material encounters with mapping in different contexts. This needs to consider how the material forms of mapping might make a difference and perhaps explore the kinds of affordance these enable, *and* disable, and the contributions of the material in everyday problem-solving with maps.

The Political Economy of Mapping

A major methodological element of map studies should be to explore the political economy of contemporary mapping. In the late 1980s social constructivist research began to interrogate the power of mapping and its historical implication in capitalist modes of production. Similarly, there were a number of studies on the use of cartography in the propaganda of nation states and others (e.g. Monmonier 1996a). However, a political-economic approach is very rarely taken in studies of contemporary mapping, despite the fact that the vast bulk of mapping, measured in terms of volume, scale and spatial coverage, is still produced and owned by government institutions and large corporations. This concentration of spatial power is likely to remain the case into the future as well, notwithstanding the current fashion and fascination with 'open' maps made with volunteer effort. So tracing the monetary and political structures underlying the production of maps used in everyday practice is worthwhile. The fact that we seem to have more 'free' access (i.e. underpinned by advertising revenue) to detailed mapping than ever before, via Internet portals masks continuing limits to availability of large-scale data that stem from official and corporate secrecy. Decisions on where capital is being invested to produce updated and new maps, data and delivery systems affects, in practical and political terms, how the world is going to be envisioned cartographically in the future, but is opaque to scrutiny. Who controls what gets mapped when you enter a mundane geographical search query on the Web, or type a postcode destination into the find menu on your satnav, or text 'locate' on your phone? Tracing out patterns of capital investment, government subsidies, licencing fees and profits that circulate continuously, but unseen, through maps can reveal the wider power structures in which everyday mapping practice is situated, many of which are several steps removed from moments of use.

Affective Understandings of Mapping

Research methods also need to consider mapping as practices. Two of us have argued elsewhere that new insights will emerge if mapping is studied processionally rather than representationally. From that perspective, there is a need for research that examines contemporary map creation as a performance of space and the affective power flowing from of-the-moment map use in diverse contexts.

There is a burgeoning body of research on the affective nature of spaces in human geography that is clearly relevant to practices of mapping. This kind of research might consider: the emotional capacity of maps to do work in the world; the kinds of action and affect enabled in everyday mapping activities; and the role affect might play in enacting solutions to spatial problems. Thinking affectively could also grant insights in how people map, by focusing attention on the relations between design and its deployment, which would help professional mapmakers to create a wider range of products and interfaces capable of evoking a greater variety of actions and responses beyond the often taken-for-granted neutrality of the map as problem-solving artefact.

Thinking about what affective maps are and might be like has already begun. Experimental examples that tap into feelings have been produced, particularly by artists. In epistemological terms several scholars have begun to see the exciting and innovative potential for making mapping that encompasses affective qualities of space. For example, the recent work of Mei-Po Kwan and collaborators (e.g. Kwan 2007) enacts a feminist re-imaging of GIS as an affective and emotional alternative to neutral science, and Margaret Pearce (2008) has translated the sense of place from the narrative of trapper's diaries into affective maps of their journeys in eighteenth-century Canada.

Ethnography and Novel Evaluation of Mapping

The need to capture *how* maps emerge into the world to do their work necessitates more announced means of evaluation than has typically been employed in academic cartographic research to date. Studying mapping needs to progress outside controlled laboratory environments and to seek deeper ethnographic understanding of mapping in the 'wild', so to speak. Here the focus moves from measured responses to tests towards situated observations and participation in the mapping process. Ethnographically a map is not a map because it looks like a map, rather mapping is defined by how maps are used in practice and how they perform space. Capturing everyday mapping performance and attempting to interpolate multiple and opaque meanings is challenging conceptually and time-consuming empirically. Gaining access to natural, vernacular and everyday settings to observe situated mapping activities requires creative solutions and negotiation for scholars whose experience has mainly focused on bringing people into their labs for testing. But computer anthropologists and human–computer interaction (HCI) researchers have successfully moved in this direction in their research on how people (mis)use computers (Dix *et al.* 2004). An insightful step in this direction for map studies, which draws on experiences from HCI research is demonstrated in Barry Brown and Eric Laurier's (2005) work on the use of mapping in everyday wayfinding, in which they observe real-world navigational behaviour of people travelling in their cars. Beyond academic studies per se, another constructive illustration of the ethnographic method is Stephen Gill's (2004) photography project, which is really a visual essay resembling in many ways the mundane essence of mapping.

One area that seems ripe for such an approach is the study of the cultural practices of open-source mapping. Here, ethnographic methods could be profitably used to study key activists through participant observation of mapmaking work (such as OpenStreetMap). Work is also needed to examine the organizational structures of open-source mapping projects, the incentives for participants and the mechanisms for creating trust in the wiki production of cartographic knowledge. These could be studied as actor-networks, drawing partly on data contained in online discussion lists and blogs, to reveal the complex and contested ways that new mappings are brought into the world. It should also be possible directly to analyse the authorship of the map, because map data itself can tell stories of its own manufacture. This effort at mapping the mappers begins to lift the lid on the tradition-ally anonymous authorship and authority. Interestingly, this kind of analysis of authorship has already begun to reveal a lack of broad democratic participation in some open-source mapping projects (cf. Haklay 2008).

In addition, there needs to be more ethnomethodology in map studies. Such studies would focus on the use and practices of digital mapping systems and tools, and would research how technologies are used by different people, instead of how the systems have been designed to work. Studies would be small-scale and focused rather than generalist in nature. This kind of research could usefully study incomplete and failed mapping practices, and conflicted activities to reveal social contexts and the embodied experience of cartographic problem solving. A pragmatic end-goal of such local field studies is to reconstruct the conditions under which mapping is deployed, so as to help in the design of future map systems.

Besides ethnographic studies out in the field, we suggest that future map studies should move beyond conventional evaluative methods for revealing the effectiveness of cartographic representations, to look at how people manipulate and play with maps. Online three-dimensional virtual worlds and multiplayer games might become useful experimental and experiential spaces for such map evaluation. Processes of testing can be made more engaging and perhaps fun, but with the capacity for comprehensive and rigorous data capture of how users do what they do. Some steps in this direction have been taken by Michael Batty's team at the Centre for Advanced Spatial Analysis in their evaluation of thematic maps, geometric building models and spatial simulations inside virtual worlds.

THE MOMENTS OF MAPPING

In this third section of a manifesto for map studies we want to think through when and where mapping really matters. How can scholars identify some of the significant times and places of mapping practice that need to be examined in detail? Instead of the usual and sometimes sterile enumeration of particular sectors, contexts, cultures, places or even types of map or product, we argue that a focus on key processes is more likely to reveal critical aspects of mapping. As such, we offer a tentative list of mapping moments that we think are significant and worthy of study: (i) places and times of failures, (ii) points of change, (iii) time–space rhythms of map performance, (iv) the memories of mapping, (v) academic praxis; and (vi) newly creative engagement with mapping practice.

Moments of Mapping Failure

The moment when things go wrong often highlights how things really work, a point often overlooked in everyday life. For example, how a software glitch in an air traffic control system leads to the grounding or rerouting of all planes flying in that sector (Dodge and Kitchin 2004). These moments of failure are revealing of the world in process. As Graham and Thrift (2007) discuss, infrastructures – and as noted above mapping is in many respects an informational infrastructure of contemporary capitalism – are often most easily exposed to critical scrutiny when they fail; '[p]erhaps we should have been looking at breakdown and failure as no longer atypical and therefore only worth addressing if they result in catastrophe and, instead, at breakdown and failure as the means by which societies learn and learn to re-produce'.

Many breakdowns in utility and reliability of digital mapping can be related to errors in software code that brings the map to the screen. Often these breakdowns are more a failure in understanding and interpretation between human and computer. The rapid rise in the use of in-car satellite navigation with its novel dynamic map of the driven world coming into being just beyond the windscreen is a fascinating illustration of this interpretative failure that has led to a considerable amount of press coverage. Map studies might seek to get behind the headlines of these satnav 'cockup' stories to reveal how people cope with this of-the-moment wayfinding mapping combined with turn-by-turn voice instructions. As such, investigating the processes of getting lost may well be more productive than researching successful navigation!

Moments of Change and Decision Making

Where mapping is involved in decision making it does so because it makes a difference. Identifying when maps appear in these processes and assessing the contributions they make is, we would argue, a potentially rich field of research, which might allow researchers to track between representational and non-representational approaches to the world in ways that are 'more-than-representational', linking practices to artefacts and material culture (Lorimer 2005). Monmonier (1996b) offers a useful starting point with its consideration of 'carto-controversies': moments and processes where mapping has been strongly contested. The role mapping plays in the construction and maintenance of different global world orders, and its contributions to moments of change such as revolutions, boundary disputes or regime change is seriously under-researched. Productive examples illustrating this potential are Crampton's (2006) work on the role of mapping in the inquiry at the end of World War I and Campbell's (1999) consideration of mapping in the Dayton Peace Accord after the Bosnian conflict. The role of maps in navigation and travel is also clearly amenable to this kind of treatment. Here map studies could usefully draw on the experience of mobilities researchers with their focus on the contingent and relational ways in which space is produced through movement. The iconic power of mapping has also been an important force in the progress of intellectual decisions, with visualization at times coming to represent change in intellectual fashion, and at times being strongly influential in changing ways of understanding ideas in many different disciplines. In geography for example, two of the authors are identifying the 'Maps that Matter', charting the ways in which ideas come to be embodied in map form and how this has a lasting impact ion the world of ideas.

The Rhythms of Mapping

Map studies could also focus on the shape of the patterns of mapping in time–space using the notion of rhythm analysis (developed, in part, by Lefebvre 2004). This theoretical perspective is beginning to pick up traction in human geography, because as Edensor and Holloway (2008) argue '[i]t foregrounds the processual, dynamic and complexity of both space and time, and their imbrication with each other.... rhythmanalysis can highlight the experience of both mobility and situatedness, and the ways in which they are blended'. The rhythms of how mapping appears and disappears in everyday activities could be a productive area to research, for example, the meanings of the repeating nightly viewing of the weather map on television, always subtly different, but reassuringly the same. The extent to which mapping always depicts novelty, bringing possible futures into the present and offering alternatives, itself has a temporality, frequency and spatiallity.

Willim (2007: 8) also argues for a more temporally dynamic approach to the analysis of mapping software, noting: [t]he uses of these more dynamic technologies transform social and cultural patterns and processes. The software-based map of GPS-devices represent space not only as distances and spatial relations but also as rhythmic patterns. These technologies may combine spatial and temporal representations in new ways which highlights human experience of the spatial as something also temporal.

Memories of the Moments of Mapping

Mapping has always evoked memories, leaving traces behind of its reading that resonate in the everyday experience of individuals in different societies. Anthropological approaches to mapping argue strongly that these traces play important but understated roles in the construction of identities, in senses of place and in practical wayfinding skills (Ingold 2000). Memories of paper mapping have been captured in narrative. The digital transition affords new research possibilities for investigating these traces of past practice. What we see as a stable map interface on our screens is really a provisional instantiation of algorithms and data, fundamentally ephemeral and unstable, made-of-the-moment and disappearing as quickly as electrons are switched and pixels fade. These fleeting map interfaces, that emerge from software spaces, leave new kinds of traces of their presence in the world, a pattern memory of their creation preserved in automatically generated logs of the executing code. These logs can themselves be rendered visually, as maps of map memories revealing when and where people are mapping their worlds. As an example that illustrates, in a rudimentary fashion, the potential of these map memories is the 'heatmap' created by Fisher (2007) showing the differential interest levels of users of Microsoft's Virtual Earth mapping systems. The previously apparently fixed map interface can itself be charted as the memories embedded in its construction are themselves also available: for example, the explosive growth of OpenStreetMap is mapped as an animation, made up of individual mapping stories brought together into a moving set of mobile memories.

The degree to which significant moments of mapping are automatically captured in memories of map use and construction needs to be researched. This empirical work would inevitably have serious ethical implications because of the risks that these memories reveal much more than intended. It also seems likely that the nation state and corporations will be interested in the surveillant potential of individual logs of geographical search and online mapping. The mundane, yet intimate, scope of tracking of social lives from our moments of mapping is part of a wider concern that the world of code does not forget.

Mapping Ourselves – Moments in Academic Practices

As an introspective moment, map studies could explore how academics, including geographers, deploy maps in their everyday praxis, in university laboratories, their offices and lecture halls. Ongoing questioning of the relation between academic geography and the map could be a productive area to research, leading to a more critical geography of cartography, exploring more than simply publications and curriculae. It can be argued that there has been disappointingly little development in terms of progressive and creative *use* of maps by human geographers in their researches; Perkins (2004: 385) laments: '[d]espite arguments for a social cartography employing visualizations to destabilize accepted categories most geographers prefer to write theory rather than employ critical visualization'. The humanistic cartography of Danny Dorling is a notable exception to this. Dorling (2005) has argued for socially informed mapping to educate the next generation of geographers and also to influence public policy by more effectively and creatively highlighting the extent of social inequalities across space; '[m]aps are powerful images', acknowledges Dorling (1998: 287), but this can be exploited in a progressive way, '[f]or people who want to change the way we think about the world, changing our maps is often a necessary first step'. Map studies needs to explore these educative moments of mapping in schools and universities.

Creative Moments

A common current in post-structural thought emphasizes that the world may be better theorized as a series of interlinked and constantly changing flows, as a network of possibilities, as a series of bounded possibilities in which change is the only constant and where immanence comes to replace essence (Massey 2005). Map studies needs to create new ways of mapping this context. We live in a time of unprecedented mapping possibilities, in which more people than ever before are engaging in mapping, making their own maps and deploying mapping in novel ways. Artists are deploying the map more than ever before to explore our relationship to the world. Writers use cartographic metaphors to express many different ideas about place. Filmmakers constantly return to mapping as a motif for the human condition. But this mass everyday explosion of mapping is largely taking place outside of the world of map studies. We argue that the creative possibilities of all this new mapping ought to inform our studies too, and that we ought not to separate the analytical from the creative. People studying maps in creative ways need to be more creative in their mapping activities as well. The world is changing and the way we understand these changes is itself making new worlds. Mapping is part of this process: maps are products of the world and they produce the world. Such changes demand a new manifesto – new ways of thinking, researching and creating maps. For too long, much mapmaking and research has replicated old certainties, focusing on areas, scales and themes, deploying rather tired existing ways of imagining the world and simply applying these to interactive, animated and multimediated contexts, instead of exploring the full potential of new contexts, styles and technologies. As we have argued in this chapter, and as the various chapters in this volume demonstrate, rethinking the modes, methods and moments of maps offers a myriad of new, productive ways to progress cartographic theory and praxis.

As we have collectively argued and illustrated, alternatives need to be made and worked through that push cartography beyond the pursuit of refining itself as a set of ontic knowledges. Our arguments in this concluding chapter have accordingly highlighted *what* aspects of these changing intellectual landscapes may be particularly worthy of attention, identifying some possible ways forward, flagging up some of the many possible options in *how* the new terrains may be studied, and trying to contextualize this manifesto by stressing that all research needs to be situated, placed and timed. Research and rethinking are both processes, and although in the words of the song, the future's not ours to see, mapping has always been particularly good at bringing it home, offering a route through the infinity of possible outcomes. So to conclude this narrative demands a call for action – a new manifesto: rethink and remake your map studies and practice!

THINKING ABOUT MAPS

Given the long history of mapmaking and its scientific and scholarly traditions one might expect the study of cartography and mapping theory to be relatively moribund pursuits with long established and static ways of thinking about and creating maps. This, however, could not be further from the truth. As historians of cartography have amply demonstrated, cartographic theory and praxis have varied enormously across time and space, and especially in recent years. As conceptions and philosophies of space and scientific endeavour have shifted so has how people come to know and map the world.

Philosophical thought concerning the nature of maps is of importance because it dictates how we think about, produce and use maps; it shapes our assumptions about how we can know and measure the world, how maps work, their techniques, aesthetics, ethics, ideology, what they tell us about the world, the work they do in the world, and our capacity as humans to engage in mapping. Mapping is epistemological but also deeply ontological – it is both a way of thinking about the world, offering a framework for knowledge, and a set of assertions about the world itself. This philosophical distinction between the nature of the knowledge claims that mapping is able to make, and the status of the practice and artefact itself, is intellectually fundamental to any thinking about mapping.

In this opening chapter we explore the philosophical terrain of contemporary cartography, setting out some of the reasons as to why there is a diverse constellation of map theories vying for attention and charting some significant ways in which maps have been recently theorized. It is certainly the case that maps are enjoying something of a renaissance in terms of their popularity, particularly given the various new means of production and distribution. New mapping technologies have gained the attention of industry, government and to some extent the general public keen to capitalize on the growing power, richness and flexibility of maps as organizational tools, modes of analysis and, above all, compelling visual images with rhetorical power. It is also the case that maps have become the centre of attention for a diverse range of scholars from across the humanities and social sciences interested in maps in and of themselves and how maps can ontologically and epistemologically inform other visual and representational modes of knowing and praxis. From a scientific perspective, a growing number of researchers in computer science and engineering are considering aspects of automation of design, algorithmic efficiency, visualization technology and human interaction in map production and consumption.

These initiatives have ensured that mapping theory over the past twenty years has enjoyed a productive period of philosophical and practical development and reflection. Rather than be exhaustive, our aim is to demonstrate the vitality of present thinking and practice, drawing widely from the literature and signposting relevant contributions among the chapters that follow. We start our discussion by first considering the dimensions across which philosophical differences are constituted. We then detail how maps have been theorized from within a representational approach, followed by an examination of the ontological and epistemological challenges of post-representational conceptions of mapping.

DIMENSIONS ACROSS WHICH MAP THEORY IS CONSTITUTED

A useful way of starting to understand how and why map theory varies is to explore some of the dimensions across which philosophical debate is made. Table illustrates some important binary distinctions that strongly influence views on the epistemological and ontological status of mapping: judging a philosophy against these distinctions provides an often unspoken set of rules for knowing the world, or in our case, for arguing about the status of mapping. These distinctions are clearly related to each other. An emphasis upon the map as representation, for example, is also often strongly associated with the quest for general explanation, with a progressive search for order, with Cartesian distinctions between the map and the territory it claims to represent, with rationality, and indeed with the very act of setting up dualistic categories. By exploring how these dimensions work we can begin to rethink mapping and explain the complex variety of approaches described later in this book.

The mind–body distinction is often a fundamental influence on how people think about the world. If the mind is conceptualized as separate from the body then instrumental reason becomes possible: the map can be separated from the messy and subjective contingencies that flow from an embodied view of mapping. As such, science and reason become possible and a god-like view from nowhere can represent the world in an objective fashion, like a uniform topographic survey. On the other hand assuming a unity of mind and body and emphasizing the idea of embodied knowing focuses attention on different, more hybrid and subjective qualities of mapping, rendering problematic distinctions between the observer and observed.

Table: Rules for knowing the world: binary opposites around which ideas coalesce

Mind	***Body***	***Structure***	***Agency***
Empirical	Theoretical	Process	Form
Absolute	Relative	Production	Consumption
Nomothetic	Ideographic	Representation	Practice
Ideological	Material	Functional	Symbolic
Subjective	Objective	Immutable	Fluid
Essence	Immanence	Text	Context
Static	Becoming	Map	Territory

The question of whether geographic knowledge is unique or whether the world might be subject to more general theorizing also has fundamental implications for mapping. An ideographic emphasis on uniqueness has frequently pervaded theorizing about mapping in the history of cartography: if each map were different, and described a unique place, searching for general principles that might govern design, or explain use would be doomed to fail. Instead, mapping becomes the ultimate expression of descriptive endeavour, an empirical technique for documenting difference. Artistic approaches to mapping that privilege the subjective may be strongly compatible with this kind of interpretation. On the other hand a more nomothetic approach, which emphasizes laws and denies idiosyncratic difference risks reifying artificially theorized models or generalizations while at the same time offering the possibility of scientific universalization. Many of the approaches described in the chapters by Goodchild and Gartner in this volume subscribe to this quest for order. Debate continues around the nature of map generalization and whether mapping is holistic or fragmentary, stochastic or regular, invariant or contingent, natural or cultural, objective or subjective, functional or symbolic, and so on. It is clear, however, that since World War II a number of different scientific orthodoxies have pervaded the world of Western academic cartographic research which almost all trade on the notion of searching for a common, universal approach. Yet, paradoxically, everyday ideas of geography and mapping as ideographic and empirical survive.

As we examine in detail later in the chapter, the idea of viewing maps as texts, discourses or practices emerged in the late 1980s, in stark opposition to the more practical and technologically driven search for generalization. These new theoretical ways of understanding mapping often emphasized the discursive power of the medium, stressing deconstruction, and the social and cultural work that cartography achieves. Here, the power of mapping becomes a more important consideration than the empirical search for verifiable generalization, and the chapters in this volume by Crampton, Harris and Hazen, and Propen consider some of these alternative approaches.

Structural explanations of the significance of mapping have also strongly influenced understandings of maps. Insights drawn might stem from class relations, from cultural practice, from psychoanalysis, or linguistics: for example, semiotic approaches to mapping have been a powerful and influential way of approaching the medium and its messages for academic researchers. There is an ongoing debate in relation to mapping over how the agency of an individual might be reconciled with this kind of approach, given that structural approaches often posit fundamental and inevitable forces underpinning all maps. There is also a continuing debate over the philosophical basis of the structural critique. For example, is it grounded in a materialist view of the world, or in a more ideological reading of the human condition.

The distinction between forces producing the world and the forces consuming it also has a strong resonance in philosophical debates around mapping. The cultural turn in academic geography encouraged a growing emphasis on the contexts in which maps operate, encouraging a shift away from theorizing about production and towards philosophies of mapping grounded in consumption. Here, the map reader becomes as important as the mapmaker. Technological change that reduced the significance of barriers to accessing data, and the democratization of cartographic practice have also encouraged this changed emphasis. Associated with this shift has been the increasingly announced drift towards poststructuralist ways of knowing the world, which distrust all-encompassing knowledge claims. Instead of a belief in absolute space, or a socially constructed world, an alternative way of understanding mapping has emphasized relativity and contingency in a universe where notions of reality come to be replaced by simulation and in which the play of images replaces visual work, or in which speed of change itself gains agency.

REPRESENTATIONAL CARTOGRAPHY

It is usually accepted that cartography as a scientific endeavour and industry seeks to represent as faithfully as possible the spatial arrangements of phenomena on the surface of the earth. The science of cartography aims to accurately capture relevant features and their spatial relations and to re-present a scaled abstraction of that through the medium of a map. Maps seek to be truth documents; they represent the world as it really is with a known degree of precision. Cartography as an academic and scientific pursuit then largely consists of theorizing how best to represent and communicate that truth.

This quest for producing truth documents has been the preoccupation for Western cartographers since the late Middle Ages, and especially with the need for accurate maps with respect to navigation, fighting wars and regulating property ownership. It was only in the 1950s, however, that the first sustained attempts began to emerge in the US to reposition and remould academic cartography as an entirely scientific pursuit. Up until then the history of cartography was a story of progress. Over time maps had become more and more precise, cartographic knowledge improved, and implicitly it was assumed that everything could be known and mapped within a Cartesian framework. The artefact and individual innovation were what mattered. Space, following Kant, became conceived as a container with an explicit geometry that was filled with people and things, and cartography sought to represent that geometry. Scientific principles of collecting and mapping data emerged, but cartography was often seen as much of an art as a science, the product of the individual skill and eye of the cartographer. Mapping science was practical and applied and numerous small advances built a discipline.

In the latter part of the twentieth century, US scholar Arthur Robinson and his collaborators sought to re-cast cartography, focusing in particular on systematically detailing map design principles with the map user in mind. His aim was to create a science of cartography that would produce what he termed 'map effectiveness' – that is, maps that capture and portray relevant information in a way that the map reader can analyse and interpret. Robinson suggested that an instrumental approach to mapping grounded in experimental psychology might be the best way for cartography to gain intellectual respectability and develop a rigorously derived and empirically tested body of generalizations appropriate for growing the new subject scientifically. Robinson adopted a view of the mind as an information-processing device. Drawing upon Claude Shannon's work in information theory, complexity of meaning was simplified into an approach focusing on input, transfer and output of information about the world. Social context was deemed to be irrelevant; the world existed independent of the observer and maps sought only to map the world. The cartographer was separate from the user and optimal maps could be produced to meet different needs.

The aims of the cartographer were normative – to reduce error in the representation and to increase map effectiveness through good design. Research thus sought to improve map designs by carefully controlled scientific experimentation that focused on issues such as how to represent location, direction and distance; how to select information; how best to symbolize these data; how to combine these symbols together; and what kind of map to publish. Framed by an empiricist ideology, the research agenda of cartography then was to reduce signal distortion in the communication of data to users. Art and beauty had no place in this functional cartographic universe.

Out of this context in the late 1960s and 1970s emerged an increasingly sophisticated series of attempts to develop and position cartographic communi-cation models as the dominant theoretical framework to direct academic research. Communication models encouraged researchers to look beyond a functional analysis of map design, exploring filters that might hinder the encoding and decoding of spatial information. For researchers such as Grant Head (1984) or Hansgeorg Schlichtmann (1979) the map artefact became the focus of study, with an emphasis on the semiotic power of the map as opposed to its functional capacity, while Christopher Board (1981) showed how the map could be conceived as a conceptual, as well as a functional, model of the world. As models of cartographic communication multiplied so attention also increasingly focused on the map reader, with cognitive research seeking to understand how maps worked, in the sense of how readers interpreted and employed the knowledge maps sought to convey. Drawing on behavioural geography, it was assumed that map reading depended in large part upon cognitive structures and processes and research sought to understand how people came to know the world around them and how they made choices and decisions based on that knowledge. This approach is exemplified in the work of Reginald Golledge (1999), Robert Lloyd (2005) and Cynthia Brewer. Here the map user is conceived as an apolitical recipient of knowledge and the cartographer as a technician striving to deliver spatially precise, value-free representations that were the product of carefully controlled laboratory-based experiments that gradually and incrementally improved cartographic knowledge and praxis. Most research investigated the filters in the centre of this system concerned with the cartographers' design practice, and the initial stages of readers extracting information from the map. Little work addressed either what should be mapped or how mapping was employed socially because this was beyond the philosophical remit for valid research.

Other strands of scientific research into mapping emphasized the technologies that might be employed. Waldo Tobler's (1976) analytical cartography emerged in the early 1970s, offering a purely mathematical way of knowing the world, and laying the foundations for the emergence of geographic information science. This analytical approach sought progress through the application of mathematical models and the subsequent application of technology so as to create new conceptual bases for mapping the world. Over time, conceptual and technically driven developments in computer graphics, computation and user interfaces have begun to fundamentally transmute the role of the map from a finished product to a situation where the map is displayed within a visual toolbox to be used interactively for exploratory data analysis. This changing conceptualization of the map is at the heart of the emerging field of geovisualization, which in the last decade or so has been one of the leading areas of applied cartographic research. Although distinctly positivist epistemologies underlie most of the geovisualization research, some have tried to open up the scope of visualization in more politically progressive directions, for example, Craine and Aitken's chapter in this volume, which considers the emotional energy latent in cinematic qualities of maps, and Kwan's (2007) work in fusing geospatial technologies with feminist theory to map affect and emotional geographies.

In other contexts different theoretical positions were adopted. For example, the French disciplinary tradition was much less influenced by Robinsonian functionalism and empirical research. Semiotic approaches were much more influential in this context, and may be traced back to the influential theories of Jacques Bertin. In 1967 Bertin derived from first principles a set of visual variables that might be manipulated by designers concerned with the effective design of mapping and other visualizations.

By the mid 1980s the cartographic communication model as an organizing framework for academic research was beginning to wane. Technological changes rendered problematic a single authoritative view of the world at a time when data were becoming much more readily available, and when technologies for the manipulation and dissemination of mapping were also being significantly changed. Users could become mappers and many possible mappings could be made. Digital mapping technologies separated display from printing and removed the constraint of fixed specifications. GIS increasingly supplanted many technical aspects of cartographic compilation and production. Digital position, elevation and attribute data could be captured from remotely sensed sources, and easily stored and manipulated in a digital form. Imagery could be generated to provide frequent updates of changing contexts. Maps could become animated. From the late 1990s the Internet has allowed maps to be evermore widely shared and disseminated at low cost. Mapping needed to be understood as much more of a process than was possible in communication models.

In the face of these profound challenges a second dominant approach to mapping research had replaced cartographic communication by the mid 1990s as the scientific orthodoxy. The linear inevitability of communication was supplanted by a multifaceted and multilayered merging of cognitive and semiotic approaches, centred on representational theory, and strongly influenced by the work of Alan MacEachren (1995). Articulating ideas grounded in Peircean semiotics, this approach recognized the need for a much less literal and functional positioning of maps. The iconic diagrammatic description of this approach is the notion of 'cartography cubed'. The dimensions of interactivity, the kind of knowledge, and the social nature of the process show the three key ways in which scientific understanding has been repositioned. Mapping can now be investigated as collaborative, the social context beyond map reading per se can be charted, and the process of knowing explored. And mapping is one of many kinds of visualization. However, mapping is still about revealing truth through a scientific approach reliant upon Western ways of seeing and upon technologies of vision; it still depends upon scientific experimentation and a representational view of the world.

POST-REPRESENTATIONAL CARTOGRAPHY

Despite the obvious advances of the various social constructivist approaches in rethinking maps, more recent work has sought to further refine cartographic thought and to construct post-representational theories of mapping. Here, scholars are concerned that the critique developed by Harley and others did not go far enough in rethinking the ontological bases for cartography, which for them has too long been straitjacketed by representational thinking. As Denis Wood (1993) and Jeremy Crampton (2003) outline, Harley's application of Foucault to cartography is limited. Harley's observations, although opening a new view onto cartography, stopped short of following Foucault's line of inquiry to its logical conclusion. Instead, Crampton (2003: 7) argues that Harley's writings 'remained mired in the modernist conception of maps as documents charged with "confessing" the truth of the landscape'. In other words, Harley believed that the truth of the landscape could still be revealed if one took account of the ideology inherent in the representation. The problem was not the map per se, but 'the bad things people *did* with maps' (Wood 1993: 50, original emphasis); the map conveys an inherent truth as the map remains ideologically neutral, with ideology bound to the subject of the map and not the map itself. Harley's strategy was then to identify the politics of representation in order to circumnavigate them (to reveal the truth lurking underneath), not fully appreciating, as with Foucault's observations, that there is no escaping the entangling of power/knowledge. Crampton's solution to the limitations of Harley's social constructivist thinking is to extend the use of Foucault and to draw on the ideas of Heidegger and other critical cartographers such as Edney (1993).

In short, Crampton (2003: 7) outlines a 'non-confessional understanding of spatial representation' wherein maps instead of 'being interpreted as objects at a distance from the world, regarding that world from nowhere, that they be understood as being in the world, as open to the disclosure of things'. Such a shift, Crampton argues, necessitates a move from understanding cartography as a set of ontic knowledges to examining its ontological terms. Ontic knowledge consists of the examination of how a topic should proceed from within its own framework where the ontological assumptions about how the world can be known and measured are implicitly secure and beyond doubt (Crampton 2003). In other words, there is a core foundational knowledge – a taken for granted ontology – that unquestioningly underpins ontic knowledge.

With respect to cartography this foundational ontology is that the world can be objectively and truthfully mapped using scientific techniques that capture and display spatial information. Cartography in these terms is purely technical and develops by asking self-referential, procedural questions of itself that aim to refine and improve how maps are designed and communicate. In these terms a book like Robinson *et al.* (1995) is a technical manual that does not question the ontological assumptions of the form of mapping advocated, rather it is a 'how to do "proper" cartography' book that in itself perpetuates the security of cartography's ontic knowledge. In this sense, Harley's questioning of maps is also ontical, as his project sought to highlight the ideology inherent in maps rather than to question the project of mapping per se; 'it provided an epistemological avenue into the map, but still left open the question of the ontology of the map' (Crampton 2003: 90). In contrast, Crampton details that examining cartography ontologically consists of questioning the project of cartography itself.

Such a view leads to Crampton, following Edney (1993), to argue for the development of a non-progressivist history of cartography; the development of a historical ontology that rather than being teleological (wherein a monolithic view of the history of cartographic practices is adopted that sees cartography on a single path leading to more and more complete, accurate and truthful maps) is contingent and relational (wherein mapping – and truth – is seen as contingent on the social, cultural and technical relations at particular times and places). Maps from this perspective are historical products operating within 'a certain horizon of possibilities' (Crampton 2003: 51). It thus follows that maps created in the present are products of the here-and-now, no better than maps of previous generations, but rather different to them. Defining a map is dependent on when and where the map was created, as what constitutes a map has changed over time. For Crampton (2003: 51) this means that a politics of mapping should move beyond a 'critique of existing maps' to consist of 'a more sweeping project of examining and breaking through the boundaries on how maps are, and our projects and practices with them'; it is about exploring the 'being of maps'; how maps are conceptually framed in order to make sense of the world. Several other cartographic theorists have been following similar lines of enquiry to Crampton in seeking to transfer map theory from ontic knowledge to ontology and it is to them that we now turn.

Maps as Inscriptions

John Pickles (2004) has sought to extend cartographic theory beyond ontic status by conceiving of maps as inscriptions as opposed to representations or constructions. His work focuses on 'the work that maps do, how they act to shape our understanding of the world, and how they code that world'. As such his aim is to chart the 'practices, institutions and discourses' of maps and their social roles within historical, social and political contexts using a poststructural framework that understands maps as complex, multivocal and contested, and which rejects the notion of some 'truth' that can be uncovered by exposing ideological intent. Pickles' detailed argument unpicks the science of representation, calling for a post-representational cartography that understands maps not as mirrors of nature, but as producers of nature. To paraphrase Heisenberg (1959, cited in Pickles 2004), Pickles argues that cartography does not simply describe and explain the world; it is part of the interplay between the world and ourselves; it describes the world as exposed to our method of questioning.

For Pickles, maps work neither denotatively (shaped by the cartographic representation, labelling, embedded with other material such as explanatory text, etc.) or connotatively (what the mapper brings to the representation in terms of skills, knowledges, etc.) but as a fusion of the two. Pickles thus proposes a hermeneutic approach that interprets maps as unstable and complex texts, texts that are not authored or read in simple ways. Rather than a determinate reading of the power of maps that seeks to uncover in a literal sense the authorial and ideological intent of a map (who made the map and for wha purpose), Pickles expresses caution in fixing responsibility in such a manner, recognizing the multiple, institutional and contextual nature of mapping. Similarly, the power of maps is diffuse, reliant on actors embedded in contexts to mobilize thei *potential* effects: 'All texts are... embedded within chains o signification: meaning is dialogic, polyphonic and multivocal - open to, and demanding of us, a process of ceaseles contextualization and recontextualization'.

Alongside a hermeneutic analysis of maps, Pickles propose that a post-representational cartography consists of the writin of denaturalized histories of cartography and the production de-ontologized cartography. Denatural-ized histories reveal th historicizing and contextualizing conditions that have shape cartographic practices to 'explore the ways in which particula machines, disciplines, styles of reasoning, conceptual system bodies of knowledge, social actors of different scales... and forth, have been aligned at particular times and particula places'. In other words, they consist of genealogies of ho cartography has been naturalized and institutionalized acro space and time as particular forms of scientific practices a knowledge. A de-ontologized cartography is on the one ha about accepting counter-mappings as having equal ontologic status as scientific cartographic, and on the other, deconstructing, reading differently, and reconfiguring scientific cartography.

Maps as Propositions

Like Pickles, Crampton and others, Wood and Fels (2008) extend the notion of a map as social construction to argue that the map itself, its very make-up and construction – its self-presentation and design, its symbol set and categorisation, its attendant text and supporting discourse – is ideologically loaded to convey particular messages.

A map does not simply represent the world; it produces the world. They argue that maps produce the world by making propositions that are placed in the space of the map. Maps achieve their work by exclaiming such propositions and Wood and Fels define this process as one of 'posting' information on map. Posting is the means by which an attribute is recognized as valid (e.g. some class of the natural world) and is spatialized. It is the means by which the *nature* of maps (is – category) and the nature of *maps* (there – sign) conjoin to create a unified spatial ontology (this is there). However, the map extends beyond spatial ontology by enabling higher order propositions (this is there and *therefore it is also*; Wood and Fels 2008) to link things in places into a relational grid.

Wood and Fels argue that the power of this spatial propositional framework is affirmed through its call to authority – by being an objective reference object that is prescriptive not descriptive. So the map produces and reaffirms territory rather than just describing it. Authority is conveyed through what they term the paramap. A paramap is the combination of perimap and epimap. The perimap consists of the production surrounding a map: the quality of the paper, the professionalism of the design, the title, legend, scale, cartouches, its presentation and so on. The epimap consists of the discourse circulating a map designed to shape its reception: advertisements, letters to reviewers, endorsements, lectures, articles, etc. Together, the perimap and epimap work to position the map in a certain way and to lend it the authority to do work in the world.

Because maps are prescriptive systems of propositions, Wood and Fels contend that map creation should not solely be about presenting information through attractive spatial representations as advocated by the majority of cartographic textbooks (which borrow heavily from graphic design traditions). Instead they suggest map design should be about the 'construction of meaning as a basis for action'. They propose turning to cognitive linguistics to rethink map design as a form of 'cognitive cartographics'. Cognitive linguistics examines the ways in which words activate neural assemblages and open up 'thinking spaces' in the mind within which meaning is constructed by linking present information with past knowledge. They contend that maps perform like words, by firing up thinking spaces. Employing cognitive cartographics, they suggest, will create a non-representational approach to map design focused on the construction of meaning rather than graphic design and the nature of signs. It will also enable cartographic theory to move beyond the compartmentalized thinking that has divided mapmaking from map use by providing a more holistic framework. In other words, both map design and map reading can be understood through a cognitive cartographics framework. These ideas are developed in Krygier and Wood's chapter in this volume.

Maps as Immutable Mobiles and Actants

In his book *Science in Action* Bruno Latour (1987) used the example of cartography to explore how the cultures and mechanisms involved in production of Western scientific knowledge gained their power and authority to make truth claims about the world that in turn are employed to do work in the world. He cogently argued that the assemblage of cartographic theory, mapping technologies, and disciplinary regimes of trade and service (e.g. sea captains all taught the same principles and practices of surveying, recording and bringing back spatial data) worked together to enable information from distant places to be accumulated in a cyclical and systematic fashion and for maps to enable appropriate action at a distance (maps informed their readers as to local conditions and guided their safe navigation).

As the scientific basis of mapmaking and map use became conventionalized, Latour argues that maps increasingly took on the status of immutable mobiles. That is, the mechanisms used to generate cartographic information and the form maps took (in terms of scale, legend, symbols, projection, etc.) became familiar and standardized through protocols so that the map became a stable, combinable and transferable form of knowledge that is portable across space and time. As such, a map produced in South America by Argentinian cartographers is decipherable to someone from another country because it shares common principles that render it legible. Moreover, spatial data transported from South America in the form of latitude and longitude can be used to update charts of the area or be combined with other information, despite the fact that the cartographer is unlikely to have ever visited the area they are mapping.

Mapping then is seemingly transformed into a 'universal' scientific practice and maps become mobile and immutable artefacts through which the world can be known and a vehicle through which spatial knowledge can be transported into new contexts. What is mapped, how it is mapped, and the power of maps is the result of Western science's ability to set the parameters and to dominate the debate about legitimate forms of knowledge. As Latour notes, however, cartographic theory and praxis is seemingly immutable in nature because it disciplines its practitioners and silences other local mapping knowledges. And yet, immutable Western cartographic practice is itself similarly the product of localized practices that are deemed appropriate within a limited circle of practitioners and mapping agencies, who exercise powerful claims to scientific objectivity and truth. The immutability of maps is then at one level a powerful illusion, but one that readily does work in the world.

Latour contends that the immutability, combinability and mobility of maps allowed exploration, trade and ultimately colonialism to develop by allowing control to be exerted from afar and knowledges about new territories to be effectively transported globally. Maps became a vital part in the cycle of knowledge accumulation that allowed explorers to '*bring* the lands *back with them*' and to successfully send others in their footsteps. Latour thus argues that the European cartographers of the Renaissance produced centres of calculation (key sites of cartographic practice) that came to dominate the world. In so doing, maps he suggests do not simply represent space at a particular time, but produce new spaces – times. Maps open up new possibilities – such as international trade and territorial conquest – and thus create new geographies and histories.

To understand maps then, Latour suggests that it is necessary to unpick the cultures, technologies and mechanics of how a particular form of mapping came to gain immutability and mobility to reveal its contingencies and relationalities. Following on from his work, the development of Actor-Network Theory (ANT) in science studies has provided a framework for considering how maps work in concert with other actants and actors to transform the world. ANT involves the tracing out of the context and instruments of mapping – its assemblage – not just cartographic praxis. For example, understanding the road system, Latour argues, cannot be fully realized by looking at infrastructure and vehicles alone, it also needs to consider civil engineering, plans of roads, standards for signage, garages, mechanics, drivers, political lobbying, funding, spare parts and so on.

Maps do not have meaning or action on their own; they are part of an assemblage of people, discursive processes and material things. They are deployed in an actor-network of practices rather than existing as de-corporalized, a priori, non-ideological knowledge objects. ANT then seeks to provide a broader and richer understanding of the creation of maps through particular actor-networks and the use of maps as actants within various actor-networks (e.g. land conservation) by considering the diverse, day-to-day practices of, and the interactions and the circulation of ideas and power between, various actors (people, texts, objects and money) (Perkins 2006). In so doing, ANT identifies the nature of 'boundary objects' (objects such as technical standards that enable the sharing of information across networks), 'centres of calculation' (locations such as mapping agencies where observations are accumulated, synthesized and analysed), 'inscription devices' (technical artefacts that record and translate information such as tables of coordinates or satellite imagery), 'obligatory points of passage' (a site in a network that exerts control and influence such as government department), 'programs of action' (the resources required for an actor to perform certain roles) and 'trials by strength' (how competing visions and processes within the network compete for superiority) (cf. Martin 2000). From this perspective, the stories of mapping always need to be con-sidered as historically contingent actor-networks; as timed, placed, cultured and negotiated; a Web of interacting possibilities in which the world is complex and nothing is inevitable. The focus shifts from what the map represents to how it is produced and how it produces work in the world (Perkins 2006).

From Ontology to Ontogenesis

In recent years, there has been a move towards considering cartography from a relational perspective, treating maps not as unified representations but as constellations of ongoing processes. Here it is recognized that maps are produced and used through multiple sets of practices. Spatial data are surveyed, processed and cleaned; geometric shapes are drafted, revised, updated, copied, digitized and scanned; information is selected for inclusion, generalized and symbolized. A map is then worked upon by the world and does work in the world. It might be folded or rolled, converted to another file format, embedded in other media; it might be packaged, marketed, sold, bought, used, stored, collected, re-used, thrown away or recycled; it might be read in different ways in different contexts; it might be employed to plan a journey, make money, play a game or teach moral values. Mapmaking and map use are understood as processual in nature, being both embodied and dynamic.

Mapping can then be conceptualized as a suite of cultural practices involving action and affects. This kind of approach reflects a philosophical shift towards performance and mobility and away from essence and material stability. This rethinking of cartography is supported by historical and contemporary work. Researchers concerned with historical contexts increasingly stress the interplay between place, times, actions and ideas. Mapping in different cultures reflects multiple traditions including an internal or cognitive set of behaviours involving thinking about space; a material culture in which mapping is recorded as an artefact or object; and a performance tradition where space may be enacted through gesture, ritual, song, speech dance or poetry. In any cultural context there will be a different blend of these elements. Interpreting mapping then means considering the context in which mapping takes place; the way it is invoked as part of diverse practices to do work in the world. Instead of focusing on artefacts, aesthetics, human agency, or the politics of mapping, research focuses on how maps are constituted in and through diverse, discursive and material processes.

Arguments presently emerging in the literature extend both the notion of maps as processes and the ontological thought underpinning cartography by problematizing the ontological security enjoyed by maps. The idea that a map represents spatial truth might have been challenged and rethought in a number of different ways, but a map is nonetheless understood as a coherent, stable product – *a* map; a map has an undeniable essence that can be interrogated and from which one can derive understanding. Moreover, the maps and mapping practices maintain and reinforce dualities with respect to their conceptualization – production–consumption, author–reader, design– use, representation–practice, map–space. This position has been rejected by those adopting performative and ontogenetic understandings of mapping. Maps rather are understood as always in a state of becoming; as always mapping; as simultaneously being produced *and* consumed, authored *and* read, designed *and* used, serving as a representation *and* practice; as mutually constituting map/space in a dyadic relationship.

James Corner (1999) argues that cartographic theory has been hampered by a preoccupation to view maps in terms of what they represent and mean rather than what they do. Drawing on poststructural theory, he problematizes the conception of maps as representations that are separate and proceeding from territory. Following Baudrillard, Corner argues that a territory does not precede a map, but that space becomes territory through bounding practices that include mapping. Moreover, given that places are planned and built on the basis of maps, so that space is itself a representation of the map, the 'differentiation between the real and the representation is no longer meaningful'. Maps and territories are co-constructed. Space is constituted through mapping practices, among many others, so that maps are not a reflection of the world, but a re-creation of it; mapping activates territory.

Corner develops an understanding of maps as unfolding potential; as conduits of possibilities; as the sites of imagination and action in the world. The 'function of maps is not to depict but to enable'; 'mappings do not *represent geographies* of ideas; rather they *effect* actualization'. Mapping involves *processes* of 'gathering, working, reworking, assembling, relating, sifting,... speculating and so on... [that] allow certain sets of possibility to become actual'. In this sense, maps remake 'territory over and over again, each time with new and diverse consequences'. Corner explains that maps engender such re-territorializations because they are doubly projective: they both capture elements from the world and also project back a variety of effects through their use. As such, the agency of maps lies not in 'their reproduction or imposition, but in uncovering realities previously unseen or unimagined'. He thus suggests that cartographic research and practice need to focus on mapping actions and mapping effects and not solely on the construction of maps per se. He charts four practices of mapping – drift, layering, game-space and rhizome – to illustrate how the processes of mapping and the ongoing construction of space entwine. To take one of these, Corner (1999: 244) argues that the map acts as a rhizome because it is infinitely open with many diverse entry points and exits that enable 'a plurality of readings, uses and effects', opening up milieus to new possibilities of action. So a 'standard' topographic map sheet from the Ordnance Survey, for example, has 'multiple entryways, diverse uses and applications, infinite routes and networks, and potentially endless surfaces of engagement' that when enacted brings the world into being in new ways.

Tim Ingold (2000) also develops an approach to mapping grounded in cultural practice. He makes a distinction between mapping, mapmaking and map-use and argues that map-use (navigation) is to navigate by means of a map, plotting a course between one location to another in space. Mapping, in terms of wayfinding practices, however, consists of moving from one place to another in a region. He argues that maps that chart peoples' experiences of movement – such as sketch maps, indigenous maps – are expressions of mapping. For him, because these mappings refer to the itineraries of their inhabitants they do not detail locations in space but histories of movement that constitute place. Such movements consist of passages through vistas, rather than an abstracted Cartesian landscape and therefore encode mobility as opposed to location. As such, the resulting mappings are 'not so much representations of space as condensed histories' and therefore un-maplike. They are un-maplike because the knowledge they portray is bound to the place where they are made, unlike Western cartographic practice, which seeks to be non-indexical – that is a view from nowhere. However, as Turnbull (1989) and others have noted, the non-indexical nature of maps is an illusion – they are always a view from somewhere bound within the practices and knowledges of their makers. Western cartography, according to Ingold (2000: 203), thus 'transforms everywhere-as-region, the world as experienced by a mobile inhabitant, into everywhere-as-space, the imaginary "bird's-eye view" of a transcendent consciousness'. In so doing, people and their experiences are obliterated from the map, and the structure of the world is fixed without regard to the movements and actions of its inhabitants – 'the world it describes is not a world in the making, but one ready-made for life to occupy'; 'in the cartographic world... all is still and silent'. Maps as reminders of paths and expressions of experience, as they were conceived in the European Middle Ages, morphed into supposed representations of space through the application of scientific principles. The issue is, however, that people live in the everywhere-as-region and know as they go – they are constantly mapping as they move through places employing a form of process cartography – so there is a disconnect between Western notions of a map, and the everyday ways in which people come to know and be in the world. This leads to a paradox – the more a map 'aims to furnish a precise and comprehensive representation of reality, the less true to life this representation appears'. For Ingold, we need to simultaneously understand and value the process cartography of mapping and critique and reform representational modes of cartography.

Vincent Del Casino and Stephen Hanna (2005) draw on poststructural theory, and in particular the ideas of Deleuze and Guattari and Judith Butler, to argue that maps are in a constant state of becoming; that they are 'mobile subjects' whose meaning emerges through socio-spatial practices of use that mutate with context and is contested and intertextual. For them the map is not fixed at the moment of initial construction, but is in constant modification where each encounter with the map produces new meanings and engagements with the world. Del Casino and Hanna (2005: 36) state that '[m]aps are both representations and practices... simultaneously. Neither is fully inscribed with meaning as representations nor fully acted out as practices'. In so doing, they argue that maps are not 'simply visual objects ripe for deconstruction.... Maps... are tactile, olfactory, sensed objects/subjects mediated by the multiplicity of knowledges we bring to and take from them through our everyday interactions and representational and discursive practices'. Maps and spaces co-produce each other through spatial practices to create what they term 'map spaces', wherein it is impossible to disentangle fully how the map does work in the world from how the world shapes how the map is performed – they are co-constitutive. Del Casino and Hanna (2005) illustrate their arguments by an examination of how visitors produce the historic town of Fredericksburg in Virginia, by deploying tourist maps, along with other texts and narratives (such as a guided tour), which together shape how people interact with the space and the town. They show that the real is read back into the map, making it more legible. Tourists are both consumers and producers of the map; authors and readers. Meaning emerges through action and action is shaped by meaning in a complex, recursive and intertextual performativity. The tourist map of Fredericksburg then is never complete, but is always mobile; always being produced by tourists and producing Fredericksburg.

CONCLUSION

Mapping, its theory, praxis and technologies, is a rapidly changing and exciting field of study. Intellect, capital, culture and innovation are reshaping how maps are made, used and thought about. In this book we are particularly concerned with exploring the diverse constellation of contemporary mapping theories. As we have so far demonstrated, the theories of mapping consist of a set of winding and contested journeys through philosophical and practical terrains. These journeys are far from over and the philosophical under-pinnings of maps remain a fertile ground in which to explore issues of space, representation and praxis. The chapters that follow provide detailed examinations into contemporary cartographic theory. They highlight that there are many rich ways of rethinking maps both ontologically and epistemo-logically. It is certainly not clear if any of these different modes of thought will emerge to become paradigmatic and it may be the case that we are entering a period characterized by theoretical diversity and exchange. For us, such a period will continue to be highly productive in terms of thinking through the nature and role of maps, their production and use, and the work that they do in the world. There is much rethinking yet to be done!

5

Geography of Population, Distribution, Density and Growth

The studies concerning population distribution and density assume significance for less developed countries, because in their case the forces of demographic transition have a direct bearing on the direction and pace of the process of development.

SALIENT FEATURES OF INDIAN DEMOGRAPHY

The striking features of Indian demography are as follows:

Population too large for Area

While being one of the most popular counties of the world, occupying the second place after China and accounting for 16% of the world population, India, however accounts for only 2.42% of the total world area.

Overwhelming Proportion of Rural

Population About 74% of the population lives in rural areas. This indicates a massive dependence on agriculture and other rural industries.

Fast Rate of Population Growth

Although the average annual exponential growth rate for the 1981-91 decade has dropped to 2.14% from 2.22% in 1971-81, it still remains very high. The cities or towns have registered even a higher growth. This has happened because the urban centres have expanded in area and have encroached upon the surrounding villages, as people continue to pour into urban centres in search of jobs and better living.

Declining Proportion of Women

India's population is by and large male-dominated. The proportion of women has been declining all through the twentieth century. This may be attributed more to the sociological factors which explain the low preference for the female child in the family. In the absence of proper attention, the female child falls an easy prey to diseases caused by under-nutrition. A large number of women also die during child-birth.

High Percentage of Non-workers

Only 36% of our population can be classified as worker-this includes the population below 15 years of (i.e., child labour), otherwise this figure would have been even lower. While 52.5% of the males are workers, only 20% of females work. In advanced countries, females account for as much as 40% of the workforce, reaching nearly the 50% mark in countries like Denmark, Finland, USA and Japan. In India, thus a high percentage of below 15years population (nearly 36% of the total) and low rates of labour participation among women are responsible for a high percentage of the non-working population.

Lop-sided Age Structure

About one-half of our population is less than 20 years of age. Such a large population of youth has its own social, economic and political implications.

Ethnic Diversity

Apart from the problems associated with its size, the problem of ethnic diversity with its size, the problem of ethnic diversity with which the country was characterized has also divested the Indian society of social cohesion which has affected the pace of socio-economic advancement of the country adversely. Above all, the concentration of religious minorities in the strategically located peripheral areas is also not without its social, economic and political implications.

ASPECTS OF SPATIAL DISTRIBUTION

India's population, according to the 1991 census is 846.30 million (439.23 million males and 407.07 million females). This includes the projected population of 7.72 million of Jammu and Kashmir. However the spatial distribution of population within the country is highly uneven. These contrasts are obvious even at the level of states and are further sharpened at the level of districts. The 1991 census was not held in J&K. The population projections of J&K as on March 1, 1991 made by the Standing Committee of Experts on population Projection (October 1989) is given.

Uttar Pradesh as the largest population followed by Bihar, Maharashtra, West Bengal and Andhra Pradesh in the same order. These five states together share among themselves more than one-half of the country's population. More than one-fourth of our people live in two states of Uttar Pradesh and Bihar alone. Uttar Pradesh has more people than the two largest states of Madhya Pradesh and Rajasthan. The three southern states of Kerala, Karnataka and Tamil Nadu together have just as many people as Uttar Pradesh alone. In fact, more people live in Delhi than in the state of Jammu and Kashmir or in all the union territories put together.

The uneven nature of the distribution of population becomes more evident when we try to find out as to what proportion of India's population lives in each state of the Indian Union. This may be described as the 'Index of Concentration'. This index is 16.44% for Uttar Pradesh, 0.14% for Nagaland, 0.21% for Meghalaya and 0.91 for Jammu and Kashmir. The highly corwded state of West Bengal accommodates 8.04% of the country's population, while the shares of the agriculturally developed states of Punjab and Haryana are 2.40% and 1.94% respectively.

A closer examination of the census data shows that the states of the Indian Union have an unequal share not only in population but also in area. In fact, it seems that there is little relationship between area and population. Which Madhya Pradesh is the largest state and account for about 14% of the total area of the country; it accommodates only 7.82% of the population. The two large states of Rajasthan and Andhra Pradesh together have 19% of the country's area butonly 13% of its population.

SEX RATIO

In any study of the population, the analysis of the sex composition plays a vital role. The sex composition of the population is affected by the differentials in the population is affected by the differential in the mortality conditions of males and females, sex selective migration and the sex ratio at birth.

Sex ratio is defined as the number of females per 1000 males. In India, it has generally been adverse to women. The ratio has also declined over the years except in 1981 when it slightly improved to 934 from 930. In 1991, it fell by seven points to be at 927 per thousand males. But Kerala represented a different spectrum. The state has higher number of females than males, 1,036 females for thousand males.

In the Indian context, a sex ratio of 950 and above can be considered as favourable to females. The states and union territories coming under this category besides Kerala are Himachal Pradesh (976), Andhra Pradesh (972), Goa (967), Karnataka (960), Manipur (958), Orissa (971), Tamil Nadu (974), Dadra and Nagar Haveli (952), Daman and Diu (969) and Pondicherry (979). Chandigarh accounted for the lowest number of females (790) per thousand males. For the trends of decline of the sex-ratio during previous decades.

Sex Ratio (1901-1991)

Census year	Sex Ratio
1901	972
1911	964
1921	955
1931	950
1941	945
1951	046
1961	941
1971	930
1981	934
1991	927

If we consider the sex ratio in context of specific regions, the overall picture is gloomy except for the south and western coastal areas, the Uttarakhand hill districts of Uttar Pradesh and a pocket of four districts in Himachal Pradesh along with sizeable pocket of underdeveloped areas in Madhya Pradesh and the south western coastal district of Orissa. These areas in Madhya Pradesh and Orissa are largely on female lives, conferring on them corresponding social equity and status.

AGE STRUCTURE

Age structure refers to the composition of a nation by different age groups. There are three types of age structures, viz. (i) the West European type in which children constitute less than 30 percent, and 15 percent of the population are old; (ii) population the North American type where 35-40 percent of the population are children and 10 percent, old people; and (iii) the Brazilian type with 45-55 percent of the population being children, and old people constituting only 4-8 percent of the total population. The type of age structure has a direct influence on the future of a nation, since both extremes, i.e., old age dependencies as well as young age dependency prove to be a severe burden on the economy of a country. There are different methods of analysing age composition.

Age Pyramids

Also known as age and sex pyramid, the method is commonly used. The age pyramid on its vertical axis represents age group at a regular interval of, say, 5 years, starting from 0 to 5 and ending according to the age structure of the population under study. The horizontal axis represents the total population or populations of males and females separately. Under normal situations, the number of persons in each successive year is less than the number in the preceding year; therefore the age composition represents the shape of a pyramid. The developing countries, characterized by high birth rate and high death rate, have a broad-base pyramid, while the developed countries in the last stage of demographic transition have a narrow-base age pyramid.

Age Groups

The population categoriesed into various age groups allows geographers to dra regional comparisons on choropleth maps. In general, the population is divided into three braod age groups: (a) the young, (b) the adults, (c) the old. The most popular standardized break point is 15 to 60. So, three broad age groups emerge: 0-14; 15-59, 60 and above.

Age Indices

Such ratios are calculated with the help of three age groups on a broad basis, e.g. ratio between the aged and the adults, the young and the aged and so on. Therefore numerous such ratios exist. The ratio between the adults and the young plus aged is called dependency ratio.

DEPENDENCY RATIO

The dependency ratio is computed by dividing the number of children plus old people by the number of adults and multiplying it by hundred. It is mainly governed by the age structure of the population. The Oxford Dictionary of Geography defines dependency ratio as the ratio between the number of people in a population between the ages of 15 and 64 and the dependent population: children (0-14) and elderly people (65 and over). Dependency ratio quantifies the ratio between the economically active population and the dependent population. The age-limits for dependency ratio are arbitrary in different countries of the world. Generally developing countries are characterized by higher dependency ratios owing to higher population growth and lack of employment opportunities, mainly. As per the 1991 census, the total number of persons in age group 0-14 and 60+ were 369.05 million. Such a huge population is dependent on 464.83 million people of India. The national average of dependency ratio is 794 persons. Taking the overall scenario into consideration, the North Indian states reveal a very high dependency ratio compared to the states of South India.

The lower Ganga plains of Uttar Pradesh and adjoin Bihar have extremely high dependency ration (900-974). According to the 1991 census, the lowest range (674 and below) of dependency ratio is found in Kerala and Tamil Nadu; Goa and Andaman & Nicobar Islands witness a dependency ratio of less than 674 674. As per state/union territory level, the highest value is found in Bihar (907) followed by Uttar Pradesh (905) whereas Goa has the lowest dependency ratio (556).

DENSITY OF POPULATION

A ratio of population to area may be a better measure of variation in the distribution of population. One such measure is the 'density of population', expressed as number of people per unit area, for example, a square kilometre or a hectare. However, it is a crude measure, and is referred to as the 'arithmetic density'. It is crude because the entire area of a country or a state is taken into consideration while calculating the density. In fact, the population lives only in the selected areas which are productive, rich in natural resources and accessible to man. The hilly and the rugged terrain, swampy, marshy and forested tracts as well s the areas covered by water bodies are just not suited for human habitation. Because of the limitation of the arithmetic density, densities are sometimes calculated for the rural population or agricultural population. In calculating the density, a cultivated area is considered. A ratio of population to cultivated area is described in France as 'physiological density'. This measure of density gives us an idea as to how many people are dependent on each hectare of cultivated land. It is a highly meaningful index, particularly for countries whose economies are largely dependent on agriculture.

The analysis of population density of the country discussed her is, however, based on the 'arithmetic density'-defined as the number of persons per square kilometre. The population density has gone up from 216 in 1981 to 267 persons in 1991 (excluding Assam and Jammu and Kashmir). In 1901, it was 77 persons. Thus, it implies an addition of 51 persons per square kilometre for the country. This addition in a short span of ten years is really alarming.

From among the various states, West Bengal occupied the first rank with the highest density of 767 persons per sq km. It was followed by Kerala (749), Bihar (497), Uttar Pradesh (473), Tamil Nadu (429), Punjab (403), Haryana (372), Goa (316) and Assam (286) in this order. Thus Kerala drifted to the second position during 1981-91 in terms of population density mainly due to it is controlled growth of population. However, these nine states had a density higher than the national average of 267. At the other end of the scale was Arunachal Pradesh which, among various states, had the lowest density of only 10 persons per sq km. there were eight states in the country which had a density less than 100 person's per sq km. These states included Mizoram (33), Sikkim (57), Nagaland (73), Jammu and Kashmir (76), Meghalaya (78), Manipur (82) and Himachal Pradesh (92). Thus, the states having low density were either the hill states or had a large proportion of mountainous areas.

As regards the union territories, with the exception of Andman and Nicobar islands (34), all the union territories had a higher density than the national average of 267. Delhi, with a density of 6352 persons per sq km was the most densely populated region of the country. The unions territories are mostly highly urbanized and hence display a high degree of population concentration. The sparsely populated territory of Andaman and Nicobar Islands consists of a large number of widely spread, poorly connected islands which are located at a great distance from the mainland. The ten most densely populated districts of the country include Calcutta, Chennai, Greater Mumbai, Hyderabad, Delhi, Chandigarh, Mahe, haora, Kanpur Nagar and Bangalore in this order. These districts together account for 5% of the country's total population, but, on an average, have a density of 5,791 persons/sq km. It all the districts in the country are arranged in a descending order in terms of their density and average quartile values of densities are calculated, the following are observed:

Each quartile has 107 districts (excluding the districts of Jammu and Kashmir and Assam for which data are not yet available). The first quartile districts (having densities above 522) account for 36% of the country's population and cover 12% of the country's area. On an average, these districts together have a density of 844 persons/sq km. The districts in the second quartile (having densities between 271 and 522) account for 28% of the country's population and 20% of its area. These districts together have an average density of 383 persons. The wide gap in densities between, the first and the second quartiles signifies a high degree of variability in population density from one region to another.

The third quartile districts (densities between 155 to 2700 account for about 25% of the country's population and 3% of its area. The average density for these districts works out to be 204. The districts in the fourth quartile have densities below 155 and accommodate 11% of the country's population. These districts account for as much as 35% of the country's area with an average density of 83.

CAUSES OF RAPID POPULATION GROWTH

The main reasons why population growth is rapid are as follows:

High Birth Rates and Declining Death: According to the 1991 census, birth rate in India was 30.5, while the death rate was 9.4. As a result, the survival rate has been increasing. To arrest this trend, the birth rates will have to be brought down further.

Near Universal Incidence of Marriage: According to one survey, in the 40-44 years age group, the percentage of women who never married was merely 0.55%. Because of universal marriage of women, the number of children born per couple is very large.

Early Marriage of Girls: The survey also revealed that 44% of the women is 15-19 years age-group and 90% in the 20-24 years age group are married. This implies more chances of bearing children for women in the early reproductive years-thus leading to high birth rates.

Economic Backwardness

Because of a high percentage of rural population and a high incidence of rural poverty more children considered a resource. A high infant mortality rate also encourages the poor to produce more children.

Climatic Factors

The tropical climate makes for early puberty and conservative social institutions lead to an early marriage of women.

LITERACY

Education is a key factor in socio-economic development. A reasonable level of literacy achieves the following objectives. It increases the receptivity of the population to modern ideas and improved techniques and enlarges their mental horizon. It promotes increased participation of citizens in the affairs of the country. It results in greater awareness of available opportunities and mobility of labour. It produces skilled and trained personnel needed by economy and society. It promotes science and technology and, even more importantly, a scientific outlook. It generates national and development consciousness. For the purpose of census, a person is deemed as literate if he or she can read and write any language, with understanding. In the 1991 census, the question on literacy was canvassed only for population aged seven years and above, unlike earlier censuses which took into account population of five years and above for this purpose.

The final results reveal that there has been an increase in literacy in the country. The literacy rate, according to the 1991 census, is 52.21% (64.13% for males and 39.29% for females). Kerala retained its position by being on top with a 89.81 % literacy rate in the country. Bihar stood at the bottom with a literacy rate of 38.48% with Rajasthan with a percentage of 20.44% as compared to 54.99% among the males.

The average literacy rates, however, conceal many sharp inequalities. First, and quite glaring, is the wide difference between rural and urban areas. Secondly, there is large difference between males and females. Female literacy rate was 25% below that of the male literacy rate in 1991. Thirdly, there are enormous interstate differences in literacy rates. In 1991, Kerala stood at one end with the overall literacy rate of 89.81% (male: 96.62%, female: 86.17%) and Rajasthan at the other with 38.55% (male: 54.99%, female: 20.44%). The maximum difference-that between Kerala's urban male population and Rajasthan's rural female population was 84%.

One straight forward message from these trends is that, if India continues at the present rate of growth of literacy, it will keep on adding to the number of illiterates. Earlier estimates by such a reputed source as the World Bank had suggested that if India continued at present rates, by 2000 AD, it would have the rather dubious distinction of being the home of more than half the illiterate population in the world.

IMPLICATIONS OF LOW LITERACY RATES

Such a poor performance has, of course, many serious implications. There is enough evidence now to show that high literacy-rates-especially high female literacy rates-are associated with low rates of population growth. Kerala is an outstanding example where high (especially female) literacy rates have gone hand is hand not only with low rates of growth of population, but with superior performance I terms of a number of health indicators, such as infant mortality rates, death rates of growth of population, but with superior performance in terms of a number of health indicators, such as infant mortality rates, death rates, sex ratio and so on. In sharp contrast, abysmally low rural female literacy rates are associated with both high population growth rates and poorer performance in terms of health indicators-as the case of Bihar, Rajasthan, Uttar Pradesh and Madhya Pradesh demonstrates.

PERFORMANCE OF STATES IN LITERACY

From the analysis of the performance of states in literacy during the last decade, the following points emerge-Only three states-Kerala, Tamil Nadu and Maharashtra-have crossed the 50% marks in female literacy rates. Haryana has shown the greatest improvement in terms of overall as well as female literacy rates.

Bihar shows the least progress in male, female and total literacy rates. Male-Female literacy differentials have narrowed in all states except Rajasthan. While this is encouraging, the pattern of decline is not. Thus, the states which perform the worst in terms of literacy rates-Bihar, Rajasthan, Madhya Pradesh, Uttar Pradesh and Andhra Pradesh-are also the ones which have recorded minimum improvement in the matter of male-female differentials. The states which have shown significant decline in male-female literacy differential are also the ones which have consistently had above average literacy rates for all categories-persons, males and females. Male-female differential are comparatively low in the three regions inhabited predominantly by tribal-Meghalaya, Mizoram and Nagaland.

MEASURE TO ARREST LOW LITERACY RATES

The states with low literacy rates tend to have low enrolment-retention rates among girls which depress the overall figures for these states. The most vulnerable classes (especially for girls) for non-starter and drop-outs are Scheduled Castes, Scheduled Tribes, those living in remote and backward areas and the children of recent migrants to towns. Thus, socio-economic compulsions, rather than non-availability of schools, are mainly responsible for the children keeping out of schools. The programmes like mid-day meals, free books, uniforms and stationary have had limited impact. The following steps are suggested to ensure full enrolment of the 6-14 year ago group-Lag in enrolment of girls be removed.

Overall enrolment percentage in educationally backward states is brought to the national level. Innovative measures are evolved to check the drop-out rates. Quality, relevance and effectiveness of primary education are improved. To improve literacy levels among children, the government launched 'Operation Blackboard' in 1987-88 which, according to the current norms, aims at equipping each primary and upper primary school with three reasonably large, all weather rooks; at least three teacher per school, one of them being a lady teacher; separate titles for boys and girls; adequate learning and teaching material such as maps, charts, toys and too old for work experience.

The government also provides non-formal education facilities for the children in tribal, hilly, desert and remote areas and in urban slums, where quite a number of children work. To attain higher levels of literacy among the adult population, the National Adult Education Programme was taken up in 1978. The Sixth Plan set the target of reaching 100% literacy in the 15-35 years age group. Ink1988, a National Literacy Mission was launched to impart functional literacy to the adult population in 15-35 years age group. The National Literacy Mission Campaigns are area-specific, time-bound, volunteer based, cost-effective and outcome oriented. These campaigns also aim at universal enrolment and retention of children, small family norms, immunization, maternity protection, communal harmony and environment protection. The Mission Campaigns aim to cover 345 districts by the end of the 8 Plan.

PROBLEMS ASSOCIATED WITH HIGH POPULATION GROWTH

The large population of India and its continued growth at an annual rate well above 2% has created many problems;

Scope for Decline in Death Rates

With ever increasing provision of health services, there is a scope for further decline of the death rates. If the birth rates do not show similar declines, the population growth rates will go further up.

Tendency for Rise in Proportion of Women in the Reproductive Age

According to the 1991 census, 36% of the population is below 15 years. Women in this age group will contribute to the reproductive age section in future. This will lead to increase in overall birth rates due to an ever expanding

High Birth Rate Depresses Per Capita Income

Income During 1950-51 to 1990-91 period, the national income rose by 223% (average annual rate-4.21%), but the per capita income rose by 52.8% only (average annual rate-2.23%). This is because the population rose by 223% (average annual rate-2.14%) during this period. Low rates of per capita income mean low rates of savings and of investments which depress the growth of national income as a whole.

High Birth Rates a Strain on Mother's Health and Norms Activity

This results in lower productivity of the population.

High Population Growth Means increased Pressure on Land

As the total area of the country is fixed, the rapid growth of population has increased pressure on land, especially cultivable land. In India, only 46% of the total land is available for agricultural purposes, while 70% of the population depends on agricultural land is responsible for high unemployment rates among rural people.

Inter-Regional Migration

Rapid population growth causes migration of people from denser regions like Kerala and West Bengal to less dense regions. This causes increased demands for infrastructure and civic amenities in areas which receive migrating populations.

Environmental Implications

Because of growth of population, there is an increased

demand for food, clothing, shelter, industrial and consumer goods. This creates pressure on natural resources and leads to increased use of fertilizers, pesticides, irrigation measures, machines, power etc. This coupled with rapid deforestation to clear land for human settlement, growing slums, poor sanitation, soil erosion, air and water pollution causes a great strain on our natural resources and gives way to an unsustainable mode of development. Growing concerns on environmental degradation are related to high levels of population growth.

Increasing Pressure on Civic Amenities and the Social Problems

Because of high population growth rates, and migrations in search of employment to urban areas, there is immense of employment to urban areas, there is immense pressure on public facilities like transport, hospitals, educational institutions, water supply, electricity, sanitation etc. Because of growing socio-economic disparities and large floating populations in urban areas, social problems arise, such as crime against women and the elderly, drug abuse, child delinquency, vulgar consumerism etc. Similarly, high rates of unemployment among youth, rising prices and demands for higher wages are other problems associated with high rates of population growth.

INDIA AND THE DEMOGRAPHIC TRANSITION

India entered the second stage of demographic transition mainly after 1951 when the death rates declined while the birth rates were still high. But the Indian situation showed slight deviation from the industrialized countries. In India, the decline in death rates occurred before there was a change in the basic economic structure or the consequent rise in living standards. Thus, there is no guarantee that a fall in birth rates will occur automatically. There is a high probability that in absence of deliberate efforts, it will not be so.

According to the projection of the Standing Committee of planning Commission of Population Projects, from 1986-91 onwards, the birth rates will decline faster than the death rates, thus the growth rate will show a steady decline. According to theses projections, the following trends will follow:

	19986-91	2006 AD
Birth Rate	30.9%	23%
Death Rate	10.8%	7.8%
Decadal Growth Rate	20.1%	15.2%
Annual Growth Rate	2.01%	1.52

INDIA'S POPULATION POLICY

Although family planning efforts in India started as early as 1953, it was accorded high priority only after the 1961 census which showed a population growth much higher than was expected. Following are the highlights of India's population Policy-

Policy Emphasis on Reducing Birth

The policy emphasizes on broad-based targeting and laying down of firm demographic targets.

A Voluntary and Comprehensive Family Planning Programme

The objective of population control is to be achieved by persuasion. Family Planning is viewed as an integral part of the national effort for betterment of the life of the people. The family planning programme is integrated with the health of family, especially that of women and children.

Targets for Reducing Population Growth

	Annual Growth	Birth Rate
1981-86	2.1%	33.2 per 1000
1986-90	1.9%	29.7 per 1000
1990-95	1.71%	26.7 per 1000
1996-2000	1.53 %	23.7 per 1000

Methods for Reducing Birth Rates-Cafeteria Approach: This means introducing a wide range of direct and indirect methods to select from, such as IUD, sterilization, condoms, oral pills, raising the marriage age and social pressures etc. for bringing down the birth rate.

Incentives for population control methods: These incentives include cash incentives, advance salary increment, 'green card' schemes which give preferences in housing, education and government services.

Propagation and Education: Population study has been included as a subject in schools and adult education programmes. Special steps are being taken to reach the target groups, backward areas and the urban slums.

Organisational and Research Efforts: This is a 100% centrally funded area, implemented by the states. Under this, training institutes are created which train the workers and medical personnel. Research is being undertaking in the field of demography, communications, reproductive biology and fertility control.

GOVERNMENT MEASURES TO CONTROL POPULATION THROUGH SUCCESSIVE PLANS

India realized the interrelationship between population and development from the very beginning of its development planning. The First Five Year Plan, which was launched in 1951, clearly spelt out this linkage. The plan document stated-the higher the rate of population growth, the larger the efforts needed to raise per capita living standards.

India launched its national family welfare programme as a part of its First Five Year Plan. During the first tow plans, the achievements were limited. The health infrastructure, which formed the delivery system for the family planning programme, was still developing. The choice of the contraceptives was limited to a few barrier and chemical methods, and natural methods like the rhythm method and coitus interrupters. Sterilization for males and females was still not a popular contraceptive choice.

The 1961 census showed that the population growth rate in India between 1951 and 1961 had gone up to 2% per annum as compared to only 1.2% during the previous decade. During the Third Plan period (1961-66), the pace of development of health infrastructure was therefore stepped up. The programme got a tremendous boost with the creation of a separate department of Family Planning in the Health Ministry in 1966. An extension approach was adopted, as against the 'clinic approach' of the previous two plans, to increase the outreach of services and improve awareness and knowledge about family planning among the masses.

The 1971 census was alarming as it showed an all-time high rate of population growth in the country. Several important policy decisions were taken and action initiated to give the family planning programme greater thrust and a new direction. Maternal and child health services were made part of the programme. During the Sixth Five Plan, population control was specifically mentioned as one of the plan objectives, and integrated in the twenty-point programme.

A landmark in the population policy of the country was a draft statement on Population Policy, issued in the Parliament in 1976, expressing the government's determination to control population growth. Increasing the legal age of marriage (from 15 to 18 years for girls and from 18 to 21 years for boys), freezing the population central assistance to states for development were some important decisions taken by the government following the 1976 draft population policy statement. After the Seventh Plan (1985-90) was finalized, a revised strategy was adopted for the family planning programme. It emphasized on increasing the minimum age for marriage of women, making them literate, enhancing their status by increased economic and employment opportunities, improving the health of mothers and children, greater coordination and linkages with poverty alleviation programmes and greater involvement of the NGOs in the family planning programmes.

Human Development was adopted as the ultimate goal of the Eighth Five Year Plan. Population control was listed as one of the priorities.

POPULATION PROBLEMS OF DEVELOPING COUNTRIES

This is directly linked to low productivity levels in countries like India, Pakistan, China, Myanmmar, Nepal, Indonesia, Malaysia, Philippines etc. Low productivity means slow growth which is the root cause of rapid population growth in these countries. This is the strange case with many countries having abundant natural resources which lie untapped for want of human resources. These countries in clued Brazil, Colombia, Peru, Zaire, Russian Siberia, Kazhakhastan, Uzbekistan, Turkmnistan, Krighistan and Tazhikistan.

Disproportionate Share of Young Population

This is because of improved health facilities. This younger section puts tremendous pressure on a comparatively small working population. Lack of development of secondary and tertiary sectors leaves limited employment opportunities for the skilled and the educated that move to more developed towns or to foreign countries in search of better job opportunities. This results in a distorted demographic structure in both the countries.

Undernourishment and Lack of Hygiene

Low standards of living and poor living condition are responsible for this. As a result, incidence of diseases is high leading to high rates of mortality, especially among children and pregnant mothers. The developing countries are characterized by agrarian based subsistence production. Traditional and obsolete methods and implements for cultivation, lack of capital for investment, fragmented holdings and semi-feudal tenancy relations make the base of this type of economy very weak.

Weak Industrial Base

Lack of capital, outdated technology and inadequate skilled manpower have resulted in a weak industrial base in most of the developed countries. This has prevented any substantial improvement in living standards of populations of these countries. Inward looking attitudes restrict flow of awareness regarding birth control, family planning etc. Caste system inhibits social mobility in societies like India.

Underpopulated Pockets

These may exist either within populated countries or as separate countries. This type of situation, especially in the first case, leads to rural-urban disparity. Also, it becomes uneconomical to invest in physical and social infrastructure in such countries. Any investment in agriculture or in industry involves long gestation periods in such pockets. Industry faces the problem of shortage of skilled manpower and insufficient market, even if high standards of living prevail. Many under populated countries have hostile climatic or topographical conditions. Such conditions obstruct development and it is both difficult and expensive to overcome these problems.

Population Problems of Developed Countries

The developed countries are characterized by high levels of industrialization and urbanization, high per capita incomes, dependence of a major part of the workforce on secondary and tertiary activities, an efficient and productive agricultural sector. The problems faced by these countries, I relation to population, are discussed below.

This happens because of low death rates and high rates of life expectancy. As a result a large section of population is above sixty years of age and is dependent on the relatively small workforce. Also, financial problems arise on account of pensions, health services, etc.

Shortage of Labour

As standards of education improve, the children remain longer at school and join the workforce later. This implies slow expansion of the workforce. As a result, many countries of Europe face shortage of labour. High wage rates disrupt the overall economic pattern. Search for better living conditions leads to distorted demographic structures, especially in rural areas, and neglect of the agricultural sector.

Congestion in Towns

As towns expand, the pressure on civic amenities, transport, housing etc. increase. Pollution and social tensions lead to heart disease, breathing problems, lung and skin problems etc.

Unregulated growth of urban centres leads to growth of slums which create many social and environmental problems. The highly productive agricultural land is encroached by urban houses, roads and industries. Thus, the developing and the developed countries share many of the problems related to population. But, the problems of low population developing countries and the high population developing countries differ substantially.

DISTRIBUTION OF THE POPULATION

India is essentially an agricultural country. According to the last Census nearly 200 millions of the people were engaged directly in agricultural or pastoral occupations. These people arc necessarily scattered over the land and not congregated together in towns. Many more are indirectly employed on the land, being engaged in ministering to the needs of the agriculturists proper. These also are scattered over the country. India has no great mineral resources, and even what she has are as yet but little worked. Nor are there any great manufactures to draw the people together in towns. Small manufactures there are in plenty, and some have their centres in particular localities. But in no sense can India, or any Province of India, be called a manufacturing country. The result of this is that the vast majority of the people live in hamlets or villages, and the towns and cities are comparatively few, and for the most part small. This is best seen by comparing.

India with a great manufacturing country like England. While in India, out of a population of 294 millions, only 270 millions—or considerably less than 10 per cent.—live in towns of 5,000 inhabitants and over, in England 77 per cent, of the total population live in such towns. In the one case over 90 per cent, of the people are scattered over the land, but in the other only 23 per cent. India is thus emphatically a land of villages.

In ancient days these villages were generally self-contained and self-organised communities. They had but little communication with the outside world and needed little. Living upon the soil, the majority of their people were cultivators, but the simple handicrafts, etc.. necessary for the independent life of an agricultural community were represented in every village, and all occupations passed from father to son. In ordinary years, when nature was propitious, such villagers had few inducements to look beyond their own narrow borders. Roads were few; travelling difficult and dangerous; and, except when some religious festival drew them to some famous shrine, they spent their quiet and laborious days among their own people. In many parts of India this is still to a large extent the case, but in others it is rapidly passing away. Better roads, and other means of communication, the spread—even among the illiterate—of some knowledge of the world beyond, the increase of their means, and the opening of outside markets for their produce, are all enlarging the outlook of the people, breaking down their village exclusiveness, and bringing them into touch with a wider world. But these influences do not tend to substitute town life for village life, nor will they ever do so. So long as India remains, as she must remain, an agricultural country, the vast majority of her people must live upon the land they till.

In modern days the growth of towns on particular sites is almost always due to one or more of three reasons. This last is an essentially modern cause of towns, and is due to the increase in the facilities of travel, and of the wealth and leisure of the people. It is naturally, therefore, most operative in Europe and America, where a multitude of towns trace their growth and prosperity to no other cause. But it has also been operative in India, and such hill stations as Simla, Darjeeling, Ootacamund, etc., owe their existence to it alone. Such towns are, however, of less importance than those whose origin is to be ascribed to the other causes named. Though they may grow to considerable size and wealth, and may be, as in India, summer seats of Government, 'they exercise no great influence on the development and destiny of a people.

But while in these modern days most towns are indebted to commerce or manufacture for their prosperity, very different reasons may have led originally to their foundation. In ancient times (i) political and (2) religious considerations had more to do with the founding of towns in India than had commerce. At various periods the country has been overrun by foreign invaders, and at others has been broken up into a multitude of States almost ceaselessly at war with one another. In such times, wherever a powerful chief settled, people flocked to him, partly for defence and partly for trade; and a town soon grew up, which became his capital and the seat of his government. The site of such a town was chosen not so much for commercial as for military reasons. It had, indeed, to be situated, if possible, in some place to which the supplies needed by his retainers and army could be easily brought; but it was still more needful that it should be in a good strategic position, well adapted both for defence and as a base for attack. A large number of Indian towns had this origin. Many others owed their origin to religion. The presence of a famous shrine, or the proximity of a sacred river, attracted annually multitudes of pilgrims, whose requirements in the way of accommodation and provisions afforded lucrative employment for a large resident population.

When once a town has been founded, no matter what its origin may have been, tends to build up for itself a trade and thus to maintain itself in prosperity, even though the circumstances in which it had its rise should quite pass away. Religious change in India is so exceedingly slow, that towns which grew up at first for the convenience of pilgrims are often preserved in prosperity for many centuries by the conditions which gave them birth. We have illustrations of this in Benares and Puri. Puri exists solely for the sake of pilgrims, and though Benares has now an additional importance, due to other and modern causes, yet its shrines and pilgrims are still the chief sources of its fame and wealth.

Political changes in India have, however, been as rapid as religious changes have been slow, but British rule has now given peace to the whole country. Many towns, therefore, that had a strategical origin are now flourishing trade centres. In most cases they possessed from the first, as we have seen, a certain suitability of position for trading purposes. When they became centres of environment, and seats of a large population, roads were pushed out in every direction, and other means of communication opened up, till in course of time they became the recognised emporia for large districts. When their political importance declined, their trade still maintained them and became a more enduring cause of prosperity and wealth. Under British rule such towns have frequently become centres of civil or military administration, and have regained much of their old greatness. Delhi, Lucknow, Allahabad, Poona, and a host of others are examples. When, however, such ancient military towns were not well situated for trade, and did not become the natural and accepted commercial centres of considerable districts, any change in the political circumstances which gave them birth generally led to their decline, and sometimes to their complete extinction. Kanauj, Ajodhya, and Seringapatam are illustrations of this.

Of the ancient towns in India which owe their origin to commerce, comparatively few are of any size or great importance. India has always had a considerable foreign trade, and though even in ancient times the bulk of it was, no doubt, carried by sea, it gave rise to no sea-port of any magnitude that has survived to modern days. This was mainly due to the fact that the trade was carried in foreign ships, and the people of India themselves never took largely to navigation. Further, the trade being chiefly on the West Coast, where the accumulation of sand washed up by the sea is greatest, such ancient ports as there were have either been obliterated or have become inland towns. Even the later ports of Surat, Cambay, and Goa, which enjoyed the earlier trade round the Cape of Good Hope, have greatly suffered from this cause, and the bulk of their trade has now passed to Bombay. Overland commerce has, however, left more permanent marks on many of the towns of the north and northwest. Shikarpur has for ages controlled the trade across the Bolan Pass; Dera Ismail Khan, and, further inland, Shahpur and Multan, that by the Gonial; Peshawar, than by the Khyber; and Jullundur and Amritsar, that through Kashmir to Tibet. All these towns owe much to the fact that for centuries they have been the natural and recognized centres for the trade carried on across these ancient mountain routes. Inland trading towns grew up in early times, chiefly along the great waterways of the Ganges and Indus, or where trade routes crossed one another.

THE DENSITY OF POPULATION

In an agricultural country like India, which does not import its food but grows it, the population of every considerable area tends to increase till it approaches the maximum that the produce of the land can feed.

But the abundance of the harvests depends upon the nature of the soil and the sufficiency and regularity of the water supply. And, since in most places the water supply is almost entirely due to the rainfall, it follows that, as a general rule and within certain limits, the density of the population varies with the average rainfall. Of course, there are many exceptions to this. The rainfall may be so irregular that, though the country may have a large annual average, it may, nevertheless, be burnt up for the greater part of the year and flooded for a few weeks. Such an irregular rainfall as this would not greatly promote agriculture. Or, though the rainfall is large and regular, the land itself may consist of rocky and barren hills. Both the produce and the population will then be low. On the other hand, a country which has a scanty rainfall may be well watered by irrigation, and therefore fertile. But if sufficiently large areas be taken, it will be found that regions of ampler rainfall are also regions of denser population.

It should be noted, however, that this connection only holds good in agricultural countries. Wherever other industries are largely developed, whether mining or manufacture, a population is often found far larger than any that the land itself could support. The wealth made by these industries enables such countries to import much of their food from other lands. The following map, which shows the density of the population in the several States and Provinces of the Empire, illustrates in part this relation between rainfall and population.

At one time Dravidian forms of speech probably occupied the whole country. That is at least suggested by the fact that scattered tribes, speaking Dravidian tongues, are still found as far north as Baluchistan in the west and Chota Nagpur in" the east. Now, however, the vernacular languages of at least four-fifths of the Indian people belong to the Aryan family. This is precisely what might have been expected. Whenever a stronger people, more advanced in all the arts, and with a more developed language, dispossess a weaker race, the latter will in course of time adopt the language of their conquerors, even though, through intermarriage, the races themselves may coalesce. The superseded tongue may contribute any number of words to the new language which the conquered must adopt, but ultimately the language which survives will be, in idiom, form and structure, the language of the conquerors. This process has gone on largely in India. Though Dravidian blood still prevails in some degree almost up to the Himalayas, and in comparative purity as far north as Central India, Dravidian languages are, with the exception of a few scattered remnants, confined to those parts of South India over which the waves of Aryan immigration never swept in force.

The principal Dravidian languages are Telugu, Tamil, Kanarese, and Malayalam, which are spoken respectively by about 2, 3,4, and 6 millions of people, inhabiting an area which forms a solid linguistic block in southeast India. Gond is spoken by over a million people, chiefly in the Central Provinces; Tulu by over half a million in South Kanara; Kurukh, or Oraon, by about the same number on the hills of Chota Nagpur. And Kandh by nearly as many on the hills of Orissa. There are many other Dravidian languages spoken by smaller numbers, the most interesting of which is Brahi, spoken by an isolated group in eastern Baluchistan.

Santali and Kol, the languages of the Santhals and Kols, who number nearly three millions and are found in Bihar, Chota Nagpur and Orissa, arc the chief languages of the Munda Sub-Family. There are several other members of this group, but less known, and spoken by smaller numbers. These languages used to be called Kolarian, and the Kolarians were believed by some to have entered India from the northeast. The group is, however, essentially Dravidian, and is probably identical in origin with the Dravidian languages of the South.

The Aryan languages spoken in India fall into two classes, the Irano-Aryan, or Iranian, which prevail west of the Indus, and of which Baloch, Pashto, and Persian are the chief examples, and the Indo-Aryan which prevail from the Indus to the confines of Burma, and southwards till they meet the Dravidian languages of the peninsula

All the chief Indo-Aryan languages are Sanscritic in their character, Sanscrit, the great classical language of India, having in all probability been developed into the form in which it is found in the Vedas long after the final Aryan immigrants had settled in the " Middle Land." A comparison of these languages suggests that they were introduced into India at two different periods, probably separated by several centuries; that the earliest wave of immigrants, coming, most likely, from the west, spread over the greater part of western and northern India before the arrival of the second wave; and that these latter, coming most probably across the northern frontier, forced their way into the middle of the previous settlers, and, as they grew in numbers, drove them gradually to the east, south and west, and to some extent also to the north. Dr. Grierson, the head of the Linguistic Survey of India, calls the languages whose origin is to be traced to these later settlers, the Inner Indo-Aryan languages, and those that appear to have sjirung from the language of the earlier settlers, the Outer Indo-Aryan languages. The localities in which these various languages are spoken are shown on the map on the following page. It should be remembered, however, that neighbouring languages shade off into one another by almost imperceptible gradations, and though the boundaries are of necessity sharply defined on a map, they are not so in reality.

Most of these languages have numerous dialects, sometimes exhibiting a very wide degree of divergence. The only one of these that we need notice is Hindustani, the chief dialect of Western Hindi. Hindustani is spoken more or less all over India, and particularly by the Muhammadans, and is often spoken of as the lingua franca of India. Urdu is literary Hindustani, written in the Persian character, and often greatly modified by the introduction of Persian words. The prevalence of Hindustani throughout India is due to the widespread influence of the Mughal Empire, and to the fact that Muhammadans are numerous in every' Province.

In the extreme north of India are tribes speaking Non-Sanscritic Indo-Aryan languages. They are few in number, however, and none of their dialects have native characters. The Indo-Chinese languages spoken in India, of which by far the most important group is the Tibeto-Burman, are very numerous, including no fewer than 92 of the 147 languages enumerated in the Census Report. They are spoken, however, by a comparatively small fraction of the people, less than twelve millions in all, including the people of Burma and the border mountains, the Khasi and Garo Hills, and the slopes of the Himalayas. Burmese, the most cultivated of these languages, is spoken by about 11 millions. Karen and Shan, spoken by tribes bearing the same names, are closely related to Chinese, and are each spoken by about a million people. The rest of the languages of this group are spoken by mere handfuls of people. Comparatively little is known as yet about many of the Indo-Chinese languages.

CONSEQUENCES OF POPULATION GROWTH

The already densely populated developing countries contribute to over 95% of the population growth and rapid population growth could lead to environmental deterioration. Developed countries are less densely populated and contribute very little to population growth; however, they cause massive ecological damage by the wasteful, unnecessary and unbalanced consumption the consequences of which could adversely affect both the developed and the developing countries. The review on "Promotion of sustainable development: challenges for environmental policies" in the Economic Survey 1998-99 had covered in detail the major environmental problems, and policy options for improvement; the present review will only briefly touch upon some of the important ecological consequences of demographic transition.

In many developing countries continued population growth has resulted in pressure on land, fragmentation of land holding, collapsing fisheries, shrinking forests, rising temperatures, loss of plant and animal species. Global warming due to increasing use of fossil fuels (mainly by the developed countries) could have serious effects on the populous coastal regions in developing countries, their food production and essential water supplies. The Intergovernmental Panel on Climate Change has projected that, if current greenhouse gas emission trends continue, the mean global surface temperature will rise from 1 to 3.5 degrees Celsius in the next century. The panel's best estimate scenario projects a sea-level rise of 15 to 95 centimetres by 2100. The ecological impact of rising oceans would include increased flooding, coastal erosion, salination of aquifers and coastal crop land and displacement of millions of people living near the coast. Patterns of precipitation are also likely to change, which combined with increased average temperatures, could substantially alter the relative agricultural productivity of different regions. Greenhouse gas emissions are closely linked to both population growth and development. Slower population growth in developing countries and ecologically sustainable lifestyles in developed countries would make reduction in green house gas emission easier to achieve and provide more time and options for adaptation to climate change. Rapid population growth, developmental activities either to meet the growing population or the growing needs of the population as well as changing lifestyles and consumption patterns pose major challenge to preservation and promotion of ecological balance in India. Some of the major ecological adverse effects reported in India include:

- severe pressure on the forests due to both the rate of resource use and the nature of use. The per capita forest biomass in the country is only about 6 tons as against the global average of 82 tons.
- adverse effect on species diversity:
- conversion of habitat to some other land use such as agriculture, urban development, forestry operation. Some 70-80 % of fresh water marshes and lakes in the Gangetic flood plains has been lost in the last 50 years.
- Tropical deforestation and destruction of mangroves for commercial needs and fuel wood. The country's mangrove areas have reduced from 700,000 ha to 453,000 ha in the last 50 years.
- Intense grazing by domestic livestock
- Poaching and illegal harvesting of wildlife.
- Increase in agricultural area, high use of chemical fertilizers pesticides and weedicides; water stagnation, soil erosion, soil salinity and low productivity.
- High level of biomass burning causing large-scale indoor pollution.
- Encroachment on habitat for rail and road construction thereby fragmenting the habitat increase in commercial

activities such as mining and unsustainable resource extraction.

- Degradation of coastal and other aquatic ecosystems from domestic sewage, pesticides, fertilizers and industrial effluents.
- Over fishing in water bodies and introduction of weeds and exotic species.
- Diversion of water for domestic, industrial and agricultural uses leading to increased river pollution and decrease in self-cleaning properties of rivers.
- Increasing water requirement leading to tapping deeper aquifers which have high content of arsenic or fluoride resulting health problems.
- Disturbance from increased recreational activity and tourism causing pollution of natural ecosystems with wastes left behind by people.

The United Nations Conference on Environment and Development (1992) acknowledged population growth, rising income levels, changing technologies, increasing consumption pattern will all have adverse impact on environment. Ensuring that there is no further deterioration depends on choices made by the population about family size, life styles, environmental protection and equity.

Availability of appropriate technology and commitment towards ensuring sustainable development is increasing throughout the world. Because of these, it might be possible to initiate steps to see that the natural carrying capacity of the environment is not damaged beyond recovery and ecological balance is to a large extent maintained. It is imperative that the environmental sustainability of all developmental projects is taken care of by appropriate inputs at the planning, implementation, monitoring and evaluation stages.

URBANIZATION

The proportion of people in developing countries who live in cities has almost doubled since 1960 (from less than 22 per cent to more than 40 per cent), while in more developed regions the urban share has grown from 61 per cent to 76 per cent.

Urbanization is projected to continue well into the next century. By 2030, it is expected that nearly 5 billion (61 per cent) of the world's 8.1 billion people will live in cities. India shares this global trend toward urbanisation

Globally, the number of cities with 10 million or more inhabitants is increasing rapidly, and most of these new "megacities" are in developing regions. In 1960, only New York and Tokyo had more than 10 million people. By 1999, the number of megacities had grown to 17(13 in developing countries). It is projected that there will be 26 megacities by 2015, (18 in Asia; of these five in India); more than 10 per cent of the world's population will live in these cities (1.7% in 1950). India's urban population has doubled from 109 million to 218 million during the last two decades and is estimated to reach 300 million by 2000 AD. As a consequence cities are facing the problem of expanding urban slums.

Like many other demographic changes, urbanization has both positive and negative effects. Cities and towns have become the engines of social change and rapid economic development. Urbanisation is associated with improved access to education, employment, health care; these result in increase in age at marriage, reduction in family size and improvement in health indices. As people have moved towards and into cities, information has flowed outward. Better communication and transportation now link urban and rural areas both economically and socially creating an urban-rural continuum of communities with improvement in some aspects of lifestyle of both. The ever increasing reach of mass media communicate new ideas, points of reference, and available options are becoming more widely recognized, appreciated and sought. This phenomenon has affected health care, including reproductive health, in many ways. For instance, radio and television programmes that discuss gender equity, family size preference and family planning options are now reaching formerly isolated rural populations. This can create demand for services for mothers and children, higher contraceptive use, and fewer unwanted pregnancies, smaller healthier families and lead to more rapid population stabilisation.

But the rapid growth of urban population also poses some serious challenges. Urban population growth has outpaced the development of basic minimum services; housing, water supply, sewerage and solid waste disposal are far from adequate; increasing waste generation at home, offices and industries, coupled with poor waste disposal facilities result in rapid environmental deterioration. Increasing automobiles add to air pollution. All these have adverse effect on ecology and health. Poverty persists in urban and peri-urban areas; awareness about the glaring inequities in close urban setting may lead to social unrest.

RURAL POPULATION AND THEIR DEVELOPMENT

Over seventy per cent of India's population still lives in rural areas. There are substantial differences between the states in the proportion of rural and urban population (varying from almost 90 per cent in Assam and Bihar to 61 per cent in Maharashtra).

Agriculture is the largest and one of the most important sector of the rural economy and contributes both to economic growth and employment. Its contribution to the Gross Domestic Product has declined over the last five decades but agriculture still remains the source of livelihood for over 70 per cent of the country's population.

A large proportion of the rural work force is small and consists of marginal farmers and landless agricultural labourers. There is substantial under employment among these people; both wages and productivity are low. These in turn result in poverty; it is estimated that 320 million people are still living below the poverty line in rural India.

Though poverty has declined over the last three decades, the number of rural poor has in fact increased due to the population growth. Poor tend to have larger families which puts enormous burden on their meagre resources, and prevent them from breaking out of the shackles of poverty. In States like Tamil Nadu where replacement level of fertility has been attained, population growth rates are much lower than in many other States; but the population density is high and so there is a pressure on land. In States like Rajasthan, Uttar Pradesh, Bihar and Madhya Pradesh population is growing rapidly, resulting in increasing pressure on land and resulting land fragmentation.

Low productivity of small land holders leads to poverty, low energy intake and under nutrition, and this, in turn, prevents the development thus creating a vicious circle. In most of the states non-farm employment in rural areas has not grown very much and cannot absorb the growing labour force.

Those who are getting educated specially beyond the primary level, may not wish to do manual agricultural work. They would like better opportunities and more remunerative employment. In this context, it is imperative that programmes for skill development, vocational training and technical education are taken up on a large scale in order to generate productive employment in rural areas. The entire gamut of existing poverty alleviation and employment generation programmes may have to be restructured to meet the newly emerging types of demand for employment.

Rural poor have inadequate access to basic minimum services, because of poor connectivity, lack of awareness, inadequate and poorly functional infrastructure. There are ongoing efforts to improve these, but with the growing aspirations of the younger, educated population these efforts may prove to be inadequate to meet the increasing needs both in terms of type and quality of services. Greater education, awareness and better standard of living among the growing younger age group population would create the required consciousness among them that smaller families are desirable; if all the felt needs for health and family welfare services are fully met, it will be possible to enable them to attain their reproductive goals, achieve substantial decline in the family size and improve quality of life.

Water Supply

In many parts of developed and developing world, water demand substantially exceeds sustainable water supply. It is estimated that currently 430 millions (8% of the global population) are living in countries affected by water stress; by 2020 about one fourth of the global population may be facing chronic and recurring shortage of fresh water. In India, water withdrawal is estimated to be twice the rate of aquifer recharge; as a result water tables are falling by one to three meters every year; tapping deeper aquifers have resulted in larger population groups being exposed to newer health hazards such as high fluoride or arsenic content in drinking water.

At the other end of the spectrum, excessive use of water has led to water logging and increasing salinity in some parts of the country. Eventually, both lack of water and water logging could have adverse impact on India's food production.

There is very little arable agricultural land which remains unexpected and in many areas, agricultural technology improvement may not be able to ensure further increase in yield per hectare. It is, therefore, imperative that research in biotechnology for improving development of foodgrains strains that would tolerate salinity and those which would require less water gets high priority. Simultaneously, a movement towards making water harvesting, storage and its need based use part of every citizens life should be taken up.

Food Security

Technological innovations in agriculture and increase in area under cultivation have ensured that so far, food production has kept pace with the population growth. Evolution of global and national food security systems have improved access to food. It is estimated that the global population will grow to 9 billion by 2050 and the food production will double; improvement in purchasing power and changing dietary habits (shift to animal products) may further add to the requirement of food grains. Thus, in the next five decades, the food and nutrition security could become critical in many parts of the world especially in the developing countries and pockets of poverty in the developed countries.

In India one of the major achievements in the last fifty years has been the green revolution and self-sufficiency in food production. Food grain production has increased from 50.82 in

1950-51 to 200.88 million tons in 1998-99 (Prov.). It is a matter of concern that while the cereal production has been growing steadily at a rate higher than the population growth rates, the coarse grain and pulse production has not shown a similar increase.

Consequently there has been a reduction in the per capita availability of pulses (from 60.7 grams in 1951 to 34 grams per day in 1996) and coarse grains. Over the last five decades there has been a decline in the per capita availability of pulses. During the last few years the country has imported pulses to meet the requirement. There has been a sharp and sustained increase in cost of pulses, so there is substantial decline in per capita pulses consumption among poorer segment of population. This in turn could have an adverse impact on their protein intake. The pulse component of the "Pulses and Oil Seeds Mission" need to receive a major thrust in terms of R&D and other inputs, so that essential pulse requirement of growing population is fully met.

Rising cost of pulses had a beneficial effect also. Till eighties in central India wages of landless labourers were given in the form Kesari Dal which was cheaper than cereals or coarse grains. Consumption of staple diet of Kesari Dal led to crippling disease of neuro lathyrism.

Over the last three decades the rising cost of pulses has made Kesari Dal more expensive than wheat or rice and hence it is no longer given to labourers as wages for work done; as a result the disease has virtually disappeared from Central India. Over years the coarse grain production has remained stagnant and per capita availability of coarse grain has under gone substantial reduction; there has been a shift away from coarse grains to rice and wheat consumption even among poorer segment of population. One of the benefits of this change is virtual elimination of pellagra which was widely prevalent among low income group population in Deccan Plateau whose staple food was sorghum.

Coarse grains are less expensive than rice and wheat; they can thus provide higher calories for the same cost as compared to rice and wheat. Coarse grains which are locally produced and procured if made available through TPDS at subsidised rate, may not only substantially bring down the subsidy cost without any reduction in calories provided but also improve "targetting"-as only the most needy are likely to access these coarse grains. Another area of concern is the lack of sufficient focus and thrust in horticulture; because of this, availability of vegetables especially green leafy vegetables and yellow/red vegetables throughout the year at affordable cost both in urban and rural areas has remained an unfulfilled dream. Health and nutrition education emphasizing the importance of consuming these inexpensive rich sources of micronutrients will not result in any change in food habits unless there is harnessing and effective management of horticultural resources in the country to meet the growing needs of the people at affordable cost. States like Tamil Nadu and Himachal Pradesh have initiated some efforts in this direction; similar efforts need be taken up in other states also.

6

Geography of Urban Planning

URBAN GEOGRAPHY

Urban geography is the study of urban areas. That is the study of areas which have a high concentration of buildings and infrastructure. These are areas where the majority of economic activities are in the secondary sector and tertiary sectors. They often have a high population density. Urban geography is that branch of science, which deals the study of urban areas, in terms of concentration, infrastructure, economy, and environmental impacts.

It can be considered a part of the larger field of human geography. However, it can often overlap with other fields such as anthropology and urban sociology. Urban geographers seek to understand how factors interact over space, what function they serve and their interrelationships. Urban geographers also look at the development of settlements. Therefore, it involves planning city expansion and improvements. Urban geography, then, attempts to account for the human and environmental impacts of the change. Urban geography focuses on the city in the context of space throughout countries and continents. Urban geography forms the theoretical basis for a number of professions including urban planning, site selection, real estate development, crime pattern analysis and logistical analysis.

Areas of Study

There are essentially two approaches to urban geography.

The study of problems relating to the spatial distribution of cities themselves and the complex patterns of movement, flows and linkages that bind them in space. Studies in this category are concerned with the *city system*. Secondly there is the study of patterns of distribution and interaction within cities, essentially the study of their inner structure. Studies in this category are concerned with the *city as a system*. A succinct way to define urban geography that recognizes the link between these two approaches within the subject is then, that "urban geography is the study of cities as systems within a system of cities."

Site and Situation

Site describes the location of a city with respect to its soil, water supply and relief, or more still the actual point on which a settlement is built while situation describes the surrounding area of the city such as other settlements, rivers, mountains and communication. Locations for cities are usually chosen for good reasons. Benefits of certain locations can include:

- A wet area: water is a constant necessity for urban areas and is difficult to transport. For this reason many cities are located near or adjacent to rivers.
- A dry area: in wet areas a dry area offers protection from flooding and marshland.
- Easy access to building materials: stone, wood or clay are necessary for the construction of cities and are difficult to transport long distances.
- A strategic defensive position: historically many cities have been constructed on high ground in order to make attack more difficult and to give a good view of surrounding land (for example, Quebec City). River meanders are also used as partial moats. Some cities were also built in swampy areas for the same reason (for example, Paris).
- fuel supply: most cities were initially constructed near wood for burning and cooking. Today many cities are constructed near coal, oil and gas mines to make use of those resources (for example: Newcastle, Glasgow, Pittsburgh, Essen).

- A food supply: cities need some nearby land to be suitable for animal grazing or crop growing
- A travel intersection point and bridging points: it is often useful for a city to be located at the intersection of rivers, roads or train lines in order to facilitate travel and trade. Bridging points are shallow areas that allow easy construction of bridges, (for example: London, Cologne).
- Historically many cities grew at so-called "break-of-bulk" points along navigable rivers, where a local obstacle such as rapids required trade goods to be trans-shipped from larger boats to smaller boats, for example: Chicago, Montreal.
- Shelter and aspect: it is desirable to construct cities located on the side of a slope that is protected from incoming winds, and in a direction that receives maximum sun exposure.

CITIES AS CENTRES OF MANUFACTURING AND SERVICES

Cities differ in their economic makeup, their social and demographic characteristics and the roles they play within the city system. These differences can be traced back to regional variations in the local resources on which growth was based during the early development of the urban pattern and in part the subsequent shifts in the competitive advantage of regions brought about by changing locational forces affecting regional specialization within the framework of the market economy. Recognition of different city types necessitates their classification, and it is to this important aspect of urban geography that we now turn. Emphasis is on *functional town classification* and the basic underlying dimensions of the city system.

The purpose of classifying cities is twofold. On the one hand, it is undertaken in order to search reality for hypotheses. In this context, the recognition of different types of cities on the basis of, for example, their functional specialization may enable the identification of spatial regularities in the distribution and structure of urban functions and the formulation of hypotheses about the resulting patterns. On the other hand, classification is undertaken to structure reality in order to test specific hypotheses that have already been formulated. For example, to test the hypotheses that cities with a diversified economy grow at a faster rate then those with a more specialized economic base, cities must first be classified so that diversified and specialized cities can be differentiated.

The simplest way to classify cities is to identify the distinctive role they play in the city system. There are three distinct roles.

1. *Central places* functioning primarily as service centres for local hinterlands.
2. *Transportation* cities performing break-of-bulk and allied functions for larger regions.
3. *Specialized-function* cities are dominated by one activity such as mining, manufacturing or recreation and serving national and international markets. The composition of a cities labour force has traditionally been regarded as the best indicator of functional specialization, and different city types have been most frequently identified from the analysis of employment profiles. Specialization in a given activity is said to exist when employment in it exceeds some critical level.

The relationship between the city system and the development of manufacturing has become very apparent. The rapid growth and spread of cities within the heartland-hinterland framework after 1870 was conditioned to a large extent by industrial developments and that the decentralization of population within the urban system in recent years is related in large part to the movement of employment in manufacturing away from the traditional industrial centres. Manufacturing is found in nearly all cities, but its importance is measured by the proportion of total earnings received by the inhabitants of an urban area. When 25 percent or more of the total earnings in an urban region are derived from manufacturing, that urban areas is arbitrarily designated as a manufacturing centre.

The location of manufacturing is affected by myriad economic and non-economic factors, such as the nature of the material inputs, the factors of production, the market and transportation costs. Other important influences include agglomeration and external economies, public policy and personal preferences. Although it is difficult to evaluate precisely the effect of the market on the location of manufacturing activities, two considerations are involved: the nature of and demand for the product and transportation costs.

BEHAVIOURAL GEOGRAPHY

Behavioural geography is an approach to human geography that examines human behaviour using a disaggregate approach. Behavioural geographers focus on the cognitive processes underlying spatial reasoning, decision making, and behaviour. In addition, behavioural geography is an ideology/approach in human geography that makes use of the methods and assumptions of behaviourism to determine the cognitive processes involved in an individual's perception of, and/or response and reaction to its environment.

Behavioural geography is that branch of human science, which deals with the study of cognitive processes with its response to its environment, through behaviourism.

Issues in Behavioural Geography

Because of the name it is often assumed to have its roots in behaviourism. While some behavioural geographers clearly have roots in behaviourism due to the emphasis on cognition, most can be seen as cognitively oriented. Indeed, it seems that behaviourism interest is more recent and growing This is particularly true in the area of human landscaping. Behavioural geography is an approach to human geography that examines human behaviour using a disaggregate approach. It draws from early, behaviourist works such as Tolman's concepts of "cognitive maps". More cognitively oriented, behavioural geographers focus on the cognitive processes underlying spatial reasoning, decision making, and behaviour. More behaviourally oriented geographers are materialists and look at the role of basic learning processes and how they influence the lanscape patterns or even group identity.

The cognitive processes include environmental perception

and cognition, way finding, the construction of cognitive maps, place attachment, the development of attitudes about space and place, decisions and behaviour based on imperfect knowledge of one's environs, and numerous other topics. The approach adopted in behavioural geography is closely related to that of psychology, but draws on research findings from a multitude of other disciplines including economics, sociology, anthropology, transportation planning, and many others.

URBAN PLANNING

Urban, city, and town planning integrates land use planning and transportation planning to improve the built, economic and social environments of communities. Regional planning deals with a still larger environment, at a less detailed level. Urban planning can include urban renewal, by adapting urban planning methods to existing cities suffering from decay and lack of investment.

History

Agriculture and other techniques facilitated larger populations than the very small communities of the Paleolithic. They may have led to stronger, more coercive governments at the same time. The pre-Classical and Classical ages saw a number of cities laid out according to fixed plans, though many tended to develop organically. Designed cities were characteristic of the Mesopotamian, Harrapan, and Egyptian civilizations of the third millennium BCE.

Distinct characteristics of urban planning from remains of the cities of Harappa, Lothal, and Mohenjodaro in the Indus Valley Civilization (in modern-day northwestern India and Pakistan) lead archeologists to conclude that they are the earliest examples of deliberately planned and managed cities. The streets of many of these early cities were paved and laid out at right angles in a grid pattern, with a hierarchy of streets from major boulevards to residential alleys. Archaeological evidence suggests that many Harrapan houses were laid out to protect from noise and enhance residential privacy; many also had their own water wells, probably for both sanitary and ritual purposes. These ancient cities were unique in that they often had drainage systems, seemingly tied to a well-developed ideal of urban sanitation.

The Greek Hippodamus (c. 407 BC) has been dubbed the "Father of City Planning" for his design of Miletus; Alexander commissioned him to lay out his new city of Alexandria, the grandest example of idealized urban planning of the Mediterranean world, where the city's regularity was facilitated by its level site near a mouth of the Nile. The Hippodamian, or grid plan, was the basis for subsequent Greek and Roman cities.

The ancient Romans used a consolidated scheme for city planning, developed for military defence and civil convenience. The basic plan consisted of a central forum with city services, surrounded by a compact, rectilinear grid of streets, and wrapped in a wall for defence. To reduce travel times, two diagonal streets crossed the square grid, passing through the central square. A river usually flowed through the city, providing water, transport, and sewage disposal. Many European towns, such as Turin, preserve the remains of these schemes. The Romans had a very logical way of designing their cities. They laid out the streets at right angles, in the form of a square grid. All roads were equal in width and length, except for two, which formed the center of the grid and intersected in the middle. One ran east–west, the other north–south. They were slightly wider than the others. All roads were made of carefully fitted stones and smaller, hard-packed stones. Bridges were constructed where needed. Each square marked by four roads was called an *insula*, the Roman equivalent of a modern city block.

Each insula was 80 yards (73 m) square, with the land within it divided. As the city developed, each insula would eventually be filled with buildings of various shapes and sizes and crisscrossed with back roads and alleys. Most insulae were given to the first settlers of a Roman city, but each person had to pay to construct his own house. The city was surrounded by a wall to protect it from invaders and to mark the city limits. Areas outside city limits were left open as farmland. At the end of each main road was a large gateway with watchtowers. A portcullis covered the opening when the city was under siege, and additional watchtowers were constructed along the city walls. An aqueduct was built outside the city walls.

The collapse of Roman civilization saw the end of Roman urban planning, among other arts. Urban development in the Middle Ages, characteristically focused on a fortress, a fortified abbey, or a (sometimes abandoned) Roman nucleus, occurred "like the annular rings of a tree", whether in an extended village or the center of a larger city. Since the new center was often on high, defensible ground, the city plan took on an organic character, following the irregularities of elevation contours like the shapes that result from agricultural terracing.

The ideal of wide streets and orderly cities was not lost, however. A few medieval cities were admired for their wide thoroughfares and orderly arrangements, but the juridical chaos of medieval cities (where the administration of streets was sometimes passed down through noble families), and the characteristic tenacity of medieval Europeans in legal matters prevented frequent or large-scale urban planning until the Renaissance and the strengthening of all central governments, from city-states to the kings of France, characteristic of that epoch.

Florence was an early model of the new urban planning, which took on a star-shaped layout adapted from the new star fort, designed to resist cannon fire. This model was widely imitated, reflecting the enormous cultural power of Florence in this age; "[t]he Renaissance was hypnotized by one city type which for a century and a half— from Filarete to Scamozzi— was impressed upon utopian schemes: this is the star-shaped city". Radial streets extend outward from a defined center of military, communal or spiritual power. Only in ideal cities did a centrally planned structure stand at the heart, as in Raphael's *Sposalizio* (*Illustration*) of 1504. As built, the unique example of a rationally planned *quattrocento* new city center, that of Vigevano (1493–95), resembles a closed space instead, surrounded by arcading.

Filarete's ideal city, building on Leone Battista Alberti's *De re aedificatoria*, was named "Sforzinda" in compliment to his patron; its twelve-pointed shape, circumscribable by a "perfect"

Pythagorean figure, the circle, took no heed of its undulating terrain in Filarete's manuscript. This process occurred in cities, but ordinarily not in the industrial suburbs characteristic of this era, which remained disorderly and characterized by crowding and organic growth.

Following the 1695 bombardment of Brussels by the French troops of King Louis XIV, in which a large part of the city center was destroyed, Governor Max Emanuel proposed using the reconstruction to completely change the layout and architectural style of the city. His plan was to transform the medieval city into a city of the new baroque style, modeled on Turin, with a logical street layout, with straight avenues offering long, uninterrupted views flanked by buildings of a uniform size. This plan was opposed by residents and municipal authorities, who wanted a rapid reconstruction, did not have the resources for grandiose proposals, and resented what they considered the imposition of a new, foreign, architectural style. In the actual reconstruction, the general layout of the city was conserved, but it was not identical to that before the cataclysm. Despite the necessity of rapid reconstruction and the lack of financial means, authorities did take several measures to improve traffic flow, sanitation, and the aesthetics of the city. Many streets were made as wide as possible to improve traffic flow.

In the 1990s, the University of Kentucky voted the Italian town of Todi as the ideal city and "most livable town in the world", the place where man and nature, history and tradition, come together to create a site of excellence. In Italy, other examples of ideal cities planned according to scientific methods are Urbino, Pienza, Ferrara, San Giovanni Valdarno, and San Lorenzo Nuovo.

Many Central American civilizations also planned their cities, including sewage systems and running water. In Mexico, Tenochtitlan was the capital of the Aztec empire, built on an island in Lake Texcocc in what is now the Federal District in central Mexico. At its height, Tenochtitlan was one of the largest cities in the world, with over 200,000 inhabitants. Shibam in Yemen features over 500 tower houses, each rising 5 to 11 storeys high, with each floor being an apartment occupied by a single family. The city has some of the tallest mudbrick houses in the world, some over 100 feet (30 meters) high.

In the developed countries of Western Europe, North America, Japan, and Australasia, planning and architecture can be said to have gone through various paradigms or stages of consensus in the last 200 years. Firstly, there was the industrialised city of the 19th century, where building was largely controlled by businesses and wealthy elites. Around 1900, a movement began for providing citizens, especially factory workers, with healthier environments. The concept of the garden city arose and several model towns were built, such as Letchworth and Welwyn Garden City in Hertfordshire, UK, the world's first garden cities. These were small in size, typically providing for a few thousand residents.

In the 1920s, the ideas of modernism began to surface in urban planning. Based on the ideas of Le Corbusier and using new skyscraper-building techniques, the modernist city stood for the elimination of disorder, congestion, and the small scale, replacing them with preplanned and widely spaced freeways and tower blocks set within gardens. There were plans for large-scale rebuilding of cities in this era, such as the *Plan Voisin* (based on Le Corbusier's Ville Contemporaine), which proposed clearing and rebuilding most of central Paris. No large-scale plans were implemented until after World War II, however. Throughout the late 1940s and 1950s, housing shortages caused by wartime destruction led many cities to subsidize housing blocks. Planners used the opportunity to implement the modernist ideal of towers surrounded by gardens. The most prominent example of an entire modernist city is Brasilia in Brazil, constructed between 1950 and 1960.

Reaction

By the late 1960s and early 1970s, many planners felt that modernism's clean lines and lack of human scale sapped vitality from the community, blaming them for high crime rates and social problems. Modernist planning fell into decline in the 1970s when the construction of cheap, uniform tower blocks ended in most countries, such as Britain and France. Since then many have been demolished and replaced by other housing types. Rather than attempting to eliminate all disorder, planning now concentrates on individualism and diversity in society and the economy; this is the post-modernist era.

Minimally planned cities still exist. Houston is a large city (with a metropolitan population of 5.5 million) in a developed country without a comprehensive zoning ordinance. Houston does, however, restrict development densities and mandate parking, even though specific land uses are not regulated. Also, private-sector developers in Houston use subdivision covenants and deed restrictions to effect land-use restrictions resembling zoning laws. Houston voters have rejected comprehensive zoning ordinances three times since 1948. Even without traditional zoning, metropolitan Houston displays large-scale land-use patterns resembling zoned regions comparable in age and population, such as Dallas. This suggests that non-regulatory factors such as urban infrastructure and financing may be as important as zoning laws in shaping urban form.

Sustainable Development and Sustainability

Sustainable development and sustainability influence today's urban planners. Some planners argue that modern lifestyles use too many natural resources, polluting or destroying ecosystems, increasing social inequality, creating urban heat islands, and causing climate change. Many urban planners, therefore, advocate sustainable cities. However, sustainable development is a recent, controversial concept. Wheeler, in his 1998 article, defines sustainable urban development as "development that improves the long-term social and ecological health of cities and towns." He sketches a 'sustainable' city's features: compact, efficient land use; less automobile use, yet better access; efficient resource use; less pollution and waste; the restoration of natural systems; good housing and living environments; a healthy social ecology; a sustainable economy; community participation and involvement; and preservation of local culture and wisdom.

Because of political and governance structures in most jurisdictions, sustainable planning measures must be widely supported before they can affect institutions and regions. Actual implementation is often a complex compromise. Collaborative Strategic Goal Oriented Programming (CoSGOP) is a collaborative and communicative way of strategic programming, decision-making, implementation, and monitoring oriented towards defined and specific goals. It is based on sound analysis of available information, emphasizes stakeholder participation, works to create awareness among actors, and is oriented towards managing development processes. It was adopted as a theoretical framework for analyzing redevelopment processes in large urban distressed areas in European cities.

Background of CoSGOP'

CoSGOP is derived from goal-oriented planning (Gesellschaft für Technische Zusammenarbeit-GTZ 1988), which was oriented towards the elaboration and implementation of projects based on a logical framework, which was useful for embedding a specific project in a wider development frame and defining its major elements. This approach had weaknesses: its logical rules were strictly applied and the expert language did not encourage participation. CoSGOP introduced a new approach characterized by communication with and active involvement of stakeholders and those to be affected by the program; strategic planning based on the identification of strengths and weakness, opportunities and threats, as well as on scenario-building and visioning; the definition of goals as the basis for action; and long-term, flexible programming of interventions by stakeholders.

Elements of CoSGOP

CoSGOP is not a planning method but a process model. It provides a framework for communication and joint decision-making, in a structured process characterized by feedback loops. It also facilitates stakeholder learning. The essential elements of CoSGOP are analysis of stakeholders (identifying stakeholders' perceptions of problems, interests, and expectations); analysis of problems and potentials (including objective problems and problems and potentials perceived by stakeholders); development of goals, improvement priorities, and alternatives (requiring intensive communication and active stakeholder participation); specification of an improvement program and its main activities (based on priorities defined with the stakeholders); assessment of possible impacts of the improvement program; definition and detailed specification of key projects and their implementation; continuous monitoring of improvement activities, feedback, and adjustment of the programme (including technical and economic information and perceptions of stakeholders).

Application

CoSGOP has been applied in European cross-border policy programming, as well in local and regional development programming. In 2004, the CoSGOP model was applied in the LUDA Project, starting with an analysis of the European experience of urban regeneration projects.

Collaborative Planning in the United States

Collaborative planning arose in the US in response to the inadequacy of traditional public participation techniques to provide real opportunities for the public to make decisions affecting their communities. Collaborative planning is a method designed to empower stakeholders by elevating them to the level of decision-makers through direct engagement and dialogue between stakeholders and public agencies, to solicit ideas, active involvement, and participation in the community planning process. Active public involvement can help planners achieve better outcomes by making them aware of the public's needs and preferences and by using local knowledge to inform projects. When properly administered, collaboration can result in more meaningful participation and better, more creative outcomes to persistent problems than can traditional participation methods. It enables planners to make decisions that reflect community needs and values, it fosters faith in the wisdom and utility of the resulting project, and the community is given a personal stake in its success.

Experiences in Portland and Seattle have demonstrated that successful collaborative planning depends on a number of interrelated factors: the process must be truly inclusive, with all stakeholders and affected groups invited to the table; the community must have final decision-making authority; full government commitment (of both financial and intellectual resources) must be manifest; participants should be given clear objectives by planning staff, who facilitate the process by providing guidance, consultancy, expert opinions, and research; and facilitators should be trained in conflict resolution and community organization.

ASPECTS OF PLANNING

In developed countries, there has been a backlash against excessive human-made clutter in the visual environment, such as signposts, signs, and hoardings. Other issues that generate strong debate among urban designers are tensions between peripheral growth, housing density and new settlements. There are also debates about the mixing tenures and land uses, versus distinguishing geographic zones where different uses dominate. Regardless, all successful urban planning considers urban character, local identity, respects heritage, pedestrians, traffic, utilities and natural hazards. Planners can help manage the growth of cities, applying tools like zoning and growth management to manage the uses of land. Historically, many of the cities now thought the most beautiful are the result of dense, long lasting systems of prohibitions and guidance about building sizes, uses and features These allowed substantial freedoms, yet enforce styles, safety, and often materials in practical ways. Many conventional planning techniques are being repackaged using the contemporary term smart growth.

There are some cities that have been planned from conception, and while the results often don't turn out quite as planned, evidence of the initial plan often remains.

Safety

Historically within the Middle East, Europe and the rest of the Old World, settlements were located on higher ground (for defence) and close to fresh water sources Cities have often grown onto coastal and flood plains at risk of floods and storm surges. Urban planners must consider these threats. If the dangers can be localised then the affected regions can be made into parkland or green belt, often with the added benefit of open space provision. Extreme weather, flood, or other emergencies can often be greatly mitigated with secure emergency evacuation routes and emergency operations centres. These are relatively inexpensive and unintrusive, and many consider them a reasonable precaution for any urban space. Many cities will also have planned, built safety features, such as levees, retaining walls, and shelters.

In recent years, practitioners have also been expected to maximize the accessibility of an area to people with different abilities, practicing the notion of "inclusive design," to anticipate criminal behaviour and consequently to "design-out crime" and to consider "traffic calming" or "pedestrianisation" as ways of making urban life more pleasant.

Some city planners try to control criminality with structures designed from theories such as socio-architecture or environmental determinism. Refer to Foucault and the Encyclopedia of the Prison System for more details. These theories say that an urban environment can influence individuals' obedience to social rules and level of power. The theories often say that psychological pressure develops in more densely developed, unadorned areas. This stress causes some crimes and some use of illegal drugs. The antidote is usually more individual space and better, more beautiful design in place of functionalism.

Oscar Newman's defensible space theory cites the modernist housing projects of the 1960s as an example of environmental determinism, where large blocks of flats are surrounded by shared and disassociated public areas, which are hard for residents to identify with. As those on lower incomes cannot hire others to maintain public space such as security guards or grounds keepers, and because no individual feels personally responsible, there was a general deterioration of public space leading to a sense of alienation and social disorder.

Jane Jacobs is another notable environmental determinist and is associated with the "eyes on the street" concept. By improving 'natural surveillance' of shared land and facilities of nearby residents by literally increasing the number of people who can see it, and increasing the familiarity of residents, as a collective, residents can more easily detect undesirable or criminal behavior. However, this is not a new concept. This was prevalent throughout the middle eastern world during the time of Mohamad It was not only reflected in the general structure of the outside of the home but also the inside. The "broken-windows" theory argues that small indicators of neglect, such as broken windows and unkempt lawns, promote a feeling that an area is in a state of decay. Anticipating decay, people likewise fail to maintain their own properties. The theory suggests that abandonment causes crime, rather than crime causing abandonment

Some planning methods might help an elite group to control ordinary citizens. Haussmann's renovation of Paris created a system of wide boulevards which prevented the construction of barricades in the streets and eased the movement of military troops. In Rome, the Fascists in the 1930s created *ex novo* many new suburbs in order to concentrate criminals and poorer classes away from the elegant town.

Other social theories point out that in Britain and most countries since the 18th century, the transformation of societies from rural agriculture to industry caused a difficult adaptation to urban living. These theories emphasize that many planning policies ignore personal tensions, forcing individuals to live in a condition of perpetual extraneity to their cities. Many people therefore lack the comfort of feeling "at home" when at home. Often these theorists seek a reconsideration of commonly used "standards" that rationalize the outcomes of a free (relatively unregulated) market.

Slums

The rapid urbanization of the last century caused more slums in the major cities of the world, particularly in developing countries. Planning resources and strategies are needed to address the problems of slum development. Many planners are calling for slum improvement, particularly the Commonwealth Association of Planners. When urban planners work on slums, they must cope with racial and cultural differences to ensure that racial steering does not occur. Slum were often "fixed" by clearance. However, more creative solutions are beginning to emerge such as Nairobi's "Camp of Fire" program, where established slum-dwellers promise to build proper houses, schools, and community centres without government money, in return for land on which they have been illegally squatting on for 30 years.

The "Camp of Fire" program is one of many similar projects initiated by Slum Dwellers International, which has programs in Africa, Asia, and South America. A slum, as defined by the United Nations agency UN-HABITAT, is a run-down area of a city characterized by substandard housing and squalor and lacking in tenure security. According to the United Nations, the proportion of urban dwellers living in slums decreased from 47 percent to 37 percent in the developing world between 1990 and 2005. However, due to rising population, the number of slum dwellers is rising. One billion people worldwide live in slums and the figure will likely grow to 2 billion by 2030.

The term has traditionally referred to housing areas that were once relatively affluent but which deteriorated as the original dwellers moved on to newer and better parts of the city, but has come to include the vast informal settlements found in cities in the developing world.

Many shack dwellers vigorously oppose the description of their communities as 'slums' arguing that this results in them being pathologised and then, often, subject to threats of evictions. Many academics have vigorously criticized UN-Habitat and the World Bank arguing that their 'Cities Without Slums' Campaign has led directly to a massive increase in forced evictions.

Although their characteristics vary between geographic regions, they are usually inhabited by the very poor or socially disadvantaged. Slum buildings vary from simple shacks to permanent and well-maintained structures. Most slums lack clean water, electricity, sanitation and other basic services.

Etymology

"Slum" was originally used mainly in the phrase "back slum," meaning a back room and later "back alley". The origin of this word is thought to come from the Irish phrase *'S lom* é (pron. s'lum ae) meaning 'exposed vulnerable place' The Oxford English Dictionary says it may be a "cant" word of Roma (Gypsy) origin. The etymologist Eric Partridge says flatly that it is "of unknown origin."

Other terms that are often used interchangeably with "slum" include shanty town, favela, skid row, barrio, and ghetto although each of these may have a somewhat different meaning. Slums are distinguished from shanty towns and favelas in that the latter initially are low-class settlements, whereas slums are generally constructed early on as relatively affluent or possibly a prestigious communities. The term "shanty town" also suggests that the dwellings are improvised shacks, made from scrap materials, and usually without proper sanitation, electricity, or telephone services. Skid row refers to an urban area with a high homeless population and a term is most commonly used in the United States. Barrio may refer to an upper-class area in some Spanish-speaking countries, and is only used to describe a low-class community in the United States. Ghetto refers to a neighbourhood based on shared ethnicity. By contrast, identification of an area as a slum is based solely on socio-economic criteria, not on racial, ethnic, or religious criteria.

Characteristics

The characteristics associated with slums vary from place to place. Slums are usually characterized by urban decay, high rates of poverty, illiteracy, and unemployment. They are commonly seen as "breeding grounds" for social problems such as crime, drug addiction, alcoholism, high rates of mental illness, and suicide. In many poor countries they exhibit high rates of disease due to unsanitary conditions, malnutrition, and lack of basic health care. However some like Dharavi in Mumbai are a hive of business activity such as leather work, cottage industries etc. Rural depopulation with thousands arriving daily into the cities makes slum clearance an uphill struggle. In fact one could argue that the presence of slums reflects true democracy(free movements of people)-as only a totalitarian state could 'eradicate' slums. No Indian needs a pass to enter Mumbai-however Chinese citizens need passes to enter

Shanghai and Beijing. A UN Expert Group has created an operational definition of a slum as an area that combines to various extents the following characteristics: inadequate access to safe water; inadequate access to sanitation and other infrastructure; poor structural quality of housing; overcrowding; and insecure residential status. A more complete definition of these can be found in the 2003 UN report titled "Slums of the World: The face of urban poverty in the new millennium?". The report also lists various attributes and names that are given by individual countries which are somewhat different than these UN characteristics of a slum.

Low socioeconomic status of its residents is another common characteristic given for a slum. In many slums, especially in poor countries, many live in very narrow alleys that do not allow vehicles (like ambulances and fire trucks) to pass. The lack of services such as routine garbage collection allows rubbish to accumulate in huge quantities. The lack of infrastructure is caused by the informal nature of settlement and no planning for the poor by government officials. Additionally, informal settlements often face the brunt of natural and man-made disasters, such as landslides, as well as earthquakes and tropical storms. Fires are often a serious problem.

Many slum dwellers employ themselves in the informal economy. This can include street vending, drug dealing, domestic work, and prostitution. In some slums people even recycle trash of different kinds (from household garbage to electronics) for a living-selling either the odd usable goods or stripping broken goods for parts or raw materials. Slums are often associated with Victorian Britain, particularly in industrial, northern English towns, lowland Scottish towns and Dublin City in Ireland. These were generally still inhabited until the 1940s, when the government started slum clearance and built new council houses. There are still many examples left of former slum housing in the UK, however they have generally been restored into more modern housing.

Growth and Countermeasures

Recent years have seen a dramatic growth in the number of slums as urban populations have increased in the Third

World. In April 2005, the director of UN-HABITAT stated that the global community was falling short of the Millennium Development Goals which targeted significant improvements for slum dwellers and an additional 50 million people have been added to the slums of the world in the past two years. According to a 2006 UN-HABITAT report, 327 million people live in slums in Commonwealth countries-almost one in six Commonwealth citizens. In a quarter of Commonwealth countries (11 African, 2 Asian and 1 Pacific), more than two out of three urban dwellers live in slums and many of these countries are urbanising rapidly. The number of people living in slums in India has more than doubled in the past two decades and now exceeds the entire population of Britain, the Indian Government has announced.

Many governments around the world have attempted to solve the problems of slums by clearing away old decrepit housing and replacing it with modern housing with much better sanitation. The displacement of slums is aided by the fact that many are squatter settlements whose property rights are not recognized by the state. This process is especially common in the Third World. Slum clearance often takes the form of eminent domain and urban renewal projects, and often the former residents are not welcome in the renewed housing. For example, in the Philippine slums of Smokey Mountain, located in Tondo, Manila, projects have been enforced by the Government and non-government organizations to allow urban resettlement sites for the slum dwellers. According to a UN-Habitat report, over 2 million people in the Philippines live in slums, and in the city of Manila alone, 50% of the over 11 million inhabitants live in slum areas.

Moreover new projects are often on the semi-rural peripheries of cities far from opportunities for generating livelihoods as well as schools, clinics etc. At times this has resulted in large movements of inner city slum dwellers militantly opposing relocation to formal housing on the outskirts of cities. In some countries, leaders have addressed this situation by rescuing rural property rights to support traditional sustainable agriculture, however this solution has met with open hostility from capitalists and corporations. It also tends to be relatively unpopular with the slum communities themselves, as it involves moving out of the city back into the countryside, a reverse of the rural-urban migration that originally brought many of them into the city.

Critics argue that slum clearances tend to ignore the social problems that cause slums and simply redistribute poverty to less valuable real estate. Where communities have been moved out of slum areas to newer housing, social cohesion may be lost. If the original community is moved back into newer housing after it has been built in the same location, residents of the new housing face the same problems of poverty and powerlessness. There is a growing movement to demand a global ban of 'slum clearance programmes' and other forms of mass evictions.

Alleged Positive Aspects of Slums

In recent years, some environmentalists such as Stewart Brand and organizations such as the United Nations Population Fund suggested that despite the poor living conditions, slums are positive both environmentally and socially. Because the slum is characterized by a very high density of housing, its environmental impact is smaller than that of diffuse rural communities. The fertility rate of new slum dwellers is below the replacement rate; this mitigates dangers associated with overpopulation that results from manpower-intensive subsistence agriculture, and frees up arable land for the nature, or more efficient industrialized agriculture. Slum dwellers also appear to have vastly better opportunities for getting jobs, starting small businesses and climbing out of poverty than rural inhabitants.

Decay

Urban decay is a process by which a city, or a part of a city, falls into a state of disrepair and neglect. It is characterized by depopulation, economic restructuring, property abandonment, high unemployment, fragmented families, political disenfranchisement, crime, and desolate urban landscapes. During the 1970s and 1980s, urban decay was often associated with central areas of cities in North America and Europe. During this time, changes in global economies, demographics, transportation, and policies fostered urban decay. Many planners spoke of "white flight" during this time. This pattern was different than the pattern of "outlying slums" and "suburban ghettos" found in many cities outside of North America and Western Europe, where central urban areas actually had higher real estate values.

Starting in the 1990s, many of the central urban areas in North America have been experiencing a reversal of the urban decay, with rising real estate values, smarter development, demolition of obsolete social housing and a wider variety of housing choices.

Reconstruction and Renewal

Areas devastated by war or invasion challenge urban planners. Resources are scarce. The existing population has needs. Buildings, roads, services and basic infrastructure like power, water and sewerage are often damaged, but with salvageable parts. Historic, religious or social centres also need to be preserved and re-integrated into the new city plan. A prime example of this is the capital city of Kabul, Afghanistan, which, after decades of civil war and occupation, has regions of rubble and desolation. Despite this, the indigenous population continues to live in the area, constructing makeshift homes and shops out of salvaged materials. Any reconstruction plan, such as Hisham Ashkouri's City of Light Development, needs to be sensitive to the needs of this community and its existing culture and businesses.

Urban Reconstruction Development plans must also work with government agencies as well as private interests to develop workable designs.

Transport

Transport within urbanized areas presents unique problems. The density of an urban environment increases traffic, which can harm businesses and increase pollution unless properly managed. Parking space for private vehicles requires the construction of large parking garages in high density areas. This space could often be more valuable for other development.

Good planning uses transit oriented development, which attempts to place higher densities of jobs or residents near high-volume transportation. For example, some cities permit commerce and multi-story apartment buildings only within one block of train stations and multilane boulevards, and accept single-family dwellings and parks farther away.

Floor area ratio is often used to measure density. This is the floor area of buildings divided by the land area. Ratios below 1.5 are low density. Ratios above five very high density. Most exurbs are below two, while most city centres are well above five. Walk-up apartments with basement garages can easily achieve a density of three. Skyscrapers easily achieve densities of thirty or more.

City authorities may try to encourage higher densities to reduce per-capita infrastructure costs. In the UK, recent years have seen a concerted effort to increase the density of residential development in order to better achieve sustainable development. Increasing development density has the advantage of making mass transport systems, district heating and other community facilities (schools, health centres, etc.) more viable. However critics of this approach dub the densification of development as 'town cramming' and claim that it lowers quality of life and restricts market-led choice.

Problems can often occur at residential densities between about two and five. These densities can cause traffic jams for automobiles, yet are too low to be commercially served by trains or light rail systems. The conventional solution is to use buses, but these and light rail systems may fail where automobiles and excess road network capacity are both available, achieving less than 2% ridership. The Lewis-Mogridge Position claims that increasing road space is not an effective way of relieving traffic jams as latent or induced demand invariably emerges to restore a socially-tolerable level of congestion.

Suburbanization

In some countries, declining satisfaction with the urban environment is held to blame for continuing migration to smaller towns and rural areas (so-called urban exodus). Successful urban planning supported Regional planning can bring benefits to a much larger hinterland or city region and help to reduce both congestion along transport routes and the wastage of energy implied by excessive commuting.

Environmental Factors

Environmental protection and conservation are of utmost importance to many planning systems across the world. Not only are the specific effects of development to be mitigated, but attempts are made to minimize the overall effect of development on the local and global environment. This is commonly done through the assessment of Sustainable urban infrastructure and microclimate. In Europe this process is known as a Sustainability Appraisal. In most advanced urban or village planning models, local context is critical. In many, gardening and other outdoor activities assumes a central role in the daily life of citizens. Environmental planners focus now on smaller and larger systems of resource extraction and consumption, energy production, and waste disposal. A practice known as Arcology seeks to unify the fields of ecology and architecture, using principles of landscape architecture to achieve a harmonious environment for all living things. On a small scale, the eco-village theory has become popular, as it emphasizes a traditional 100-140 person scale for communities

An urban planner can use a number of quantitative tools to forecast impacts of development on the environmental, including roadway air dispersion models to predict air quality impacts of urban highways and roadway noise models to predict noise pollution effects of urban highways. As early as the 1960s, noise pollution was addressed in the design of urban highways as well as noise barriers. The Phase I Environmental Site Assessment can be an important tool to the urban planner by identifying early in the planning process any geographic areas or parcels which have toxic constraints. Tall buildings in particular can have a substantial effect in channelling winds and shading large areas. The microclimate around the building will typically be assessed as part of the environmental impact assessment for the building.

Light and Sound

The urban canyon effect is a colloquial, non-scientific term referring to street space bordered by very high buildings. This type of environment may shade the sidewalk level from direct sunlight during most daylight hours. While an oft-decried phenomenon, it is rare except in very dense, hyper-tall urban environments, such as those found in Lower and Midtown Manhattan, Chicago's Loop and Kowloon in Hong Kong. In urban planning, sound is usually measured as a source of pollution. Another perspective on urban sounds is developed in Soundscape studies emphasising that sound aesthetics involves more than noise abatement and decibel measurements. Hedfors coined 'Sonotope' as a useful concept in urban planning to relate typical sounds to a specific place.

Light pollution has become a problem in urban residential areas, not only as it relates to its effects on the night sky, but as some lighting is so intrusive as to cause conflict in the residential areas and paradoxically intense improperly installed security lighting may pose a danger to the public, producing excessive glare. The development of the full cutoff fixture, properly installed, has reduced this problem considerably.

Process

Prior to the 1950, Urban Planning was seldom considered a unique profession. Planning focused on top-down processes by which the urban planner created the plans. The planner would know architecture, surveying, or engineering, bringing to the town planning process ideals based on these disciplines. They typically worked for national or local governments. Changes to the planning process Strategic Urban Planning over past decades have witnessed the metamorphosis of the role of the urban planner in the planning process. More citizens calling for democratic planning & development processes have played a huge role in allowing the public to make important decisions as part of the planning process. Community organizers and social workers are now very involved in planning from the grassroots level. The term advocacy planning was coined by Paul Davidoff in his influential 1965 paper, "Advocacy and Pluralism in Planning" which acknowledged the political nature of planning and urged planners to acknowledge that their actions are not value-neutral and encouraged minority and under represented voices to be part of planning decisions.

Ozawa and Seltzer (1999)advocate a communicative planning model in education to teach planners to work within the social and political context of the planning process. In their paper "Taking Our Bearings: Mapping a Relationship among Planning Practice, Theory, and Education," the authors demonstrate the importance of educating planners beyond the rational planning model in which planners make supposedly value-neutral recommendations based on science and reason. Through a survey of employers, it was found that the most highly rated skills in entry-level professional hiring are communication-based. The results suggest this view of planning as a communicative discourse as a possible bridge between theory and practice, and indicate that the education of planners needs to incorporate synthesis and communication across the curriculum.

Developers have also played huge roles in development, particularly by planning projects. Many recent developments were results of large and small-scale developers who purchased land, designed the district and constructed the development from scratch. The Melbourne Docklands, for example, was largely an initiative pushed by private developers to redevelop the waterfront into a high-end residential and commercial district.

Recent theories of urban planning, espoused, for example by .Salingaros see the city as a adaptive system that grows according to process similar to those of plants. They say that urban planning should thus take its cues from such natural processes.

7

Trends and Patterns in Internal Migration

The two main secondary sources of data on population mobility in India are the Census and the National Sample Survey (NSS). These surveys may underestimate some migration flows, such as temporary, seasonal and circulatory migration, both due to empirical and conceptual difficulties. Since such migration and commuting is predominantly employment oriented, the data underestimate the extent of labour mobility. Furthermore, migration data relate to population mobility and not worker mobility, although economic theories of migration are primarily about worker migration. It is not easy to disentangle these, firstly because definitions of migrants used in both surveys (change from birthplace and change in last usual place of residence), are not employment related. Secondly, migration surveys give only the main reason for migration, and that only at the time of migration. Secondary economic reasons could be masked, as in the case of married women, who would cite other reasons for movement. Another problem is that migration data relate to stocks of migrants and not to flows, although different policy concerns relate to stocks (of different ages) and flows. Many of these concerns can be handled only by micro surveys, which have their own problems.

Population Mobility

In one view, population mobility in India is low. Migration statistics to the early 1990s also suggest a decline in mobility.

In the 1991 census, using the change in residence concept, 27.4% of the population is considered to have migrated (that is, 232 million of the total 838 million persons), which shows a considerable decline from 30.6% in 1971 and 31.2% in 1981. This is true for male and female migrants. In the case of males, it declined from 18.1% in 1971 to 14.7% in 1991. In the case of females, it declined from 43.1% in 1971 to 41.6% in 1991.

However, recent evidence based on NSS figures for 1992–1993 and 1999–2000, and indirectly supported by the census, suggests an increase in migration rates – from 24.7% to 26.6% over that period. This evidence suggests the proportion of migrants of both sexes, in both rural and urban areas, increased during the last decade of the 20th century. Migration in India is predominantly short distance, with around 60% of migrants changing their residence within the district of enumeration and over 20% within the state of enumeration while the rest move across the state boundaries. A significant proportion of women migrates over short distances, mainly following marriage. The proportion of male lifetime migrants is low in most poor states except Madhya Pradesh and high in most developed states. For interstate migration, a similar trend is observed: developed states show high interstate immigration while poor states, except Madhya Pradesh, show low rates of total and male immigration. Rates of interstate lifetime emigration are complementary to the above trends (Srivastava, 1998).

Based on place of last residence and on place of birth, migrants are generally classified into four migration streams. Rural areas are still the main destination for migrants, but urban destinations are more important for male migrants (49% of male migrants moved to urban destinations in 1991, compared to 29.5% female migrants). Between 1992–1993 and 1999–2000, NSS data indicate an increase in urban migration, but this is mainly due to urban-urban flows.

Migration for Work

The primary motive for migration, recorded by the census as well as the NSS, is an important indicator of how mobility is influenced by conditions of the labour market. Of the 27.4%

who changed place of residence, as per 1991 census, 8.8% moved for employment reasons and 2.3% had business motives. The proportion moving due to economic motives was higher for males (27.8% moved for employment reasons, and 7.1% for business reasons), compared with females (only 1.8% moved for employment reasons and 0.5% for business reasons).

The proportion migrating for economic reasons is greater among long-distance migrants; most male migrants moving between states did so for economic reasons. Again, economic motives are more significant in urban migration streams, especially for males. While the share of interstate to total migrants was only 11.8% in 1991, such migrants comprised 28% of all economic migrants. Similarly, while 49% of male migrants were in urban areas, 69.2% of such migrants migrated for employment (Srivastava, 1998).

A distinct regional variation emerges in the work pattern of migrants. In the northeastern states and some others, migrants are mainly employed in the tertiary and secondary sector of the economy. Elsewhere, the primary sector attracts the migrant most. An analysis of the occupational division of migrant workers (other than cultivators and agricultural labourers) shows that among males, 43% are engaged in production related work. In the tertiary sector, significant proportions of male migrants are engaged as sales workers, followed by clerical and related work.

All the western states have a significant proportion of male migrants in secondary activity and in the southern and north-eastern states they are mainly engaged in the tertiary sector. In the case of female migrant workers, 40% are in production related works and a significant proportion are in technical and professional activity.

Migration for Work in the 1990s

Analysis of the recent trends of labour mobility, on the basis of NSS estimates from the 49th (1992–93) and 55th rounds (1999–00) have been carried out by Srivastava and Bhattacharya (2002) and a few central conclusions from that analysis are discussed below. This period shows a sharp increase in urban male mobility, with a significantly larger percentage of male migrants reporting economic and employment linked reasons for mobility. For other streams, there has been a decline in the percentage of migrants giving economic reasons for mobility.

A comparison of the decadal migrant streams (migrants who had migrated in the decade preceding the period of survey) shows that (a) a greater percentage of the urban migrant workers were from the non-agricultural sector (self-employed or regular employed); (b) a greater percentage of the male migrant workers were self-employed or in regular employment in 1999–00; (c) in the case of females, however, a larger percentage of decadal female migrant workers worked in 1999–00 as casual labourers (in the rural areas in agriculture). Comparing activity status before and after migration for all migrants, we find that migrants in general show much higher work participation rates for both urban and rural areas In the urban areas, the NSS 55th round figures show a significant transition towards regular employment and self-employment among males, with a small decline in the percentage of casual labour. In the rural areas, there is an increase in all three categories including casual labour, but the most significant shift is towards self-employment. In the case of female migrants, however, along with an increase in the percentage of workers to population in all three categories after migration, there is also an increase in casualisation both in rural and urban areas, but quite significantly in the former. These results, along with the decline in short duration migration, which we discuss below, suggest that the 1990s may have provided greater opportunity for labour mobility to those who were better positioned – males in urban areas and in the non-agricultural sector. However, these results are still tentative and need to be corroborated with further analysis from other sources.

Short Duration Labour Migration

Our special interest is in temporary, short duration migration, because such migrants lack stable employment and sources of livelihood at home and belong to the poorer strata. These migrants find work in agriculture, seasonal industries, or are absorbed in the amorphous urban economy, either as casual labourers or as selfemployed. They may move from one type of job to another or even from rural to urban areas. There is another category of poor and destitute migrants who have virtually no assets in the areas of origin and have lost all contact with their origin. Thus not all poor migrants would fall in the category of seasonal/short term migrants. But as discussed earlier, for one reason or another, all these categories are likely to be underestimated in data.

In terms of the duration of migration, Census of India estimates 56.2% of the migrants in 1991 were of more than 10 years standing, while 21.4% were of 1 to 9 years duration. Only 7.07 million or 3.04% of the migrants were recorded as short duration (less than one year's duration), of whom 1.37 million migrated for economic reasons. The NSS survey of 1999–00 has estimated that there was 8.64 million short duration (less than one year) (in)-migrants in 1999–00, out of whom 3.24 million had migrated for economic reasons. However, in 1992–93 the total number of estimated short duration migrants was 16.75 million, suggesting a sharp decline in the intervening years. The NSS 55th round has separately estimated (for the first time) the number of short duration outmigrants in 1999–00 (those who stayed away for a period between 2 and 6 months for work or seeking work). Generally, this category would not overlap with the category of short duration in-migrants who are expected to have stayed in their current place of residence for six months or more. A total of nearly 10.87 million people stayed away from their UPR for work/seeking work for a period between 2 and 6 months. Of these 8.45 million were resident in rural areas and 2.42 million in urban areas. Among the 8.45 million short duration out-migrant in rural areas, 3.06 million were females and 5.39 million were males.

Short-duration out-migrants constituted 2.1% of rural employed persons and 1.3% of urban employed persons. Casual labourers among them formed 3.1% and 1.5% of the casual labour force in rural and urban areas respectively.

Some informal estimates of seasonal/short term migration have been made from time to time. They broadly suggest that these flows might be underestimated in national surveys. The National Commission of Rural Labour (NCRL) made a quick estimate of such labourers based on their numbers in industries employing migrant workers. According to the NCRL, there were approximately 10 million seasonal/circular migrants in the rural areas alone. This included an estimated 4.5 million interstate migrants. There were large numbers of migrants in agriculture and plantations, brick kilns, quarries, construction sites and fish processing.

A number of field studies over the 1990s also provide rough estimates of the magnitude of seasonal migration in different parts of India. These attest to the considerable scale of such migration. Empirical research on the scale and pattern of seasonal migration of workers to the rice-producing belt of West Bengal carried out in 1999–00 suggests that the number of seasonal migrants, drawn from tribals, Muslims and other low castes, moving to Bardhaman district during aman harvesting season exceeds 500,000 and this volume has been growing since the 1980s. A study based on annual seasonal migration of tribal households from Khandesh (Dhule district, Maharashtra) to the sugarcane fields of southern Gujarat in 1988–89 estimated that every year 100,000 to 150,000 labourers are recruited from this region to work in the nine sugar co-operatives of Southern Gujarat (Teerink, 1995). Other studies in the tribal areas in MP, Rajasthan and Gujarat also indicate a very high rate of out migration, in some cases involving 60 to 80% of households.

Significant number of tribals, mainly from drought prone areas of Andhra Pradesh, Karnataka and Maharashtra, migrate to work in construction, tile factory, brick kiln and crop cutting in Maharashtra (Pandey, 1998). Saora, Munda and Santhal tribes have a long history of migration, with male only migration among the Saora (plantation cultivation in Assam and Arunachal Pradesh), whereas Mundas and Santhals migrate as household units, mainly to NALCO site in Denkanal district of Orissa (Menon, 1995). The construction industry mainly depends on migrant labour (90% of the labourers are migrants in one estimate (Vaijanyanta, 1998). Around 40,000 girls migrate from

Kerala annually to other state to work in the fishery industry (Sarodamoni, 1995).

Profile of Migrant Workers

Migration encompasses enormous economic and social diversity. Migrants are concentrated in different types of work in rural and urban areas. In the rural areas, self-employment is the predominant activity for both male and female migrant workers followed by casual work which, according to the NSS 55th round findings, engaged 33.4% of male migrant workers and 44.2% of female migrant workers in 1999–00. In urban areas, regular employment engaged 55.6% of the male workers while self-employment and casual work engaged 31.1 and 13.3% of male migrant workers respectively. In the case of females, the highest percentage were self-employed (39.7) followed by regular employment (35.1%) and casual work (25.2%) This naturally implies that there is considerable economic differentiation among migrant households. Further a little under 50% of the urban and rural migrants and more than 50% of male migrants in both sectors are in the top two consumption quintiles. Among other factors, this may reflect the higher work participation rates among migrants and the propensity of the well-off to migrate. Micro studies show a bi-modal relationship with respect to wealth/income and land: migrants cluster both at low and high levels. The NCRL report suggests that labourers and landpoor farmers have a high propensity to migrate as seasonal labourers.

Data on individual migrants gleaned from micro surveys shows a significant clustering of migrants in the 16–40 year age group. This is even more the case with poorer semi-permanent or temporary labour migrants (Srivastava 1999, and forthcoming). With respect to education, migration rates are high both among the highly educated and the least educated, and among seasonal migrants there is a high preponderance of illiterate people.

In the overall migrant population, differences across caste groups are not significant, but ST and SC migrants are more involved in short duration migrants, with migration rates among them being 2% and 1% respectively, compared with an overall rate of 0.7% for all short duration migrants (NSS, 2001). This is also corroborated by field survey data showing that low castes are predominant in short duration migration flows.

The nature of migration primarily reflects household subsistence strategies in the face of social, cultural, demographic and other constraints. Males predominate in most labour migration streams. But in a number of other cases, both men and women migrate together for work, especially among lower caste and tribals where constraints on women's participation in non-household economic activities are fewer. The pattern of labour migration (whether males alone, males and females, or females alone) is related to the social structure, the pattern of demand, and the nature of the migration process. In some sectors such as construction, brick kiln and sugarcane cutting, family migration is prevalent as it is more economical for employers. The proportion of women outmigrants (predominantly to agriculture and the construction sector) ranges from 18% to 42% in the case of some tribal areas.

Rogaly *et al* (2001), focusing on four source areas for labour migration to West Bengal's rice bowl, find male only migration in two of the source areas they studied, whereas migration from the other two areas was both by men and women. The fish processing industry has seen the migration of large numbers of single women (Sarodamoni, 1995). In the domestic maid sector, there is increasing trend of independent migration of females, A study by the Institute of Social Sciences (1991) indicates that 20% of total women migrants to Delhi are employed as domestic maids. There are also important regional differences in the pattern of female labour mobility between the northern and southern states (Singh, 1984). Among interstate economic migrants, the share of the northern states (Bihar, UP) is very large in male migration, but the southern states have a comparatively larger share in female economic migrants (Srivastava, 1998). On the whole, however, females move smaller distances for work compared to males.

Causes of Migration

Given the diversity in the nature of migration in India, the causes are also bound to vary. Migration is influenced both by the pattern of development (NCRL, 1991), and the social structure (Mosse *et al*, 2002). The National Commission on Rural Labour, focusing on seasonal migration, concluded that uneven development was the main cause of seasonal migration. Along with inter regional disparity, disparity between different socioeconomic classes and the development policy adopted since independence has accelerated the process of seasonal migration. In tribal regions, intrusion of outsiders, the pattern of settlement, displacement and deforestation, also have played a significant role.

Most migration literature makes a distinction between 'pull' and 'push' factors, which, however, do not operate in isolation of one another. Mobility occurs when workers in source areas lack suitable options for employment/livelihood, and there is some expectation of improvement in circumstances through migration. The improvement sought may be better employment or higher wages/incomes, but also maximisation of family employment or smoothing of employment/income/consumption over the year.

At one end of the migration spectrum, workers could be locked into a debt-migration cycle, where earnings from migration are used to repay debts incurred at home or in the destination areas, thereby cementing the migration cycle. At the other end, migration is largely voluntary, although shaped by their limited choices. The NCRL has recognised the existence of this continuum for poor migrants by distinguishing between rural labour migration for survival and for subsistence. The landless poor, who mostly belong to lower caste, indigenous communities, from economically backward regions, migrate for survival and constitute a significant proportion of seasonal labour flow.

The growth of intensive agriculture and commercialisation of agriculture since the late 1960s has led to peak periods of labour demand, often also coinciding with a decline in local labour deployment. In the case of labour flows to the riceproducing belt of West Bengal, wage differentials between the source and destination have been considered as the main reason for migration. Moreover, absence of non-farm employment, low agricultural production has resulted in a growth of seasonal migration. Migration decisions are influenced by both individual and household characteristics as well as the social matrix, which is best captured in social-anthropological studies. Factors such as age, education level, wealth, land owned, productivity and job opportunities influence the participation of individuals and households in migration, but so do social attitudes and supporting social networks.

Where migration is essentially involuntary, it makes little sense to use voluntaristic models to explain the phenomenon. In Dhule region (Maharashtra) sugarcane cultivation leads to high demand for labour, but landowners recruit labourers from other districts for harvesting as they can have effective control over the labour. Local labourers are thus forced to migrate with their households to South Gujarat (Teerink 1995). In Kerala, trawler-fishing has depleted marine resources. With unemployment in other industries like cashew and rubber, this has led to large scale out migration of girls (Sardamoni, 1995).

The Migrant Labour Market

Migrants at the lower end of the market comprise mostly unskilled casual labourers or those who own or hire small means of livelihood such as carts or rickshaws and are self-employed. We focus in this section primarily on migrants who work as casual labourers, although several of the conditions discussed below are also common to other categories of migrants.

Migrant labourers are exposed to large uncertainties in the potential job market. To begin with, they have little knowledge of the market and risk high job search costs. The perceived risks and costs tend to be higher the further they are from home. There are several ways in which migrants minimise risks and costs. For a number of industries, recruitment is often done through middlemen. In many cases, these middlemen are known to the job seekers and may belong to the source area. In other cases, migrants move to the destination areas on their own. This is generally the case where 'bridgeheads' have been established, lowering potential risks and costs. The movement of migrants in groups, often sharing kinship ties, also provides some protection in the context of the harsh environment in which migrants travel, seek jobs and work. Mosse *et al* (2002), based on a study of villages in the Western India Rain-fed Farming Project (WIRFFP), have shown that the incorporation of workers in the labour market in different ways may depend upon their initial status, with somewhat better-off migrants having superior social net-works and being better able to exploit bridgeheads in urban locations. As with other types of interlocked relationships, the poorer migrants trade their freedom of making individual contracts with employers to the possibility of securing advances and employment from contractors.

In the agricultural sector, labourers are sometimes directly recruited by the employer. In Punjab, labourers are often recruited by employers at the railway stations. In West Bengal, labourers are sometimes recruited at bus stands or employers often go to the source area and recruit labourers. Contractors, who often belong to same caste and community, are the other medium for recruitment in the agricultural and rural sectors (agricultural workers in Punjab, coffee plantations in Karnataka, sugarcane plantations in Gujarat, quarry workers around Delhi). In parts of Punjab, agents or traders are also active in recruitment. Labourers are hired by contractors in their village, or by their relatives and friends who have already migrated. In the urban informal sector, friends and relatives act as a network and the job market is highly segmented based around people of the same caste, religion and kinship. Social networks provide initial income support, information, accommodation, and access to jobs. However, parts of the urban unorganised sector may also be characterised by a high degree of organised migration, as in the rural areas discussed above. In the construction industry, workers are largely recruited through contractors who settle wages, retain part of their earnings apart from payments received from employer, and sometimes also play supervisory roles. In the fish processing industry in Kerala, recruitment takes place through contractors, who often use networks of older women to recruit. In the case of domestic maid servants in Delhi, a number of voluntary organisations are involved in the recruitment process. Most of the maids are from the tribal belts of Jharkhand and Chattisgarh. While a new genre of private recruitment agencies has sprung up (which continue to recruit through informal channels and make unspecified deductions from wage payments), the church also plays an active and more benign role in bringing potential employers and employees together (Neetha, 2002).

The labour process in the places of employment only partly overlaps with the process of recruitment. Workers seeking jobs independently may still find the labour processes in the destination dominated by contracting and sub-contracting relationships. Workers have to depend upon advances and irregular payments. Migrants often get lower wages than local labourers. The migrant status of the labourers accounts for 38–56% of the wage differential in Chennai city when other characteristics are accounted.

They work long and odd hours. Moreover the payments are not made on time. Piece rates are mostly prevalent which provide greater flexibility to employers (NCRL, 1991). Of course, migrants may also prefer these wage systems as they can maximise returns on a per day basis, raising the possibility of their saving part of wages. But in many cases organised migration results in credit-labour interlocking, such that the net return to labour may have no relation to wages in destination areas.

Employers often prefer migrant labourers to local labourers, as they are cheaper and do not develop social relationships with the place of destination. Women migrants fare the worst; they are generally paid less than male migrants (Pandey, 1998). In the construction industry they are viewed as assistants to their husbands, and confined to unskilled jobs. The consequent segmentation is used as a justification for low payments. Women also face greater insecurity (Viajanyanta, 1998). In the fish processing industry, they are badly exploited in terms of working condition, wages, living condition and sometimes sexually harassed (Sarodamoni, 1995).

In the public sector, wage structures also vary from project to project. As most contracts are given to private firms, they flout labour laws and minimum wage legislation. Low wages of seasonal workers are the result of instability of demand, segmented labour markets, unregulated nature and dominance of labour contractors and vulnerability of workers.

Breman (1996) has argued that the continued existence of a large mass of unorganised workers belies expectations that workers would eventually shift from the traditional to the modern sector. An examination of the major industries in the informal sector shows a steady replacement of local workers by migrants. He also finds that rural-urban migration shares a number of features in common with rural-to-rural migration. The urban and rural informal sector markets are increasingly linked through horizontal circulation as migrants may move from one to the other in search of jobs. Despite growing linkages between the urban and rural labour markets, the markets are not integrated but instead segmented in various ways. Breman (*ibid.*) shows that for locals as well as migrants, stratifications are generally preserved as workers move so that the overall tendency of the labour market is to be broken into 'circuits' of labour. Women migrant workers in urban areas are concentrated mainly in the lower segments, in household work or jobs in manufacturing, construction or personal services (Meher, 1994). According to Das (1994) chain migration also has the impact of fragmenting this market along ethnic and regional lines. In the construction sector, migrant workers are fragmented by the contracting arrangements through which they work. In focusing on the characteristics of migrant labourers, schooling and resources act as two important barriers in the poorer social groups obtaining on-job training and skills which could lead to the semipermanent jobs.

The Impact of Migration

On migrants and their families Poorer migrant workers, crowded into the lower ends of the labour market, have few entitlements *vis a vis* their employers or the public authorities in the destination areas. They have meagre personal assets and suffer a range of deprivations in the destination areas. In the source areas, migration has both negative and positive consequences for migrants and their families. Living conditions: migrant labourers, whether agricultural or non-agricultural, live in deplorable conditions. There is no provision of safe drinking water or hygienic sanitation. Most live in open spaces or makeshift shelters in spite of the Contract Labour Act which stipulates that the contractor or employer should provide suitable accommodation. Apart from seasonal workers, workers who migrate to the cities for job live in parks and pavements. Slum dwellers, who are mostly migrants, stay in deplorable conditions, with inadequate water and bad drainage. Food costs more for migrant workers who are not able to obtain temporary ration cards.

Health and Education: labourers working in harsh circumstances and living in unhygienic conditions suffer from serious occupational health problems and are vulnerable to disease. Those working in quarries, construction sites and mines suffer from various health hazards, mostly lung diseases. As the employer does not follow safety measures, accidents are quite frequent. Migrants cannot access various health and family care programmes due to their temporary status. Free public health care facilities and programmes are not accessible to them. For women workers, there is no provision of maternity leave, forcing them to resume work almost immediately after childbirth. Workers, particularly those working in tile factories and brick kilns suffer from occupational health hazards such as body ache, sunstroke and skin irritation (NCRL, 1991).

As there are no creche facilities, children often accompany their families to the workplace to be exposed to health hazards. They are also deprived of education: the schooling system at home does not take into account their migration pattern and their temporary status in the destination areas does not make them eligible for schooling there.

In the case of male-only migration, the impact on family relations and on women, children and the elderly left behind can be quite significant. The absence of men adds to material and psychological insecurity, leading to pressures and negotiations with wider family. Male out migration has been seen to influence the participation of women in the directly productive sphere of the economy as workers and decision-makers and increase the level of their interaction with the outside world. But given the patriarchal set up, women may have to cope with a number of problems which are exacerbated due to the uncertainty of the timing and magnitude of remittances on which the precarious household economy depends. This, in turn, pushes women and children from poor labouring households to participate in the labour market under adverse conditions. Thus, the impact of migration on the women can be two-sided but the strong influence of patriarchy restricts the scope of women's autonomy. The impact of male migration can be especially adverse for girls, who often have to bear additional domestic responsibilities and take care of younger siblings. The absence of male supervision further reduces their chances of acquiring education. There are several cases where women participate in the migration streams along with male members of their households. It is usual in such cases for younger siblings and older children to accompany their parents and to work along with them. Family migration usually implies migration of the younger members of the family, leaving the elderly to cope with additional responsibilities while at the same time fend for their subsistence and other basic requirements.

Changes in migrants' attitudes: Exposure to a different environment, including the stresses that it carries, has a deep impact on the attitudes, habits and awareness levels of migrant workers, depending upon the length of migration and the place to which it occurs. Changes are more dramatic in the case of urban migrants. Migrant workers develop greater awareness regarding conditions of work (Srivastava, 1999). Life style and changes in awareness may lead to a mixed impact on family members. The increased awareness which migrants, especially in urban areas, gain often helps them realise the importance of their children's education.

Impact on Source Areas

The major impacts of migration on source areas occur through changes in the labour market, income and assets, changes in the pattern of expenditure and investment. Although seasonal out migration potentially has the effect of smoothing out employment over the annual cycle, rural out migration could cause a tightening of the labour market in some circumstances. However, empirical evidence from out-migrant areas does not often attest to this. This may be because out migration often takes place in labour surplus situations. There is also evidence of the replacement of out migrant male labour by female and even child labour (Srivastava, forthcoming).

Srivastava's (1999) study of seven villages in Uttar Pradesh showed some variation over regions. While the situation in the study villages in Eastern and central Uttar Pradesh conformed to a situation of labour surplus, this was not the case in Western Uttar Pradesh where seasonal migration coincided with the agricultural peak season (*Rabi*) and employers complained of labour shortages. Significantly in all the regions studied, labourers on their part gave uncertainty of employment along with employment conditions and poor relations with their agricultural employers as the major reasons for out migration. Even if labour tightening is not an outcome, out migration may still speed up qualitative changes in existing labour relationships in rural areas, and thereby affect the pace of change. This may occur in several ways. First, there is the well-documented impact of migration on attitudes and awareness as migrant labourers and return migrants are more reluctant to accept adverse employment conditions and low wages. Secondly, out migration leads to a more diversified livelihood strategy. Combined with some increase in the income and employment portfolio of poor households, this may tend to push up acceptable level of wages (reservation wages) in rural areas and may make certain forms of labour relationships (as for example, those involving personalised dependency) less acceptable.

Out migration as a result of debt at home, or debt-interlocking (i.e. the repayment of debts through advance labour commitment) involving employers in the destination areas or their middlemen, is quite common. Such out migration may or may not eliminate the causes of debt. The reduction of personalised dependencies or interlocked relationships may also accelerate labour mobility and migration as labourers seek out alternative sources of cash income.

Remittances and effect on sending areas While the impact of out migration via the labour market has been reviewed above, the other source of changes which need to be analysed would work through changes in income, income distribution and the pattern of expenditure and investment. Although we do not have direct evidence of the value of remittances from migrants, some indirect evidence can be adduced from the NSS surveys on migration and consumption and employment/unemployment. These surveys give the percentage of out-migrants making remittances and households receiving remittances and depending upon remittances as their major source of livelihood. The former estimates depend upon the definition of out-migrants, which can vary. In 1992–93, 89% of permanent outmigrants sent remittances. The percentage of all rural households receiving remittance income is also fairly high – in some regions of the country, one-quarter to one-third of the households receive remittances. It should be noted that remittances are only one form in which resourceflows occur as a result of migration, the other being savings brought home by migrants in cash or kind. Field studies show that a majority of seasonal migrants either remit or bring home savings. In many cases, a substantial proportion of household cash income is attributed to migrant earnings. However, the cash incomes which accrue may not always add to the resource base of migrant households as some are used to adjust earlier debts.

However, it does appear that the income and consumption level of migrant households is generally higher than that of similarly placed non-migrants. But this conclusion needs to be carefully linked to migration impact as it is generally based on ex-post cross-sectional comparisons. As Mosse *et al* (2002) have noted, and as other studies testify, migrants are not only differentially placed at the entry point, their differential status also leads to different trajectories, so that changes in post-migration average incomes may provide only a limited picture of the varied set of changes. One of the few careful ethnographical studies provides some evidence of improvement in incomes of seasonal migrants as a result of migration, but these conclusions need to be supported by other studies.

The impact of migration on income and asset inequality is limited. The ethnographical study quoted above (Rogaly *et al*,

2001), finds evidence of reduced inequality, as incomes of labour households rise against non-labour households. In another context, Mosse *et al* (1997) suggest that these inequalities increase because the differentiated nature of the migration process led to the amplification of income and asset inequalities. Remittances are mainly used for purposes like consumption, repayment of loans and meeting other social obligations. These constitute, in effect the 'first charge' on migrant incomes. The evidence on investment is, however, mixed. Investment by migrant households on housing, land and consumer durables is common and migrant income is also used to finance working capital requirements in agriculture. Evidence of other productive farm or non-farm investment is scarce but a number of studies do report such investment by a small percentage of migrant and return migrant households. Thus, while studies do not fully discount for the impact of some factors such as the life cycle effect, rural out migration appears to provide some, albeit slender, evidence of an improvement in the productive potential of source areas, and the ability of some poor migrant households to acquire small surpluses and strengthen their productive base and bargaining strength in the rural economy.

The question of social and economic mobility can be examined both from the changes in worker occupations in the destination areas, as well as in the source areas. As shown earlier, a very large proportion of short duration migrants are unskilled. The question of their mobility is linked to their circumstances of migration, its duration, and is highly gendered. On the whole, a very small proportion of male migrants achieve economic mobility in the destination areas. The limited mobility occurs as migrants acquire a foothold in the destination areas, or acquire some skills, and are thus better positioned to exploit the labour market situation. In the source areas, there is a slightly greater impact on social and economic mobility, which, however, generally eludes the poorest, and in most cases, is not substantial for poor migrants.

A major linked issue, is the role of rural out migration in the material and social reproduction of rural households and the extant relationships in which they are placed. Standing

(1985) has argued that circulatory migration in particular contributes to the stability of rural production relations. He argues that circulatory labour migrations has 'safety valve' features and 'has often been a mechanism preserving a social mode of production or at least reducing the pressures on it' (*ibid).*

Temporary migration may allow households to relieve underemployment and meet debt and other obligations without having to sell assets. 'Relay migration' can also be seen as a part of the household survival strategy.

Indeed the long history of rural out migration in some of the source areas in India combined with agricultural and rural stagnation seems to corroborate the stabilising role of out migration. But labour circulation as well as other forms of rural out migration can also disrupt pre-existing production relations (Standing, *ibid*). The major impact on source areas appears to be through the labour market, with recent evidence indicating greater mobility of rural labour households leading to a less isolated and more generalised agriculture labour market and an upward pressure on wages. Further, as we have shown, there is also evidence of some impact through improvement in the resource base of the migrant households (Srivastava 1998).

Impact on Destination Areas

There are clearly multiple rationales for the use of migrant labour in destination areas. While shortages of local labour provides one important rationale, virtually all available evidence shows that recruitment of immigrants is as much motivated by strategies of labour control and wage cost reduction. Numerous cases have been documented where the same areas export and import labour to identical sectors. Migrants are preferred because their labour is easier to control and it is easier to extract labour from them under arduous conditions. Moreover, the supply of labour can be easily increased or decreased with little cost to employers and migrants can work for long and flexible hours. Flexibility of the migrant workforce is reinforced because of the role of contractors and middlemen in recruitment and supervision. The segmentation of the labour market, which also leads to greater control over both migrant and local labour, is another outcome of the process. Finally, the wage payment systems which grow around industries based predominantly on migrant labour are eminently suited to side-stepping minimum wage legislation. Thus migration reduces labour cost to employers.

The labour market outcomes generated by labour immigration facilitate a certain kind of growth and accumulation in the destination areas, although this is via what can be described as a 'low road' to capitalism. According to Breman (1996) the basic rationale for the growing informalisation, two-way mobility of labour and segmentation is to be found in the type of mercantilist capitalist development witnessed in India, just as international migration is strongly related to the structure of international capitalism. Capitalists operate in uncertain markets, under circumstances in which they are highly dependent on traders. Labour immigration is one of the strategies favoured by entrepreneurs to shift both risk and cost of production on to workers. Another reason for continued informalisation is to keep businesses away from state surveillance. Thus most enterprises in the informal sector escape regulation of any kind.

Furthermore, in such destination areas, employers rarely provide anything other than wage subsistence requirements. Migrant labourers have to fend for themselves to meet their health, shelter and other basic requirements. Although the poor condition in which labourers subsist is a result of employers not internalising the legitimate costs of hiring labour (contravening numerous laws), to society the resulting urban congestion appears to be result of unplanned mobility. The costs of population mobility have been, as a result, considered in theory in the context of large costs imposed by population concentration in large cities. The social, political and other consequences of immigration, especially where such migration is by linguistically, ethnically or regionally distinct groups, has not been considered in the growing economic literature on internal migration, but figures prominently in the corpus of sociological and political literature (cf. Weiner, 1978).

POLICY REGIME GOVERNING INTERNATIONAL LABOUR MIGRATION

The overseas employment policy regime in India mainly addresses temporary and contract migration. The most important policy instrument, the Emigration Act 1983, deals with the emigration of Indian workers for overseas employment on a contractual basis and seeks to safeguard their interest and ensure their welfare. Prior to the Act of 1983, the Emigration Act of 1922 governed the migration of Indians across national boundaries. The main purpose of this Act was to regulate and control the recruitment and emigration of unskilled agricultural workers. The Rules of the Act stipulated procedures for emigration and the steps to be taken by the foreign agents in India for the welfare of such emigrants. According to the Act, emigration of unskilled workers involved notifications for specific countries. However, since no such notification was issued by the government, the emigration of unskilled workers progressively declined between 1923 and 1947.

The Act did not specify any regulations governing the emigration of people with technical qualifications or professional expertise and therefore permanent migration to the industrialised countries, which began from the 1950s, was hardly regulated or monitored by the policy regime in India. The migration boom to the Middle East during the mid 1970s exposed the limitations of the 1922 Act in safeguarding the interests of workers emigrating for employment. This period witnessed the emergence of a large number of illegal recruiting agents who employed exploitative practices, including extortion and fraud. Workers with low skills and incomes suffered most. It was in this broader context the Emigration Act, 1983 was introduced with a view to alleviate the problems associated with emigration of unskilled and skilled workers.

The Act aims to safeguard the interests of Indians migrating abroad for employment by stipulating emigration clearance and registration of recruiting agents, and by setting up mechanisms for redressing grievances of migrants. Section 22 of the Act states that all Indian citizens seeking to migrate must obtain emigration clearances from the Office of the

Protector of Emigrants, Ministry of Labour, as an endorsement in their passports. In providing such clearances, the Protector of Emigrants is required to examine the terms and conditions of employment contracts to ensure that the wages and working conditions are not exploitative and that adequate provision has been made for travel expense, accommodation and medical care. In order to facilitate free movement of manpower, 17 categories of persons are currently exempted from the requirement to obtaining clearance and placed under emigration check not required category (ECNR category). In addition six more categories of persons with valid employment visa endorsed on their passports can also obtain ECNR endorsement.

The Emigration Act 1983 focuses on regulating overseas employment recruitment systems in India. Section 10 of the Act states that no recruiting agent can carry out the business of recruitment without a registration certificate issued by the Protector General of Emigrants. The Certificate is granted after taking into account inter-alia the recruiting agent's financial soundness, trustworthiness, adequacy of premises, experience in the field of handling manpower export, etc., and after obtaining security ranging from Rs.0.3 million to Rs.1 million in the form of Bank Guarantee. The financial security is intended to secure due performance of the terms and conditions of the Registration Certificate and also to meet the cost of repatriation of any stranded worker sent by him.

Another important aspect of the Emigration Act relates to the maximum amount that the recruiting agents are authorised to charge as fees for services rendered to the migrant. Currently this ranges from Rs.2000 for unskilled workers to Rs. 3000 for semiskilled workers to Rs.5000 for skilled workers and to Rs.10,000 for other than the above categories.

An examination of the provisions of the Emigration Act indicates that overseas employment policies in India have been largely confined to ensuring that the terms and conditions of employment conformed to certain specified norms so that agents and employers did not subject the workers to exploitation. Efforts to manage and direct export of manpower have indeed been minimal. The policy regime has also not been concerned with migration of persons with technical or professional qualifications. The Emigration Act has considerably reduced the problems encountered by migrant workers. However, there is little policy influence on the forces of market supply and demand which still largely determine the emigration of workers from India.

Problems Encountered by Migrants

Problems encountered by the migrant workers may be examined at two levels. First in relation to recruitment violations and the second in relation to working and living conditions in destination countries. Commonly reported violations are delayed deployment or nondeployment of workers, overcharging or collection of fees far in excess of authorised placement fees and illegal recruitment. Delayed deployments are often caused by factors beyond the control of the recruitment agency, such as visa delays or when the employer requests a postponement. Non-deployment is however a serious case and the magnitude of its implications are amplified if an excessive placement fee is collected from the worker. Overcharging is a serious offence and is prevalent in all labour-sending countries in Asia. What makes overcharging doubly serious is that the workers end up paying huge amounts equivalent to many months salary (Sasikumar, 2000). Minimising, if not totally eliminating, overcharging poses a serious challenge to overseas employment administrators.

Illegal recruitment is another serious violation of the rules as workers get recruited and deployed overseas without the government knowing about them. Being unlicensed, illegal recruiters are beyond the reach of the normal regulatory machinery of the national overseas employment policy. They are and should be the concern of police and other enforcement agencies. Some major problems encountered by the migrants in their countries of employment include: a) premature termination of job contracts, b) changing the clauses of contract to the disadvantage of the workers, c) delay in payment of salary, d) violation of minimum wage standards, e) freezing of fringe benefits and other perks, f) forced over-time work without returns and g) denial of permission to keep one's own passport.

Migrant labourers seldom lodge any complaint against the erring employers for the fear of losing their jobs. In cases where migrant workers decide to complain against the erring employer, they have two options. First, the employee may inform the home embassy in the country of employment. This is mainly done by people lacking the means to return home. Embassy officials sometimes seek the help and assistance of the local government to take actions against the erring employers. Apart from that, the Embassy also passes information about the complaints made to it to the Protector of Emigrants (POE) offices in India. If a registered recruiting agent recruited the complainant, then the POE refers the complaint to the concerned agent seeking explanation.

In most cases the agents maintain that it was the foreign employer who committed any violation. However, if the POE office finds the explanation unsatisfactory it proceeds with further action. Secondly, the employee registers the complaint after he/she reaches India. To facilitate the lodging of such complaints, a system of public hearing is conducted at the POE offices, where emigrants, recruiting agents, project exporters etc., can meet the most senior officer on duty to obtain information and voice their grievances. When complaints are received against foreign employers, the POE office forwards them to the Indian embassy in the concerned country of employment for taking necessary actions. As in the case of first option, if a registered agent has recruited the complainant, the POE office seeks the agent's explanation.

If the agent does not provide satisfactory explanations, a case is registered for the violation and the case is referred to the police for investigation. In some instances, the POE officials themselves conduct the inquiry. Employers against whom the complaints have been made, if found guilty through preliminary investigations, are blacklisted and this information is passed on to embassies and registered agents in order to ensure that in future labourers are not supplied to these employers. Apart from this, generally no action can be taken against foreign employers as they are governed by laws of another nation state.

Suggestions and Recommendations

Some specific suggestions relating to international labour migration are:

Developing migration information systems: One of the areas requiring immediate policy intervention is the creation of an appropriate information system on international emigration. This would enable closer surveillance and better management of emigration. The status of out-migrant data can be improved by making the registration of entry by migrant workers mandatory in the Indian missions operating in labour receiving countries. The nature of outflow data at home can be strengthened by a fuller utilisation of the data already available with government departments and recruitment agencies. A chief requirement in this connection would be the strengthening of the statistical wings of the concerned government departments.

There is also a need to use border control records for more accurate measurement of international labour migration. International experience suggests that it is possible to extract labour outflow and return flow data on key variables from embarkation/disembarkation cards. An essential first step to make use of this source is to redesign the existing arrival/departure cards to yield required information. To obtain further information, periodic airport surveys could be resorted to. Data on migration are as much essential at the state level as they are at the national level. Apart from relevant disaggregation of national data sources, it would be desirable if the National Sample Survey Organisation (NSSO) conduct detailed surveys on international migration periodically, say once in five years. To strengthen the information base abroad, an identification and networking of Indian associations operating in different Middle East countries is necessary. The Gulf crisis of 1990 had highlighted the vital role played by various Indian associations and bodies in safeguarding the interests of Indian migrants in the Gulf at a time of emergency (Sasikumar, 1995). Discussions with evacuees from Kuwait revealed that the majority of Indian migrants maintained very close liaison with community organisations even in times of stability.

Managing and directing migration flows: There is an urgent need to manage and direct migration flows from India. It is important in this context that labour markets of the major labour importing countries are closely monitored. This may be done through the establishment of a labour market monitoring authority. The authority has to carry out negotiations on various labour contracts and also study the nature of emerging skill requirements. The activities of the labour market monitoring mechanism should be linked with a comprehensive system of labour market information for all types of employment seekers.

Welfare funds: Although the issue of welfare of families of workers left behind in the home country has come to be recognised as potentially important, there are hardly any policies in this area. It may be worthwhile to consider the constitution of a 'Welfare Fund' for Indian workers abroad. Such a fund can be utilised for a wide range of welfare measures concerned with both the migrant workers and their families. The Welfare Fund could also be of vital importance to women employees in the Gulf who are largely in the category of ara-medical staff and domestic servants. The Gulf crisis of 1990 had brought to light the adverse conditions that women employees, especially the domestic servants category had to face, while their employers fled to safety. The Fund could mainly comprise of the contributions received from Indians working in the Middle East. Incentives such as attractive insurance schemes and tax relief should be offered to the migrants contributing towards the Fund.

Pre-departure orientation programmes: One of the most neglected aspects of overseas employment policy in India is the absence of any form of pre departure orientation to the intending emigrants. It is important to recognise adaptability of the workers to changed working conditions and to new socio-cultural environment. It can also influence their productivity levels. The orientation programme can include topics such as religion, the socio-cultural and political conditions of the country of employment, the do's and don'ts, the contract of employment, description of the jobsite, the duties and responsibilities of the workers, travel tips, procedure on how the workers may handle their problems at the worksite, and advice on remittance procedures. The government, registered recruitment agencies, returned associations and non-governmental organisations working among the migrant workers can participate in providing pre-departure training to the potential emigrants.

Responding to transformations in labour markets: Any policy intended to streamline the overseas labour recruitment system in India has to recognise, as a pre-condition, the important transformation that has occurred with respect to expatriate labour market in most of the labour importing countries, i.e. a transformation of expatriate labour market from being a seller's to a buyer's market.

Under the transformed expatriate labour market conditions, the expenditure incurred by the recruiting agents for the promotion and maintenance of their business has risen significantly. In order to match such a rise in expenditure, most private recruiting agents sidestep the law and charge a fee much higher than the legally prescribed limit.

It is also true that most emigrants are willing to pay an amount higher than the ones prescribed by the law as the earnings from the Gulf can easily abate losses due to extra payment. In such a context, government may take a more flexible position and reconsider the amount of maximum chargeable fee.

Financing out migration: It would also be worth establishing a government system of offering low interest loans to less well-off emigrants to finance out migration. Such a system of financing out migration may also ensure that those emigrants availing the lowinterest loans would resort to formal banking channels to transfer their remittances back home. This would further augment the foreign exchange resources, which are vital for a developing country like India.

Utilising resource flows and human capital of emigrants to strengthen development: There is an absence of any policy framework regarding the effective utilisation of financial inflows from emigrants to strengthen the development process at national or state levels.

Similarly, the existing policy regime in India hardly addresses any concerns related to the migration of persons with technical or professional expertise, many of whom are willing to make a contribution to the development process, either in their non-resident status or as returnees. These issues need close consideration at national and regional levels and effective policies need to be formulated which can integrate development concerns with the migration process.

MIGRATION IN INDIA

India as a nation has seen a high migration rate in recent years. Over 98 million people migrated from one place to another in 1990s, the highest for any decade since independence according to the 2001 census details. However in 1970s migration was slowing down. The number of migrants during 1991-2001 increased by about 22% over the previous decade an increase since 1951.

Apart from women migrating due to marriage, employment is the biggest reason for migration. The number of job seekers among all migrants has increased by 45% over the previous decade. Nearly 14 million people migrated from their place of birth in search of jobs. The overwhelming majority of these-12 million was men.

Migrants have created pressure on others who are in same job market. While freedom to migrate within the country is an enshrined right the uneven development, levels of desperation and other factors have created friction points. Most people migrate because of a combination of push and pull factors. Lack of rural employment, fragmentation of land holdings and declining public investment in agriculture create a crisis for rural Indians. Urban areas and some rural areas with industrial development or high agricultural production offer better prospects for jobs or self-employment.

Contrary to common perception the search for jobs is more often within the same state than in some other state. About 9 million persons were intra-state migrants often within the district while 5 million went to other states. The intra-state figures include people moving from villages to nearby towns and cities in search of better jobs. Over 5.7 million persons who moved in search of jobs migrated from rural to urban areas. Another 4.5 million migrated within the rural areas looking for work. The data shows that among people migrating in search of jobs, literates constitute the vast bulk over 10.6 million while illiterate migrants are about 3.3 million. Three out of four job-seeking migrants are educated males. Among literate, migrant job-seekers less than 1% was women. Nearly 40% of literate persons migrating for work had studied up to secondary level and another 32% had studied beyond. Graduates numbered over 1.8 million or about 17% while technical diploma or degree holders constituted about 8%.

About 72% do get regular work but over 11 million get less than 183 days of work in a year. This is a higher proportion than non-migrants. Independent NSS data from 1999-2000 indicates that migrant workers take up regular or casual employment or self-employment in nearly equal proportions. Around 8.1 million of the migrants were reported as available for or seeking work. The census data may not fully reflect seasonal or circulatory migration, estimated to be up to 10 million by the National Commission on Rural Labour. Seasonal migrants are usually dalits and other highly impoverished sections that go out to work in harvesting seasons or on construction sites, in brick kilns, salt mines etc. They go out to pay their debts and to survive.

8

Models of Urban Land Use and Land Allocation

Many models of urban land have been developed by economists, geographers and others and a large proportion of them can be described as bid-rent models. These assume that land using activities have different needs to locate close to the centre of the city and will bid for land accordingly. This results in a gradient of intensities of land uses and land prices which declines outwards from the centre in a more or less predictable manner. All activities are thus optimally located, such that utility, or profit, is maximised. The provenance of most of these models can be traced to the work on agricultural land published by Von Thunen in 1826, although it is Hurd (1903) who is usually given credit for applying it to urban areas.

The further development of these models can be seen through the works of Isard (1956), Beckman (1957), Wingo (1961), Alonso (1964), Muth (1969), Mills (1972) and Miyao (1981). They have been well summarised by Balchin and Kieve (1977), Hallett (1978) and Hudson and Rhind (1980), so a brief outline will suffice here. It should also be noted that, more recently, Fujita (1989) has attempted to extend them beyond the limited explanation of positivist theory into normative theory with the identification of efficient spatial structures and means of achieving them.

In essence, the bid-rent formulations rest upon the assumption that different activities will have bid-rent curves which vary in form according to their need to be at the centre of the city. This, in turn, depends upon the nature of the activities, their ability to take advantage of highly priced central sites and their sensitivity to transport costs. A number of commercial activities, for example, have very specific labour needs, customer requirements and linkages with other activities. All of these can, theoretically, best be satisfied at the centre where transport facilities maximise labour availability, customer flow and proximate linkages. Thus they will be prepared to pay high prices and will have a steep rent gradient. A number of industrial activities have (and had even more strongly in the past) a need to be close to the centre for reasons of labour availability, transport services and marketing services, but their need is less than that for commercial uses and they are less sensitive to small variations in accessibility, therefore their rent gradient is less steep and they cannot compete successfully for the very central sites. Residential activities are normally the largest user of land in the city. They may desire a fairly central location (although suburban qualities are increasingly preferred), but they cannot derive sufficient utility or profit to outbid commerce and industry. In effect, they become a residual use, consigned to the lowest levels of the bid-rent curve with locations furthest from the centre.

For all activities there will be a trade-off between the high costs of central area land and the high costs of transport incurred by locating further out, but the effects of this may be more apparent for residential uses, or for individual households within the residential sector, for whom the utility of a central location is lower. These notions of bid-rent theory, and the pattern of land use which is assumed to result, provide a degree of explanation for one of the best known models of urban structure, that of E.W.Burgess (1925). It must however be stressed that Burgess did not use rent theory as such. He was a sociologist and his model was derived from empirical observations of the way in which the city of Chicago had developed. As such, it is a hybrid of idealised land use patterns and urban social structure with a strong emphasis upon residential areas. The model is commonly represented as a purely concentric zonation of activities, but it is important to remember that, as originally developed from Chicago, it had significant additions in the form of specialised sectors.

The importance of a sectoral form of development was taken up by Hoyt (1939) in his study of residential rent levels in a large number of American cities, including Chicago. Although there are obvious difference between these two models there are also some similarities. The main difference is that Hoyt considered direction, as well as distance, from the CBD to be important in determining land use. The arrangement of the sectors was such that high income areas were protected from low income districts and from industry by buffer zones of middle income housing. The strength of the sectoral pattern which emerges should not be allowed to disguise the fact that within the sectors, Hoyt clearly identified concentric zones of differential rent and a tendency for the most fashionable residential areas to migrate outwards from the centre along specific sectors. The processes differ, in that Burgess was largely concerned with social factors such as ecological competition and migration, whereas Hoyt concentrated upon amenity value and filtering, but there is a case for suggesting that Hoyt's model should be considered as a refinement of that of Burgess rather than something which strikes off in a totally different direction. In seeking general applicability, Hoyt's model is to be preferred to that of Burgess because it is more firmly based in empirical data, being a synthesis of twenty-five cities, and because it goes further towards acknowledging that the CBD is not the only commercial focus of the city. This latter point is important because some of the rationale for identifying sectors was the growing importance of motor transport which was creating subsidiary commercial nodes, often alongside major radial roads, in the interwar period.

In a third major modelling exercise, Harris and Ullman (1945) took Hoyt's subtle recognition that the CBD was not the only focus of activity, and made it explicit in their multiple nucleii model. Again, the model is to some extent evolutionary in that it incorporates elements of Burgess and Hoyt, but it is more flexible than either. Essentially, it implies that the city has a cellular structure within which a number of specialised areas develop. Some of these may be highly nucleated, such as suburban shopping centres, but others may be quite large districts dominated by a single land use such as industry or upper-class housing. In relaxing the dominance of a single centre, and the assumptions of general accessibility to the core, the multiple nucleii model recognises the interaction of a number of locational factors. First, it gives some weight to topographical and historical features in the origins of the growth of the city, for example, in the absorption of minor settlements. Second, it recognises that different levels of retailing do not all seek a central site, some preferring suburban locations closer to their market. Third, it allows for the agglomeration economies and both the negative and positive externalities which cause certain firms or households to cluster together. These three models have become so well established in the literature on urban structure that they are normally referred to as 'the classical models'. They are all, quite clearly, North American in origin but an attempt to refine them for the British context has been made by Mann (1965). His diagrammatic model draws most heavily upon the concentric zone and sector models, but it makes passing reference to separate and more specialised areas. Importantly, it also makes allowance for public sector intervention in the form of local authority housing.

Naturally, models which have been around for such a long time will have attracted a wide measure of criticism, and the evolution of urban land use in the past three decades highlights some of their deficiencies. Some of these criticisms are valid, but in a sense unfair. For example, both Burgess and Hoyt were concerned with the rapidly growing American city of the first third of the twentieth century; to apply their models outside of this geographical and historical setting is misleading. Burgess, in particular, claimed no wide applicability for his model. Some attempt to deal with criticisms of the earlier models can be seen in the development of the later ones, notably the attempt to move away from the assumption of a single, overwhelmingly dominant central area. Similarly, there is the question of public intervention in the urban structure. At the time when Burgess was writing, the structure of the American city was almost wholly determined by market forces.

Subsequently, and especially in European cities, state intervention through planning regulations, transport policy and the provision of public sector facilities has profoundly influenced urban structure. All of these models then have severe limitations. Burgess and Hoyt, in particular, simply described the patterns which they saw; they did not provide quantifiable models and they were not very explicit in their analysis of process. For all of their shortcomings, however, the models have an enduring quality and they have undoubtedly been fruitful in shaping our understanding of patterns of urban land use and structure.

These classical models have been attempts in varying degrees to provide comprehensive statements of urban structure. If we return now to the bid-rent models, it is clear that they mainly deal with more partial views. Residential land use has been their principal focus, and a number have looked at retailing patterns, but few have examined manufacturing or other activities. Putting the various urban subsystems together has generally not been attempted except in the simulation models such as that applied by Lowry (1964) to Pittsburgh.

The seminal work of Wingo (1961), Alonso (1964) and Muth (1969) looked mainly at residential choice and this has recently been extended by Thrall (1987) in a consumption theory of land rent. He made the usual assumptions of bid-rent models, including a city populated by identical households, on an isotropic plain with all employment at the centre. Households can decide about the consumption of two goods: land and a composite of all other goods. He argued that because of higher transport costs at the periphery, disposable incomes are lower, but to compensate for this land costs are lower and people consume more of it. At the centre higher disposable incomes allow families to consume more composite goods. Some doubts must be shed upon the reality of this because wealthy suburbanites and commuters do not have to trade off consumption of land against composite goods or transport costs; they can afford more of all.

The key concepts of the bid-rent model, i.e. land values and accessibility to the centre, have been applied in a variety of circumstances to the more specialised study of urban retailing, especially with respect to the structure of the urban core. The work of Garner (1966) and Berry (1967) drew attention to the connection between different levels of the shopping hierarchy and distance from the core such that a concentric arrangement of retailing land uses occurs. The idea was further developed by Davies (1972) for the city of Coventry and here we see once again the combination of sectors and concentric rings. A detailed connection between shop types, land rents and distance from the centre, in the mainstream tradition of bidrent theory has been outlined by Scott (1970).

URBAN LAND USE IS THE IMPORTANT ROLE OF TRANSPORT

Implicit in all of these models of urban land use is the important role of transport, and it is necessary to consider two aspects. First, some reference must be made to the large scale simulation models of urban land use and transport which were developed in the united States from 1960 onwards, even though they are not primarily economic models. Second, it is useful to look at more detailed empirical examinations of the connection between transport and land costs.

The development of transport modelling created some of the prerequisites for land use modelling, (Harris 1985) and a number of massive studies of land use and transport have been undertaken, e.g. the Penn—Jersey Study and the Chicago Area Transport Study. Most of these models can be categorised as either:

1 non optimum-seeking models of disaggregated land use, e.g. Lowry (1964); or,
2 optimum-seeking models, often of a linear programme type, e.g. Herbert and Stevens (1960).

Early models took transport costs as given, but more recent ones take account of congestion, which means that travel costs are not uniform. A useful review of many of these model types was provided by Berechman and Gordon (1986). It is worth stressing that most of these models are 'non-economic' simulation models, i.e. they use rules taken from observed statistical regularities in travel and the location of activities, rather than from economic forces such as land rents and consumer preferences. Some attempt to reconcile the two categories has been made by Anas (1986). The integration of transport and land use models was explored by Putman (1983) who emphasised both the importance of transport for land use and the complexity of the relationship.

Relatively few studies have empirically tested the relationship between land use and transport, but there are a number which have shown measurable connections between transport changes and land prices. In Britain, for example, improvements in urban rail services were shown to have increased house prices in Glasgow and London (Wacher 1971), and in the Tyne and Wear area (Pickett and Perrett 1984). Similar changes were reported following the opening of the Spadina subway line in Toronto (Bajic 1983). In Australia, property prices responded to the increase in petrol prices in 1978. Up until 1978, the value of houses in the outer suburbs of Melbourne increased more rapidly than those in the inner suburbs in line with experience in most western cities. From 1978 to 1981 however there was a reversal of this pattern. Values in the inner suburbs rose by 30–50 per cent, whereas those in the outer suburbs remained static. In the USA the increases in oil prices between 1973 and 1979 also caused some adjustments, in that there was a trend towards smaller cars and a continued movement of people and industry towards the suburbs in order to decrease the journey to work distances. In Japan, on the other hand, it appears that rising transport costs have had little effect upon urban structure. Rapidly rising real incomes and the willingness of employers to subsidise commuting costs mean that urban residents can, to some extent, shrug off rising energy costs. Industry has not moved out of the cities as much as it has elsewhere because of its continuing strong links to port facilities.

Criticisms of Economic Models

A number of criticisms of individual models have already been noted, but it is also necessary to take a broader view. For simplicity, three headings will suffice—oversimplification, market failings and Marxist critiques—but, of course, there is also some overlap between these. It should not be assumed that these criticisms are always negative and destructive of the models, for in a number of cases they point the way towards better, albeit partial, understanding.

Oversimplification

In order to be meaningful, a model must be reasonably simple, but there are dangers of oversimplification. Most of the models referred to above ignore the physical setting of the city together with its inherited stock of land uses, they assume independence between land uses, they take the centre to be the point of maximum accessibility and the concentration of all employment and they assume a perfect market in which people behave in an economically rational manner deciding where to live solely on the basis of transport and land costs. Perhaps it is no wonder that Hallett (1978:16) described the bidrent models as 'a grotesque simplification of reality'.

From a geographer's viewpoint, one of the most seriously misleading assumptions is that regarding the role of the centre of the city. There are two aspects to consider. One is the unreality of assuming a single, totally dominant centre, when most cities clearly have a number of separate, perhaps specialised focal points. The second aspect concerns the changing role of the centre of the city and its decline under the impact of decentralisation and counterurbanisation. The CBD itself may still be relatively prosperous but the decline of jobs, the decentralisation of many activities and the deterioration of the urban environment have all challenged the traditional role of the central city in the wider metropolitan context. In a number of British and American cities these processes have emphasised Burgess's zone in transition. An inner city area has resulted in which the enduring problem of derelict and vacant land is evidence that demand and land prices have fallen, in some cases temporarily, to zero. Comprehensive information on land prices is not available in the UK, but robust common sense suggests that the land value surface of the declining industrial city has changed in the way indicated, with a major dip representing these depressed inner city values followed by a marked rise towards the suburbs. The severity of the fall in value at the edge of the city will depend upon the extent to which the local planning regime permits or prevents urban extension into the surrounding countryside. The declining importance of the centre as the hub about which the urban land use pattern is organised has been further demonstrated by McDonald (1984) who noted in his work on Chicago that no theoretical model explained the variation in the land use in relation to distance from the CBD. In Los Angeles too, the CBD has been shown to have relatively little importance in determining land use patterns, especially within the residential sector.

Market Failings

Even without involving the fundamental Marxist critique it can be seen that the market in urban land and property has a number of shortcomings. One of the most comprehensive criticisms concerns its failure to cater adequately for a number of social needs, in terms of the provision of land for socially desirable but unprofitable uses, and in terms of catering for economically weak social groups. But in addition to this it has a number of more detailed, intrinsic shortcomings. Balchin and Kieve describe the property market as 'one of the least efficient' and Ratcliffe (1976:10) reports that it has been described as 'chaotic, monopolistic and irrational'. There seems to be some agreement about its shortcomings and these include: the uniqueness of each site, the imperfect knowledge of both buyers and sellers, the varying motives and amounts of power of the different participants, the expense and legal complexity of transfers, the length of legal rights and property interests, the role of non-monetary factors such as sentiment, symbolism and pride of ownership, the difficulty of assessing prices in a thin market, the importance of inertia and the longevity of individual buildings. In view of all these shortcomings it is no surprise that the perfect equilibrium between supply and demand which the market theoretically provides is also something of a myth. In reality, many sites are used sub-optimally and the process of adjustment to changing conditions is quite slow. It is relatively easy to list shortcomings of the market in this fashion, but it is important also to pose the question of whether alternative systems are better at allocating urban land.

Marxist Criticisms

Notions of rent, capital and land ownership were central to the writings of Karl Marx, and although he was working in a broadly agricultural setting, a number of writers have subsequently extended his ideas into the urban context. Clearly, some caution is necessary here, for whereas agricultural land is an independent production unit, where rent is set according to the plot's own characteristics, land in the city has its usefulness and rent largely determined by its linkages with, and access to, other land, buildings and urban facilities.

The starting point for most contemporary Marxist challenges to existing land use models and the operation of the market is the assumption of very great, possibly monopoly, power in the hands of a few land owners. This enables them to manipulate or control the land market by charging absolute or monopoly rent. Harvey (1973) thus argued that in the CBD land prices do not normally depend upon locational advantage, but vice versa. Put in its extreme form, it is argued that the CBD exists not because of a genuine demand for its services, but because the land owning classes manipulate society's 'wants' to achieve high rents. Similarly, Ball (1985) suggested that simple demand is an insufficient explanation for the dense concentration of offices at the city centre. Instead, he favoured the explanation that the big investors, including pension and insurance funds, go for the development of office blocks in 'blue chip' locations in the city centre to minimise the risk of premature obsolescence. The process becomes selfreinforcing as others seek the same safe locations. Similarly, Marxists would argue that high house prices are due to high land prices rather than the liberal explanation that high demand for houses pushes up residential land prices. In practice, the argument of monopoly powers being used to determine prices is difficult to sustain in the market for new houses, because at any given time the new housing available forms only a small proportion of the total stock for sale, the great majority of which is owned by householders acting individually. Harvey went on to develop the distinction between use value and exchange value, and demonstrated that existing models treat one or the other of these, but not both together. For example, the model of Burgess, and indeed most of the contributions made by geographers, sociologists and town planners, deal with use value, whereas bid-rent models, and land economists in general, are more concerned with exchange values. He held out the possibility of a Marxist approach which would bring the two concepts together, but such a model is elusive. For Harvey, rent was not simply the key to the land use but also a prime cause of spatial conflict, production inefficiencies and social injustice.

Rent is clearly central to the Marxist interpretation, but landed capital can also use other methods to control development in order to maximise its own interests (Edel 1976). These include: 1) large estates constraining suburban growth; 2) monopoly control over building land; 3) fragmentation of ownership; 4) deliberate delays to force up prices; 5) speculative holding of land; and 6) capture of state planning controls. Clearly, there is considerable scope here for influence to be exerted over both temporal and spatial aspects of land development.

Two final comments will help to bridge the gap between the powerful, but essentially detached, criticism of Marxist theory, and the reality of land allocation processes in practice. One is that an extensive study, largely sympathetic to the Marxist view, concluded that, in Britain at least, there is no single land owning group which could be identified as a coherent faction with anything approaching monopoly powers (Massey and Catalano 1978). The second is the observation that in the quasi-Marxist societies of Eastern Europe, after several decades of absence, the benefits of a market with land pricing and wider private ownership are tentatively being re-introduced.

PUBLIC INTERVENTION

Alongside the role of the market in allocating urban land, it is also necessary to consider the impact of a wide range of public intervention measures. These vary according to the political context in which the city is set. History reveals a large number of isolated instances of regulation in Europe by monarchical or other public bodies. These include the early code of Roman law which provided a number of building regulations, the medieval controls relating to protection from fire and nuisance, the grandiose town planning layouts of the sixteenth, seventeenth and eighteenth centuries and the late-nineteenth-century housing and sanitation by-laws in Britain. Comprehensive public intervention, however, is largely a feature of the twentieth century and it has gained in scope and sophistication as the century has progressed. Today, public control in matters of urban land use is generally more elaborate and far reaching in European countries than it is in North America and Australia, but even in the latter countries where individual rights in economic terms are highly prized, the unfettered pursuit of economic gain at the expense of others is not possible. Government laws, statutes and provisions are more far reaching with respect to land than any other commodity (Goldberg and Chinloy 1984). Public intervention is closely related to political ideology and in postwar Britain it has risen or fallen according to which political party has been in power.

Public intervention in matters of urban land use comes about for many reasons, but basically they relate to failures, or presumed failures, of the market. Many of these failings have been reviewed above, but the most important ones in prompting intervention are:

1. The fact that land comes on to the market in a haphazard and unpredictable way and at no time is it in equilibrium with all land being used optimally.
2. Because of the market's emphasis upon the price mechanism, it is not good at providing for public or merit goods. Socially necessary uses such as schools, hospitals or parks thus get squeezed out.
3. Strong land owning and financial cabals can dominate weaker groups.
4. The market is not good at dealing with negative externalities such as traffic congestion, noise and noxious industries.

Public bodies thus intervene in order to overcome these problems. A wide range of instruments is available, but for simplicity they will be discussed under three broad headings: public ownership, regulatory measures and fiscal measures.

Public Ownership

Public ownership of land is closely dependent upon political ideology and it may vary from comprehensive state ownership (nationalisation) through to selective, and perhaps temporary, state or municipal involvement. Leaving aside the centrally planned economies of Eastern Europe, it is possible to trace a long history of public land ownership in Western Europe, but it is far less common in North America.

Perhaps the least controversial aspect of public land ownership is the acquisition of land for the provision of various public services such as roads, schools, hospitals parks or military establishments. Even in the relatively unfettered market conditions of the USA, this process operates, and there is also a right of 'eminent domain' whereby the federal or state government may acquire land compulsorily.

A higher level of public intervention in land ownership occurs in those countries where government or municipal bodies are heavily involved in the land development process. In Britain, public ownership of development land was an intrinsic part of the 1947 Town and Country Planning Act. It did not remain on the statute books, however, and two subsequent attempts to institute it were also repealed, the most recent being the Community Land Act of 1975, which was repealed in 1980. Only in Wales does the system remain, through the work of the Land Authority for Wales which buys, assembles and sells land for development. Selling development land for its full market value allows the authority to finance its future activities. Elsewhere in Britain, limited versions of the process also operate in certain run down inner city and industrial areas, where selective programmes such as the Urban Development Corporations, Derelict Land Grants and Partnership schemes empower public sector bodies to acquire land, assemble sites, reclaim and service land and bring it forward for development, especially by the private sector. These are not really examples of public land ownership *per se* but attempts to 'kickstart' the market.

Outside of Britain, many other European countries operate systems of public land ownership for development land. In German cities, for example, there is a relatively harmonious relationship between the free market and government intervention (Williams 1988) and both municipal and provincial governments maintain land banks for future urban development. In Scandinavia and The Netherlands municipal authorities are extensively involved in land ownership, often acting as a middle man between farmers and developers. In Stockholm a widespread system of municipal leasehold has long been in use, and as a result the city now owns three-quarters of the land within its boundary (Ratzka 1980). In almost all such cases, public ownership is combined with other fiscal or planning measures.

Regulatory Measures

Even in the broadly market economies of the west, the state has a wide array of instruments for regulating urban land use. These range from the detailed application of such specific devices as building codes and safety regulations, to the full gamut of comprehensive town planning legislation. In general, regulation stems from an attempt to reconcile two of the state's contradictory functions. These are, accumulation, i.e. the creation of favourable conditions for capital growth and investment, and legitimation, i.e. the promotion of equity and social harmony.

As practised in Britain, and most other western nations, town planning is firmly rooted in land use planning. Healey *et al.* (1988:17) suggested that 'the planning system both expresses and embodies some of the key rules of access through which agents may realise their interests in land, property, location, place and environment'. They identified development control, that is the state's power to approve or deny development, as the central focus. It is translated into a spatial pattern of land use control through the operation of district, structure and other plans which outline whether, and what kind of, development will be approved in particular locations. Successive large scale acts, such as the Town and Country Planning Acts of 1947 and 1971, and the Local Government, Planning and

Land Act of 1980 have given British local authorities wide powers to control overall urban development. In addition, a number of more specific acts, for example the New Towns Act of 1946, and a succession of housing acts have had a important influence upon land use within their own areas of concern.

The planning system established in 1947 was designed largely as a control over land uses, especially the prevention of urban sprawl and the regulation of land uses within cities. Since then, there have been many changes, especially in the 1980s, but the fundamentals, including the definition of development and the system of development control, together with the relationship between day to day control and the broad development plans, remain broadly the same. In effect, the right to develop land is nationalised, and decisions about development are taken in the public interest quite separate from issues concerning land values or ownership. Essentially, it is a permissive system, in which the planning authority can approve or refuse permission to develop, but does not, in general, initiate development itself. Blowers (1986) drew attention to the paradox of planning being focused upon land use, over which it has little control (because a developer may fail to come forward, or because refusal of development permission may be over-turned on appeal), but neglecting land values over which it does have influence by indicating both broad and specific locations approved for development. After major reorganisation of local government in the 1970s, which gave a great deal of planning power to county authorities and made the structure plan the most important document, there is now some indication of another change which will return key planning powers to the more local, district council level.

In other West European countries there are a few similarities with, but also many differences from, the British system. One of the main instruments of control over land use and development in France, Germany, The Netherlands and Denmark is a building permit issued by the local authority, and this covers both planning permission and the equivalent of the British building control. Another difference is that in these countries the local plan is a legally binding document. Clear criteria are laid down for the approval or refusal of development permission, and in general, if a proposal accords with the local plan and building regulations, it cannot be refused. This provides relatively firm guidelines and a degree of certainty for both developers and the existing users of land. Many of the rubrics are very detailed: for example, in France the *code d'urbanisme* of 1954, provides a lengthy consolidated list of legal powers and planning rules, and the local plan *(plan d'occupation des sols)* lays down zones of different land use together with other restrictions such as plot ratios. A comprehensive comparison of many West European planning systems has recently been published (Department of the Environment 1989).

In the USA the prevailing values in land use are those of private initiative and free market forces, but an increasing package of federal, state and local government measures is now involved. Garrett (1987) argued that legal considerations are important alongside economic ones in any analysis of urban land use in North America. Although the free market had, and still has, a strong hand in shaping American cities, it is possible to see, from the earliest days of large scale urban development, that a degree of centralised planning or regulation has been important. This can be seen especially in the widespread use of the grid plan which imposed an ordered pattern upon subsequent land use and urban morphology. Pierre l'Enfant's plan for Washington in 1791 for example, and the New York grid plan of 1881 have both left indelible marks on these two great cities. Concerns for health, order, clear street lines, straightforward land transactions and recognisable property lines were all important considerations in the original choice of the simple grid plan.

One of the key features of the relatively weak present day land use planning in the USA is the widespread use of zoning, a notion which partly reflects a distrust of the powers of a completely free market to allocate land effectively (Garrett 1987). Zoning of land use in the cities of the USA stems from the period between 1916 and 1926 when it was first instituted to relieve congestion of traffic and land uses within the garment district of New York. Following an important test case at Euclid,

Ohio, in 1922, zoning ordinances spread rapidly, being adopted in some form within all forty-eight states by 1946 (Goldberg and Chinloy 1984) and by 9,000 local governments in 1968 (Garrett 1987). At that stage, every major city, except Houston had accepted zoning.

LAND USE AND INTENSITY

The basic intention of zoning is to regulate land use and intensity, but in many cases it goes much further and includes layouts, plot sizes and subdivision, setbacks, shadows, aesthetics and housing type. Some idea of the scope can be gained from the very condensed summary of the zoning ordinances used by the city of Philadelphia in the 1970s. Despite the technical appearances of such regulations it can be argued that their main purpose is to express the taken for granted understanding of social order (Perin 1977), the subtext is homogeneity associated with the lowering of social conflict and the prevention of negative spillover effects. This argument then is rather different from the traditional explanations of land use planning in the UK, where the protection of weaker groups in the community and the promotion of social equity are important goals. In the UK a form of zoning is applied to land use patterns in local plans, whereby some attempt is made to keep non-conforming uses separate. Thus industry will normally be removed from, or prevented from developing in areas designated for residential development. In the USA it seems that land use zoning is at least largely about protecting individual property rights and reducing investment uncertainty by transferring some of the risk to the community. An example of this is cited by Fischel (1985) who claims that the antipathy of wealthy suburbanites to low income housing is not based upon aesthetics or the physical nature of the land use, but upon social status and especially a fear of crime.

Zoning is not the only regulatory tool affecting land use in the USA. Since 1970 there has been an extension of centralised land use regulation at state, regional and federal level and although this has a limited effect upon cities, it has grown steadily and it does show political staying power (Popper 1988). More important has been the parallel emergence of new regulatory devices at local level. In the late 1960s, land reform processes persuaded most local communities to adopt a comprehensive development or growth management plan, and although these have no statutory power they are increasingly being used for land use regulation at local level.

In the USA, as in Britain, some of the most severe challenges to planning have come in the run-down inner areas of the largest, decaying industrial cities. It is here that the land market has been in most obvious difficulties, although whether this is due to intrinsic market weaknesses or a gross distortion of the market by bureaucratic and other public intervention is debatable. At the very least it seems that the private sector has been deterred by the size and long time scale of the problem. The responses in both countries, with Britain often copying American policy, have had many similarities. Land use planning has been given a major role in the processes of job creation and revitalising the urban economy and environment. New development bodies have emerged within the context of a public-private partnership. In the USA, the role of such partnerships in rehabilitating districts of Baltimore and Pittsburgh, is well known, and the principles have been applied more recently to long-standing problem areas in a number of British cities including dockland districts in London, Manchester and Liverpool. Land use planning is only one part of a much larger scheme of revitalisation in cases such as these, but the important part which it plays has recently been reviewed by Lawless and Ramsden (1990) in the city of Sheffield.

In summary, it is possible to see that planning has a wide range of instruments for land use regulation, especially in European cities. Its operation is as much concerned with politics and social values as with economics, and for this reason it has been challenged from many directions, particularly during the 1980s when the tide seemed so often to be running against public intervention. During that decade, and currently, much of the emphasis of planning has been changed, away from regulation towards the promotion of development. Much has been expected of it, from the resolution of small scale conflicts over competing land uses to a key role in the regeneration of flagging urban economies. Certainly, there are isolated successes to be recorded, but overall it must be seen as a relatively small piece in the overall jigsaw of urban land use.

Fiscal Measures

The state may intervene in the urban land market through many fiscal measures. Essentially there are three kinds: (1) routine raising of revenue, (2) taxes or levies on land and property in order to recoup some of the enhanced value of the developed land which is considered to have been created by the community, and (3) subsidies to promote development or encourage important activities.

Routine revenue raising by means of property taxes takes a number of forms in Britain. Up until 1990, rates were levied on all property as a basic method of financing local authorities. Although they were replaced in 1989 by the Community Charge for the residential sector, a national non-domestic rate based upon notional rental values is still levied on industrial and commercial premises. Notice has been given that this Community Charge will, in turn, shortly be replaced by a new Council Charge, to be based upon domestic property values. Elsewhere, in parts of the USA for example, capital values of property are used as the basis of local taxes, and in New Zealand and Denmark, site value rating is used. The precise operation of the local land and property tax systems can have a marked effect upon attitudes towards development. For example in Britain, the absence of a tax on land which is vacant lessens the pressure to develop it, in France there is a tax regime which discourages preparing land for development, and in Japan the tax system makes it advantageous to hold financial assets in the form of land (Wijers 1988).

Major debate revolves around the extent to which the profit accruing from land development should be taxed. On the one hand is the view that the developer should be allowed to keep any profit gained from developing land to a higher use. On the other hand is the argument that it is the community which creates enhanced land values, through the general expansion of the city, or through specific actions such as granting planning permission or the provision of infrastructure, and therefore it is the community which should reap the benefit. Whilst it is true that land owners can improve the value of their land by their own actions, the value may also rise even though they do nothing. A middle ground exists by taxing the betterment in order to return some of the financial gain to the community. Basically this system, operating through changing grades of betterment levies, capital gains taxes and development land taxes, has been used in the UK since 1947. Depending on the level of taxation there are benefits for all, since the state's role is financed and the land owners keep some of the betterment, thus providing incentive for the market to continue.

Subsidies to encourage desired forms of development are the other part of the fiscal measures, and these too take a number of forms. For example, subsidies may be applied to transport to encourage the efficient operation of the urban economy, to such features as street lighting where it is administratively difficult to collect a charge, to sewerage and water supply which are capital intensive and where there may be good reasons for a state monopoly, and to education and health in order to encourage a high level of consumption. Few of these subsidies are aimed at urban land per se but they all have important implications for it. In Britain, one of the most substantial and relevant forms of subsidy is that available on housing, with income tax relief on mortgage interest for privately purchased housing and direct building and rent subsidies in the public sector. More specifically, subsidies are available in areas of development difficulty in many European countries, and to a lesser extent in the USA, through such devices as income tax and rating relief or grants to encourage investment and job creation.

FUTURE URBAN CHANGE

The nature and structure of the city are both changing, in some cases with great rapidity. In consequence, the land use pattern is also changing, but land and buildings are relatively fixed features which change more slowly than the social and economic forces around them. For this reason, land use patterns often lag behind land use processes and in extreme cases there may be a time gap of several decades between them. Different parts of the city are changing in different ways, and much depends upon the state of the local and national economies. But it should also be noted that some of the changes are so profound as to render this typology of urban areas inappropriate for the emerging, spread metropolitan regions.

The processes which are at work, and the effects which they have upon urban land use patterns. Finally, at this stage it might be appropriate to look briefly at the way in which the pattern is likely to evolve. Despite the rapidity of some of the changes of the past decade, cities can be seen as having many stabilising influences, above all in their patterns of land use, ownership and planning. Overnight transformations are not therefore likely. Cities evolve from their historic contexts, and in Europe especially, this dimension is often carefully guarded. At any point in time cities contain many remnant land use patterns and so they reflect past, as well as present, needs. Almost certainly the city a generation from now, or even two generations from now, is likely to be very similar to the city of today, although within this framework the daily way of life may be very different.

In most of the western world, the immediate historic context is one of dispersal and decentralisation. Despite small signs of renewed population growth in recently declining metropolitan cores (e.g. London), some very strong forces of dispersal are established. Given the choice, people seem determined to buy as much private space as possible, and that space is most available on, and beyond, the urban fringe. Similarly, in seeking the land, locations and images which they require, the majority of new commercial activities appear to be attracted to the urban outskirts. If, as seems clear, the structure of the city is determined by a combination of economic forces such as locational advantage, land prices and transport costs, together with social forces such as lifestyle, residential mobility, privacy and status, then an extension of growth on the major urban fringes and in attractive small town locations looks set to continue.

An unlimited continuation of these trends is, however, by no means assured. In particular, the cost and availability of energy, and the impact which this will have upon patterns of movement cannot be predicted with accuracy. Another major uncertainty is the role which planning will play. To some extent planning is an institutionalisation of underlying economic and social forces, but it is the balance between their promotion and control which is crucial. In the 1980s, planning in many western cities was diverted from its earlier, high minded concern with the creation of ideal environments, the imposition of physical order and homogeneity of land uses to promote social order, into a new pragmatism. It became more opportunistic, market led and development orientated. This is not, of itself, a wholly bad thing, but there is a negative side if the supposed advantages of development do not trickle down socially or spatially, and the distribution of benefits is grossly uneven. Although the market led approach to planning has achieved many successes in recent years, it can be argued that it does not necessarily lead to the best decisions. In particular there is the danger that it can reinforce existing biases and polarisations and neglect the need for investment in necessary public services such as education and transport.

Land use and development is inextricably linked with the social and economic forces that shape everyday life in the city. Some of these forces may appear to have a powerful life of their own, through such notions as the market or aggregated individual preferences, but through the kind of planning we chose, we can control and direct the forces. That we should do so is important, because land use and development remains one of the keys both to satisfying individual lifestyles and to the successful functioning of urban areas.

THE LAND USE - TRANSPORT SYSTEM

Urban land use comprises two elements: the nature of land use which relates to what activities are taking place where, and the level of spatial accumulation, which indicates their intensity and concentration. Most economic, social or cultural activities imply a multitude of functions, such as production, consumption and distribution. These functions take place at specific locations and are part of an activity system. Activities have a spatial imprint, therefore. Some are routine activities, because they occur regularly and are thus predictable, such as commuting and shopping. Others are institutional activities that tend to be irregular and are shaped by lifestyle (sports, leisure, etc.) or by special needs (health, etc.). Still others are production activities that are related to manufacturing and distribution, whose linkages may be local, regional or global. The behavioral patterns of individuals, institutions and firms have an imprint on land use. The representation of this imprint requires a typology of land use, which can be formal or functional:

- Formal land use representations are concerned with qualitative attributes of space such as its form, pattern and aspect and are descriptive in nature.
- Functional land use representations are concerned with the economic nature of activities such as production, consumption, residence, and transport, and are mainly a socio-economic description of space.

Land use, both in formal and functional representations, implies a set of relationships with other land uses. For instance, commercial land use involves relationships with its supplier and customers. While relationships with suppliers will dominantly be related to movements of freight, relationships with customers would include movements of passengers. Since each type of land use has its own specific mobility requirements, transportation is a factor of activity location, which in turn is associated with specific land uses. Transportation and land use interactions have often been described as a chicken-and-egg problem since it is difficult to identify the triggering cause of change. Urban transportation aims at supporting transport demands generated by the diversity of urban activities in a diversity of urban contexts. A key for understanding urban entities thus lies in the analysis of patterns and processes of the transport/land use system. This system is highly complex and involves several relationships between the transport system, spatial interaction s and land use:

- *Transport system.* Considers the set of transport infrastructures and modes that support urban movements of passengers and freight. It generally expresses the level of accessibility.

- *Spatial interactions.* Consider the nature, extent, origins and destinations of urban movements of passengers and freight. They take into consideration the attributes of the transport system as well as the land use factors that generate and attract movements.
- *Land use.* Considers the level of spatial accumulation of activities and their associated levels of mobility requirements. Land use is commonly linked with demographic and economic attributes.

Transportation and economic systems have a reciprocal relationship. In other words, transport supply and demand are mutually interdependent.

For instance, the construction of a highway interchange favors the concentration of commercial and service activities, which will generate additional transport demand, which in turn will favor the location of new activities and a reorganization of the regional spatial structure.

A transportation/land use system can be divided into three subcategories of models.

(1) Land use models are generally concerned about the spatial structure of macro-and micro-economic components, which are often correlated with transportation requirements. For instance, by using a set of economic activity variables, such as population and level of consumption, it becomes possible to calculate the generation and attraction of passengers and freight flows.

(2) Spatial interactions models are mostly concerned about the spatial distribution of movements, a function of land use (demand) and transportation infrastructure (supply). They produce flow estimates between spatial entities, symbolized by origin–destination pairs, which can be disaggregated by nature, mode and time of day.

(3) Transportation network models try to evaluate how movements are allocated over a transportation network, often of several modes, notably private and public transportation. They provide traffic estimates for any given segment of a transportation network.

Urban Land use Models

Several descriptive and analytical models of urban land use have been developed. All involve some consideration of transport in the explanations of urban land use structure:

- Von Thunen's regional land use model is probably one of the oldest relationships found between transportation, urban areas and regional land use. It was initially developed in the early nineteenth century (1826) for the analysis of agricultural land use patterns in Germany. It used the concept of economic rent to explain a spatial organization where different agricultural activities are competing for the usage of land. Although this model has conceptually little relevance to urban land use, its underlying principles have been the foundation of many models where economic considerations, namely land rent and distance-decay, shape urban land use. The core assumption of this functional land use model is that agricultural land use is segregated in concentric circles around a market. Many concordances of this model with reality have been found, notably in North America.
- The Burgess concentric model was among the first attempts to investigate spatial patterns at the urban level (1925). Although the purpose of the model was to analyze social classes, it recognized that transportation and mobility were important factors behind its spatial organization. The formal land use representation of this model is derived from commuting distance from the CBD, creating concentric circles. Each circle represents a specific socio-economic urban landscape. This model is conceptually a direct adaptation of the Von Thunen model to urban land use since it deals with a concentric representation.
- Sector and nuclei land use models were developed to take into account numerous factors overlooked by the concentric models, namely the influence of transport axes (1939) and multiple nuclei (1945) on land use and growth. Both representations consider the emerging

impacts of motorization on the urban spatial structure. The sector model is based on the recognition that communication axes, such as rail lines and major roads, guide development and thus transport has a directional effect on land use. Cities grow along major axes. The multiple nuclei model is based upon empirical evidence that many towns and nearly all large cities do not grow around one CBD, but are formed by the progressive integration of a number of separate nuclei in the urban pattern. These nodes become specialized and differentiated in the growth process and are not located in relation to any distance attribute.

- Hybrid models tried to include the concentric, sector and nuclei behavior of different processes in explaining urban land use. They are an attempt to integrate the strengths of each approach since none of these appear to provide a completely satisfactory explanation. Thus, hybrid models, such as that developed by Isard (1956), consider the concentric effect of nodes (CBDs and sub-centres) and the radial effect of transport axes, all overlain to form a land use pattern. Land rent theory was also developed to explain land use as a market where different urban activities compete for land usage at a location. The more desirable the location, the higher its rent value. Transportation, through accessibility and distance-decay, is a strong explanatory factor in the land rent and its impacts on land use. However, conventional representations of land rent are being challenged by structural modifications of contemporary cities.

Most of these models are essentially static as they explain land use patterns. They do not explicitly consider the processes that are creating or changing them.

Transportation and Urban Dynamics

Both land use and transportation are part of a dynamic system that is subject to external influences. Each component of the system is constantly evolving due to changes in technology, policy, economics, demograp' ics and even culture/values, among others. As a result, the interactions between land use and transportation are played out as the result of the many decisions made by residents, businesses and governments. The field of urban dynamics has expanded the scope of conventional land use models, which tended to be descriptive, by trying to consider the many relationships behind the evolution of the urban spatial structure. This has led to a complex modeling framework including a wide variety of components. Among the concepts supporting urban dynamics representations are retroactions, where as one component influences others. The changes will influence the initial component as feedback, either positively or negatively. The most significant components of urban dynamics are:

- *Land use*. The most stable component of urban dynamics as changes are likely to modify the land use structure over a rather long period of time. This comes as little surprise since most real estate is built to last at least several decades. The main impact of land use on urban dynamics is its function as a generator and attractor of movements.
- *Transport network*. Also considered to be a rather stable component of urban dynamics as transport infrastructures are built for the long term. This is particularly the case for large transport terminals and subway systems that can operate for a very long period of time. For instance, many railway stations are more than 100 years old. The main impact of the transport network on urban dynamics is by providing acces-sibility. Changes in the transport network will impact accessibility and movements.
- *Movements*. The most dynamic component of the system, since movements of passengers or freight reflect changes almost immediately. Movements thus tend to be an outcome of urban dynamics rather than a factor shaping them.
- *Employment and workplaces*. They account for significant inducement effects over the urban dynamics since many models often consider employment as an

exogenous factor. This is specifically the case for employment labeled as basic, or export oriented, which is linked with specific economic sectors such as manufacturing. Commuting is a direct outcome of the number of jobs and the location of workplaces.

- *Population and housing.* They act as a generator of movements as residential areas account for the origin of commuting. Since there are a wide variety of incomes, standards of living, preferences and ethnicity, this diversity is reflected in the urban spatial structure.

The issue about how to articulate these relations remains and has been the focus of substantial research.

EVOLUTION OF URBAN MOBILITY

Rapid urban development occurring across much of the globe implies increased quantities of passengers and freight moving within urban areas. Movements also tend to involve longer distances, but evidence suggests that commuting times have remained relatively stable in the twentieth century, approximately 1.2 hours per day. This means that commuting has gradually shifted to faster transport modes and consequently greater distances could be traveled using the same amount of time. Different transport technologies and infrastructures have been implemented, resulting in a wide variety of urban transport systems around the world. In developed countries, there have been three general eras of urban development, and each is associated with a different form of urban mobility:

- *The walking/horse-car era (1800–1890).* Even during the onslaught of the industrial revolution, the dominant means of getting around was on foot. Cities were typically less than 5 kilometers in diameter, making it possible to walk from the downtown to the city edge in about 30 minutes. Land use was mixed and density was high (e.g. 100 to 200 people per hectare). The city was compact and its shape was more or less circular. The development of the first public transit in the form of omnibus service extended the diameter of the city but did not change the overall urban structure. The railroad facilitated the first real change in urban morphology. These new developments, often referred to as trackside suburbs, emerged as small nodes that were physically separated from the city itself and from one another. The nodes coincided with the location of rail stations and stretched out a considerable distance from the city center, usually up to a half-hour train ride. Within the city proper, rail lines were also laid down and horse-cars introduced mass transit.

- *The electric streetcar or transit era (1890–1920s).* The invention of the electric traction motor created a revolution in urban travel. The first electric trolley line opened in 1888 in Richmond. The operating speed of the electric trolley was three times faster than that of horse-drawn vehicles. The city spread outward 20 to 30 kilometers along the streetcar lines, creating an irregular, star-shaped pattern. The urban fringes became areas of rapid residential development. Trolley corridors became commercial strips. The city core was further entrenched as a mixed-use, high density zone. Overall densities were reduced to between 50 and 100 people per hectare. Land use patterns reflected social stratification where suburban outer areas were typically middle class while the working class continued to concentrate in the central city.
- *The automobile era (1930 onward).* The automobile was introduced in European and North American cities in the 1890s, but only the wealthy could afford this innovation. From the 1920s, ownership rates increased dramatically, with lower prices made possible by Henry Ford's revolutionary assembly-line production techniques. As automobiles became more common, land development patterns changed. Developers were attracted to green-field areas located between the suburban rail axes, and the public was attracted to these single-use zones, thus avoiding the evils of the industrial city. Suburban home building companies were no longer willing to subsidize privately owned streetcar

companies to provide cheap access to their trolley-line neighborhoods. Transit companies ran into financial trouble, and eventually transit services throughout North America and Europe became subsidized, publicly owned enterprises. As time went on, commercial activities also began to suburbanize. Within a short time, the automobile was the dominant mode of travel in all cities of North America. The automobile has reduced the friction of distance considerably which has led to urban sprawl.

Urban Transit

Transit is predominantly an urban transportation mode, particularly in large urban agglomerations. The urban environment is particularly suitable for transit because it provides conditions fundamental to its efficiency, namely high density and high short distance mobility demands. Since transit is a shared public service, it potentially benefits from economies of agglomeration related to high densities and from economies of scale related to high mobility demands. The lower the density in which a transit system operates, the lower the demand, with the greater likelihood that it will be run at a loss and may have to be subsidized. Transit systems are made up of many types of services. Different modes are used to provide complementary services within the transit system and in some cases between the transit system and other transport systems.

Each of its components is designed to provide a specific array of services. Among the defining factors of urban transit are frequency, flexibility, costs and distance between stops:

- *Metro system.* A heavy rail system, often underground in central areas (parts above ground at more peripheral locations), with fixed routes, services and stations. Transfers between lines or to other components of the transit system (mainly buses and light rail) are made at connected stations. The service frequency tends to be uniform throughout the day, but increases during peak hours. Fares are commonly access driven and constant, implying that once a user has entered the system the distance traveled has no impact on the fare. However, with the computerization of many transit fare systems, zonal/distance driven fares are becoming more common.

- *Bus system.* Characterized by scheduled fixed routes and stops serviced by motorized multiple-passenger vehicles (45–80 passengers). Services are often synchronized with other heavy systems, mainly metro and transit rail, where they act as feeders. Express services, using only a limited number of stops, can also be available, notably during peak hours. Since metro and bus systems are often managed by the same transit authority, the user's fare is valid for both systems.
- *Transit rail system.* Fixed rail comes into two major categories. The first is the tram rail system, which is mainly composed of streetcars (tramways) operating in central areas. They can consist of up to four cars. The second is the commuter rail system, which is composed of passenger trains mainly developed to service peripheral/suburban areas through a heavy (faster and longer distances between stations) or light rail system (slower and shorter distances between stations). Frequency of services is strongly linked with peak hours and traffic tends to be imbalanced. Fares tend to be separate from the transit system and proportional to distance or service zones.
- *Shuttle system.* Composed of a number of privately (dominantly) owned services using small buses or vans. Shuttle routes and frequencies tend to be fixed, but can be adapted to fit new situations. They service numerous specific functions such as expanding mobility along a corridor during peak hours, linking a specific activity center (shopping mall, university campus, industrial zone, hotel, etc.) or aimed at servicing the elderly or people with disabilities.
- *Paratransit system.* A flexible and privately owned collective demand–response system composed of minibuses, vans or shared taxis commonly servicing peripheral and low density zones. Their key advantage is the possibility of a door-to-door service, less loading

and unloading time, less stops and more maneuverability in traffic. In many cities in developing countries, this system is informal, dominant and often services central areas because of inadequacies or high costs of the formal transit system.

- *Taxi system*. Comprises privately owned cars or small vans offering an on-call, individual demand–response system. Fares are commonly a function of a metered distance/time, but sometimes can be negotiated. A taxi system has no fixed routes, but is rather servicing an area where a taxi company has the right (permit) to pick up customers. Commonly, rights are issued by a municipality and several companies may be allowed to compete on the same territory. When competition is not permitted, fares are set up by regulations.

Contemporary transit systems tend to be publicly owned, implying that many decisions related to their development and operation are politically motivated. This is a sharp contrast to the past when most transit systems were private and profit driven initiatives. With the fast diffusion of the automobile in the 1950s, many transit companies faced financial difficulties, and the quality of their service declined. They were purchased by public interests, mainly for the sake of providing mobility. As such, public transit often serves more a social function of public service and a tool of social equity than any sound economic role. Transit has become dependent on government subsidies, with little if any competition permitted as wages and fares are regulated. Transit systems tend to have limited relationships with economic activities, particularly in suburban areas.

Reliance on urban transit as a mode of urban transportation tends to be high in Asia, intermediate in Europe and low in North America. Since their inception in the early nineteenth century, comprehensive urban transit systems had significant impacts on the urban form and spatial structure. Three major classes of cities can be found in terms of the relationships they have with their transit systems (Cervero, 1998):

- *Adaptive cities*. True transit-oriented cities where urban form and urban land use developments are coordinated with transit developments. While central areas are adequately serviced by a metro system and are pedestrian friendly, peripheral areas are oriented along transit rail lines.

- *Adaptive transit.* Cities where transit plays a marginal and residual role and where the automobile accounts for the dominant share of movements. The urban form is decentralized and of low density.
- *Hybrids.* Cities that have sought a balance between transit development and automobile dependency. While central areas have an adequate level of service, peripheral areas are automobile-oriented.
- Contemporary land development tends to precede the introduction of urban transit services, as opposed to concomitant developments in earlier phases of urban growth. Transit authorities operate under a service warrant. This has led to a set of considerations aimed at a higher integration of transit in the urban planning process, especially in North America, where such a tradition is not well established. Local land use impacts can be categorized in three dimensions of relationships with transit systems, including accessibility to the transit system, the convergence of local movements to transit stations and the integration of local land use with urban transit:
- *Accessibility.* The sole purpose of a transit stop is to provide accessibility to the transit system, such as stops along a bus route. Land use impacts for the stop are often minimal, if non-existent, with basic facilities to accommodate waiting time such as shelters. Accessibility defines the local market area of a transit service. For instance, for a new residential area, a minimum catchment area of 400 dwelling units or 1,000 residents within a 450-meter walk distance to a transit stop is often required for an extension of service. In a low transit use environment, accessibility to a transit stop has little if no impact on land use as access is a mere matter of convenience to a marginal segment of the

population. As the level of transit use increases, accessibility has a significant impact on local land use by favoring band-like developments along transit lines, since a growing share of the local population uses transit as a factor of urban mobility.

- *Convergence.* This generally applies to more important transit stops, notably rail and subway stations with terminal structures, including waiting areas and basic services. The transit station is a point of convergence of local traffic and often serves more than one mode. The impacts on land use are varied, ranging from park-and-ride facilities to activities that take advantage of flows, such as restaurants and convenience stores, and possibly office activities. The stations have to consider the nature and scale of movements generated. Convergence in a low level of transit use implies walking from the vicinity, basic park-and-ride possibilities and occasional drops and pickups by passenger vehicles. Transit subsystems, such as local buses, rarely converge to stops/terminals in a low transit use environment, since the demand would not justify them. As transit use increases, the convergence function may become significant, with substantial park-and-ride facilities and dedicated local transit routes collecting passengers for the stop/terminal.
- *Integration.* Large, multi-level terminals with well-integrated high-density planning designs. Local land use is consequently highly linked with the transit system, which supports a large share of the mobility. The terminal acts as a local central place with its implied hierarchy of land uses with adjacent commercial activities. Medium and low density residential areas are located further away. There are different possible levels of integration, from simple terminal design with little local impact to high integration to local land use where transit is dominant. Significant transit terminals offer opportunities to integrate local land use to transit accessibility.

From a transportation perspective, the potential benefits of better integration between transit and local land uses are reduced trip frequency and increased use of alternative modes of travel (i.e. walking, biking and transit). Evidence is often lacking to support such expectations. Community design can consequently have a significant influence on travel patterns. Land use initiatives should be coordinated with other planning and policy initiatives to cope with automobile dependence. However, there is a strong bias against transit in the general population because of negative perceptions, especially in North America, but increasingly globally. As personal mobility is a symbol of status and economic success, the users of public transit are perceived as the least successful segment of the population. This bias may prevent transit use by a segment of the population.

TYPES OF URBAN MOVEMENTS

Movements are linked to specific urban activities and their land use. Each type of land use involves the generation and attraction of a particular array of movements. This relationship is complex, but is linked to factors such as recurrence, income, urban form, spatial accumulation, level of development and technology. Urban movements are either obligatory, when they are linked to scheduled activities (such as home-to-work movements), or voluntary, when those generating it are free to decide their scheduling (such as leisure). The most common types of urban movements are:

- *Pendular movements.* These are obligatory movements involving commuting between locations of residence and work. They are highly cyclical since they are predictable and recur on a regular basis, most of the time a daily occurrence.
- *Professional movements.* These are movements linked to professional, work based activities such as meetings and customer services, dominantly taking place during work hours.
- *Personal movements.* These are voluntary movements linked to the location of commercial activities, which includes shopping and recreation.

- *Touristic movements.* Important for cities with historical and recreational features, they involve interactions between landmarks and amenities such as hotels and restaurants. They tend to be seasonal in nature or to occur at specific moments. Major sport events such as the World Cup or the Olympics are important generators of urban movements.
- *Distribution movements.* These are concerned with the distribution of freight to satisfy consumption and manufacturing requirements. They are linked to distribution centres and retail outlets.

Dense cities, which also tend to be older (such as Western European cities), are generally more transit oriented, while younger cities (such as those in the USA and Australia) tend to rely more on the automobile as the major mode for urban travel. In developing countries, cycling and walking are dominant modes, obviously because of their low costs and the lack of modern transport infrastructures. Within the United States, a greater share of work trips are made by the automobile in sprawling cities such as Phoenix and Houston than in denser cities such as New York and San Francisco.

The share of the automobile in urban trips varies in relation to location, social status, income, quality of public transit and parking availability. Mass transit is often affordable, but several social groups, such as students, the elderly and the poor are a captive market. There are important variations in mobility according to age, income, gender and disability. The so-called gender gap in mobility is the outcome of socio-economic differences as access to individual transportation is dominantly a matter of income. Consequently, in some instances modal choice is more a modal constraint linked to economic opportunities.

In central locations, there are generally few transport availability problems because private and public transport facilities are present. However, in locations outside the central core that are accessible only by the automobile, a significant share of the population is isolated if they do not own an automobile. Limited public transit and high automobile ownership costs have created a class of spatially constrained (mobility deprived) people. They neither have access to the services in the suburb nor, more importantly, to the jobs that are increasingly concentrated in those areas.

LAND AS URBAN MORPHOLOGY

Individual cities display morphologies and land use patterns which range from the very formal and carefully ordered to apparently haphazard collections of buildings, spaces and activities. The precise pattern is determined by a multiplicity of factors including the age, style and scale of development, the needs for different kinds of land and the nature of its ownership. The economic explanation of the land-use pattern must incorporate forces which extend far beyond the city's local boundaries. As Carter suggested (1983:114): 'the plan and built form of the town are direct reflections of the nature of culture on the large scale...the town epitomises in its physical nature the complex of political, economic, and social forces which characterised the period of its creation'.

As examples Carter contrasted the towns of Renaissance and Baroque Europe with their formal layout, classical architecture and defensive needs with the very different but equally rigid morphologies of the North American gridiron plan. Both were shaped by strong, centralised planning influences; in the former case the aristocratic land owners and state military architects, in the latter case by the Land Ordinance established to regulate the settlement of North America after 1785. The rationale behind the European designs can be seen in terms of the aesthetic appeal of formality, the nature and scale of contemporary warfare and the desire for pomp and ceremony. The American example, on the other hand, has been explained (Stanislawski 1946), as a reflection of the democratic principles of the time and the desire to divide and allocate land on broadly egalitarian lines. This may be true, but undoubtedly the system also owed much to the needs of simplicity and expediency in laying out numerous new settlements on largely virgin land. As with most morphological designs, these have remained remarkably enduring features of the towns in which they were applied.

A more marked contrast may be found by examining the morphologies and forms of land development which typified the explosive growth of industrial urban settlements in the nineteenth century. These forms are particlarly widespread in Britain and the rest of Europe, although they also occur commonly elsewhere. In these cases the form of development was influenced partly by detailed local factors such as ownership, location and physical resources, but overwhelmingly the shaping force was the needs of industry developing in a competitive laissez-faire environment. Little centralised planning occurred and the industrial city became dominated by its core, the needs of industry and the prevailing transport technology. As Goheen (1970:11) explained for nineteenth-century Toronto 'industry was able to demand almost any land in the city, such was its bidding power and such was the utility which manufacturing gave to the land'.

The power of industry in shaping the city was extensive for two reasons. First, manufacturing industry became the prime motor of urban growth and the dominant, although not the largest, land user in the city. But its influence went much wider. Industry reshaped the social map of the city and played a large part in determining and providing the housing needs of the urban populations. In addition, the industrialists came to dominate the civic and other institutions which shaped the political and cultural life of the city. Even wider than this, the nations which first created large urban/industrial agglomerations, notably Britain, Germany and the USA, were stamping their own imprint of development upon large parts of the rest of the world in the nineteenth and early twentieth centuries.

Second, and from a more purely academic perspective, the industrial/urban form proved to be an enduring role model for development throughout the western world, certainly up to the mid point of the present century. Much of our understanding of the city, including the derivation of a large body of urban land theory which will be reviewe, thus stems from it. Clearly, in the final quarter of the present century, the large industrial city with its traditional land use needs is undergoing profound change. One of the major underlying questions of this book therefore is the extent to which our understanding of and planning for the city, based as they are upon a largely outdated model, are valid for present day and future needs.

The typical urban morphology which emerged in the latter phases of industrial growth in the mid twentieth century carried forward many of its earlier elements, but it also introduced important changes. These will be discussed more fully later, but they need to be introduced here. Above all, the morphological anarchy of the nineteenth century became tamed by the introduction of comprehensive town planning. This had many effects, amongst which the encouragement of hierarchical forms of urban centrality, the segregation of urban land uses and the introduction of a degree of order and tidiness were important. New forms of transport permitted a greater degree of specialisation in land use and created new locational imperatives. New building standards and codes were enacted as a response to the most squalid and haphazard aspects of earlier urban conditions. Social requirements in the form of community facilities, better space standards and amenity and environmental considerations were brought to the fore. Building materials and techniques became more standardised so that a greater degree of uniformity became the norm. Huge swathes of low density housing developments, high rise office and apartment blocks, efficiently laid out industrial estates and modular schools and hospitals were replicated from one city to another. Above all, the residential suburbs, catering for car owning residents became the characteristic morphological addition to the twentieth century city.

LAND AS POWER

Traditionally, the ownership, or occupation, of land has conferred great economic and political power. Originally, this was especially true of the large agricultural estates, but the cities too proclaimed the power and wealth of the major land owners, be they individual aristocrats, the monarchy or bodies such as the church. One of the greatest social changes prompted by the Industrial Revolution in Britain, was the transfer of power from the small number of wealthy 'landed gentry' to, at first a small, and then later a growing, number of urban and industrial interests. From this point onwards the power and influence of the individual land owners declined rapidly, except for those few like the Howard de Waldens and the Dukes of Bedford, Westminster, and Portland who were fortunate enough, or shrewd enough to possess large holdings in the growing urban areas.

In the latter part of the twentieth century, land, especially in urban areas, has retained its allure as a source of wealth, power and status, but the ownership pattern has changed significantly. There are still a few individuals who have made large fortunes from urban land, but for the most part the twentieth century has seen the emergence and steady growth of three different kinds of land owning groups. The first of these is a set of institutions, including pension funds, insurance groups, investment companies and other corporate interests. These bodies are interested in urban land for a number of reasons. Most obviously, they may actually use land and buildings to accommodate their own office functions, and in this they may be looking for prestige and corporate identity as well as functional office space. Who could fail to notice for example the Woolworth or Pan Am buildings in Manhattan or the National Westminster Tower in the City of London. More significantly, however, urban land and property represents to such bodies a commodity in which wealth may be stored and which may be traded, often with good prospects for capital gain and favourable tax conditions.

The second major set of urban land owners, which has also grown markedly during this century, is located in the public sector. This includes central and local government, public utilities, state owned industries and a number of other state and quasi-state bodies. Their involvement in land ownership stems from two different reasons. First, a number of public bodies exist in order to provide services, most of which require land, e.g., for schools, hospitals, roads, and housing. Second, for reasons of social equity and planning efficiency, public sector control may be exerted over land development and urban expansion. In a number of European countries in particular there are long traditions of municipal land ownership, and state bodies are often involved in the process of land development.

The third group of owners is the growing army of individual house owners. These have been responsible for a greater fragmentation and dispersal of land holding than ever before. Their motives are twofold. Most obviously there is the status, social advantage and freedom which is conferred by home ownership, but there are also economic benefits in the form of favourable tax arrangements and the prospect of long term financial security.

There is another sense also in which land is associated with power and control. Drawing upon the work of Michel Foucault (1984), Cullen (1990) has argued that political treatises in the eighteenth century began to bracket architecture, land and space together with control and power. Foucault is interpreted as arguing that the city, its built form and the practices of those who sculpt that form are largely concerned with imposing institutions and structures of control over individuals.

LAND AS THE BASIS OF THE PLANNING SYSTEM

The two major themes outlined above, land as urban morphology and land as power, come together to form a large part of the basis of town planning. In Britain and elsewhere, the planning profession which began to emerge at the beginning of the twentieth century was concerned with many aspects of urban development, but new and more pleasing forms of urban layout and a concern to protect the interests of the weaker groups in society were central. In both of these endeavours, the use, disposition, ownership of and access to land were key factors. In short, town planning was largely synonymous with land use planning.

As far as morphology was concerned, the central task was seen as overcoming the worst aspects of the congested, and insanitary jumble of land uses which had typified the industrial city. Attempts had been made by a few enlightened industrialists in nineteenth century Britain and Germany, to build model settlements in which the needs of industry and its workers could be satisfied harmoniously, for example, at Port Sunlight near Liverpool. Early planning documents often proposed Utopian urban forms, some of which sought a return to more formal, pre-industrial layouts, whilst others attempted to deny urbanity by incorporating large amounts of open space and rural imagery. The interwar years were particularly influential, for they produced the International Congresses for Modern Architecture (CIAM). These paved the way for Le Corbusier's ideas on the Ville Radieuse with its tall blocks of flats, wide areas of public open space and careful segregation of motor vehicles and pedestrians.

Many of these ideas were taken up in practical form after the Second World War, notably by the British new town movement, but whereas other European countries were emphasising technical innovation, in Britain the focus was firmly upon the vernacular. The layout of the American city too was influenced by the modern movement but here it was given a particular character by Frank Lloyd Wright. This took development in a very different direction where the preference for individual family homes and gardens was to be combined with the freedom of the motor car in a virtually anti-urban form known as Broadacre City.

The impact of these elements of the modern movement upon the morphology and land use of today's cities has been considerable. Le Corbusier's ideas have been used, albeit in a penny-pinching form, in high density residential developments in cities throughout the world. The new town movement culminated in Britain's postwar development of more than thirty new towns, a style of urban development widely copied elsewhere and even more extensively reproduced in debased form through a multiplicity of suburban housing estates. Lloyd Wright's ideas too shaped the development in North America, and increasingly in Europe, of low density cities with out-of-town shopping centres, leisure complexes and dispersed luxury housing developments.

Following the land as power argument takes us also to the heart of the planning system. In Britain especially, but also elsewhere, planning consists largely of the three elements identified by Peter Hall (1980). A professional bureaucracy forms the centre, and this is surrounded by a number of pressure groups and politicians. The first and third of these groups seek to balance and accommodate the demands of the middle group. The system is thus inherently political and it is significant that in seeking to analyse the politics of local planning, Blowers (1980) entitled his book *The Limits of Power*.

A large part of the justification for a planning system is that it resolves competing claims over the use of resources (especially land), attempts to balance an uneven distribution of power and protects the interests of weaker groups. In a practical sense, this includes the provision of land for community facilities and for housing poorer members of society and ensuring that some checks are kept upon the dominant land using activities. Much of the development of postwar planning in Britain, notably that in the new towns, placed great emphasis upon relatively egalitarian approaches and the importance of community values. Lord Reith (New Towns Committee 1946) was quite clear that these communities should be balanced, with a contribution from every type and class of person. The success of the planning system in protecting the weak, particularly in the provision of housing and community facilities, should not be discounted, but the 'Robin Hood' view of planning taking from the rich to give to the poor is not always appropriate. In the field of urban renewal, especially, there are abundant examples where relatively weak local communities have been pushed aside by a collusion of local authority and property development interests. In recent years, the prodevelopment policies adopted by a number of governments in order to combat urban decline have tended to downgrade the power of local and community interests.

Many examples of this can be seen, especially where the rise of an office economy has required a fundamental restructuring of urban land uses and a new economic infrastructure. In the USA the needs of urban renewal in some cities have resulted in powerful corporations persuading city governments to do much of the job of land assembly and provision of infrastructure (Friedland 1982). Following the 1949

Housing Act, city and federal governments began acting effectively as brokers for private developers. In the process they biased the power struggle between the political liberals and labour leaders who wanted low cost housing to replace slums and the corporate interests who wanted commercial and high rent residential development. The situation heralded what has happened in the London Dockland redevelopment in the 1980s. Such developments may well be desirable in the interests of the overall urban economy, especially where they follow a long period of decline or dereliction, but they lend weight to Cherry's question of'Whose values are being protected, and by whom?' (1982:86).

LAND AS ENVIRONMENT

During the 1980s, there has been a renewed concern over the quality and protection of the environment. Although much of the interest has been expressed at a global scale, or has involved 'natural' landscapes, there are also many local issues concerning urban environments. Much of the original motivation for the development of suburbs came from the desire of wealthy people to construct pleasant environments which were separate from the congested city, and similar motives help to explain counterurbanisation trends today. Within the city itself, environmental concern was first translated into exclusive parks and walkways for the nobility, but by the nineteenth century municipal parks for all citizens were becoming common. Much of the imagery of planning, be it for municipal parks, garden suburbs, green belts or the design of contemporary office developments, has invoked the idea of bringing the countryside into the city.

URBAN CHANGE

The past two decades have been a period of far reaching change for urban areas in the developed nations. Almost all urban activities have been affected by the processes of change, to such an extent that even the concepts of urbanisation itself must be questioned. Naturally, there are profound consequences for our understanding of urban land issues. Perhaps the most basic factor to be confronted is that a number of powerful forces have been conspiring in those countries with market economies to direct growth away from large cities. By the middle of this century there were signs from some of the largest cities, including London, that after nearly two hundred years of rapid urban growth the rate was slackening. In the middle 1970s a reversal from urban population concentration to deconcentration was widely identified in the USA by Beale (1975), Berry (1976) and Vining and Strauss (1977) amongst others. The results of the 1981 and 1991 censuses revealed that the process was well established in Britain too, and in fact had been since the 1950s. Hall and Hay (1980) summarised the growth trends, particularly from North American evidence, as moving:

1 from larger to smaller metropolitan areas
2 from metropolitan cores to fringes
3 from urban to rural areas
4 from older manufacturing areas to newer service areas.

It soon became clear that these processes were very widespread and complex in their impact. The fact that they went beyond mere suburbanisation and local decentralisation led to the use of the term counterurbanisation. This process of counterurbanisation has been comprehensively reviewed for a large number of countries by Champion (1989). In this review, Frey (1989) suggested that it was the 1970s which represented the important decade of transition with counterurbanisation in the USA, at least, being a reaction to the economic shocks of the age. Champion concluded that by the end of the 1980s counterurbanisation was widespread but not universal. Some countries and cities continued to experience urban concentration and in others there were signs that the pace of counterurbanisation was slowing. Population figures for London, for example, suggest that some growth has resumed since 1984 and this prompts the possibility of a fresh reversal, back to the pre-turn-around pattern. Until further evidence becomes available there must remain some doubts about whether the 1970s represented a temporary hiccup in the pattern of urban growth, linked perhaps to cyclical economic depression, or signalled a long term tendency towards population dispersal and urban decline.

Whether temporary or permanent, certain explanations can be cited in this pattern of urban restructuring. First there is an economic dimension, expressed through changing patterns of urban employment. The large industrial cities of the western world have lost much of their industrial *raison d'être* in the face of competition from the newly industrialising countries in the Pacific rim and elsewhere. This has resulted in a dramatic decline in the number of industrial jobs in the urban heartlands of Britain, Germany, France and the USA. For example between 1971 and 1987 the following manufacturing job losses were recorded: London Local Labour Market Area, 602,000; Birmingham, 149,000; Glasgow, 110,000; Manchester, 103,000; Liverpool, 101,000 (Champion and Townsend 1990). The manufacturing plants which remain in these countries have been forced to change their modes of production, reduce and restructure their labour forces and choose new locations. At the same time, substantial growth has been recorded in service sector jobs; in Britain, for example, over 2.5 million service jobs were created in the period 1971–84 (ESRC 1989). Almost without exception these jobs had different labour and locational requirements from the manufacturing jobs which had previously sustained the cities, and hence they led to different land use needs.

In the social sphere too the 1970s and 1980s witnessed far reaching changes. The impact of changing age structures, family sizes and marriage patterns upon housing requirements and urban development has already been alluded to. In addition, changing lifestyle preferences, growing environmental awareness and increasing personal affluence for many encouraged people to seek work and residence in small towns with better living conditions, cleaner environments, lower crime levels and lower local government rates. In the process the size and power of the big cities has been weakened.

These two processes have been encouraged by improvements and growth in transport which has been both a prime mover and an enabling factor. In the West European countries for which statistics are readily available, traffic volume measured in millions of vehicle kilometres, increased on average by 17.5

per cent between 1984 and 1988. In the USA, starting from a much higher baseline of vehicle useage, the increase was 8.1 per cent. (International Road Federation 1989). In Great Britain, the ownership of cars and light goods vehicles increased by 23 per cent in the decade 1975–85 (Dept of Transport 1986). On the one hand transport congestion and delays in large cities have acted as a disincentive to industrial location, and on the other hand the growth in motor traffic has opened up outer suburban areas and small towns, both for industrial/office employment and for residential purposes. Even changes in the technology and handling of seaborne freight, and the dramatic decline in liner passenger traffic have hit many large port cities severely. This can be seen particularly clearly in the contemporary land use patterns of major dock areas.

Finally, government policies have played a significant part in the pattern of differential growth between large cities and other localities. In Britain, for example government policy during and after the Second World War actively encouraged the decentralisation of industry. Regional policy as variously operated in the postwar years, coupled with new town development programmes resulted in economic activity deserting the older and bigger cities in some measure. Similarly, in West Germany the regional planning policy (Kontuly and Vogelsang 1989) and in France the *villes moyennes* programme (Winchester and Ogden 1989) militated against big cities.

Alongside counterurbanisation, another major concept which helps to articulate the changing land use needs of modern urban society, is that of the postindustrial city. Hall (1988), in particular, suggested that Britain at least is well along the road to a postindustrial economy. Somewhat earlier he had suggested, along with others (Brotchie *et al.* 1985) that the microelectronic information technology revolution was beginning to produce changes in our pattern of living and working at least as profound as those produced by the Industrial Revolution, but within a shorter time frame.

The land use consequences of these trends, especially those of counterurbanisation and postindustrialism are still unclear and subject to intense speculation. But the general implications for urban and quasi-urban land patterns can be outlined. In short, the massive forces of economic and social restructuring are having, and will continue to have, profound significance for urban land. The overall pattern of change can be broken for convenience into two major components.

On the one hand, most large cities show signs of serious inner area problems. The loss of job opportunities, the concentration of deprived social groups, the collapse of the urban infrastructure, the unpopularity of many public sector developments and the difficulty of attracting private sector investment have all combined to sweep away the previous vitality of many of these areas. The immediate consequence has been to throw the inner city land market into turmoil. Land which once had a relatively high demand, and hence value, attracts little commercial interest once those traditional uses have deserted the city. As a result, vacant and underused land has become a common characteristic of such areas.

Conversely, the demand for land on the urban periphery, and in small towns throughout the outer metropolitan fringe is relatively buoyant. In Britain, Hall (1988:16) suggested that even if the major urban agglomerations succeed in stabilising their populations, the continued growth of what he terms the Golden Belt and Golden Horn regions in the southern half of the country will 'entail a voracious demand for conversion of rural land for urban purpose'. This then is the general context, a massive and relatively recent restructuring of urban areas and their economies, even to the extent that our traditional notions of the city as a settlement form must be re-examined.

9

Geographic and Demographic Setting

India is a Country of great diversity with a wide range of landform types, including major mountain ranges, deserts, rich agricultural plains, and hilly jungle regions. Indeed, the term *Indian subcontinent* aptly describes the enormous extent of the earth's surface that India occupies, and any attempt to generalize about its physiography is inaccurate. Diversity is also evident in the geographical distribution of India's ethnic and linguistic groups. In ancient times, the major river valleys of the Indo-Gangetic Plain of South Asia were among the great cradles of civilization in Asia, as were the valleys of the Tigris and Euphrates rivers in West Asia and the Huang He (Yellow River) in East Asia. As a result of thousands of years of cultural and political expansion and amalgamation, contemporary India has come to include many different natural and cultural regions.

The Himalayas (and the nations of Nepal and Bhutan) form India's northern frontier with China. Pakistan borders India to the west and Bangladesh (formerly East Pakistan) to the east. Although both were formerly part of the British Indian Empire, India and Pakistan became separate countries in 1947 and East Pakistan became independent Bangladesh in 1971. The boundaries of the Indian polity are not fully demarcated because of regional ethnic and political disputes and are the source of occasional tensions.

When the 1991 national census was taken, India's population was approximately 846.3 million. The annual population growth rate from 1981 to 1991 was 2 percent. Accounting for only 2.4 percent of the world's landmass, India is home to 16 percent of the world's population. Every sixth person in the world in the early 1990s was an Indian. It is generally assumed that India's population will surpass the 1 billion mark some time before the next census in 2001. In July 1995, the population was estimated at 936.5 million.

Some 38 percent of all Indians were officially listed as living below the poverty line in fiscal year 1991. This number represented an increase from the low mark of 26 percent in FY 1989, but the rise was believed to be only temporary by some observers. Although government-sponsored health clinics are widely available in the mid-1990s, their emphasis is on curative techniques rather than preventive medicine. However, the lack of such basic amenities as safe, potable water for much of the population is indicative of the severity of health problems. This situation has traditionally led most Indians to have large families as their only form of insurance against sickness and for their care in old age. Although family planning programs are becoming integrated with the programs of urban and rural health clinics, no official birth control programs have widespread support. The severity of the acquired immune deficiency syndrome (AIDS) epidemic in India has become increasingly apparent to health specialists, but local awareness of the causes of and ways to prevent the spread of AIDS is growing slowly.

Although many public schools are inadequate, improvements to the education system overall have been substantial since 1947. In the mid-1990s, however, only about 50 percent of children between the ages of six and fourteen are enrolled in schools. The goal of compulsory and free primary and middle school education is embodied in the Indian constitution but has been elusive. The National Policy on Education of 1986 sought to institutionalize universal primary education by setting 1990 as a target date for the education of all children up to eleven years of age. The ability of India's education system to meet this goal has been constrained by lack of adequate financial resources. Important achievements have been made, however, with implementation of the nonformal education system and adult education programs. Whereas public education is generally below standard, education standards in private schools are very high. There also are high standards among the elite institutions in the higher education system.

Principal Regions

India's total land mass is 2,973,190 square kilometers and is divided into three main geological regions: the Indo-Gangetic Plain, the Himalayas, and the Peninsula region. The Indo-Gangetic Plain and those portions of the Himalayas within India are collectively known as North India. South India consists of the peninsular region, often termed simply the Peninsula. On the basis of its physiography, India is divided into ten regions: the Indo-Gangetic Plain, the northern mountains of the Himalayas, the Central Highlands, the Deccan or Peninsular Plateau, the East Coast (Coromandel Coast in the south), the West Coast (Konkan, Kankara, and Malabar coasts), the Great Indian Desert (a geographic feature known as the Thar Desert in Pakistan) and the Rann of Kutch, the valley of the Brahmaputra in Assam, the northeastern hill ranges surrounding the Assam Valley, and the islands of the Arabian Sea and the Bay of Bengal.

Indo-Gangetic Plain

In social and economic terms, the Indo-Gangetic Plain is the most important region of India. The plain is a great alluvial crescent stretching from the Indus River system in Pakistan to the Punjab Plain (in both Pakistan and India) and the Haryana Plain to the delta of the Ganga (or Ganges) in Bangladesh (where it is called the Padma). Topographically the plain is homogeneous, with only floodplain bluffs and other related features of river erosion and changes in river channels forming important natural features.

Two narrow terrain belts, collectively known as the Terai, constitute the northern boundary of the Indo-Gangetic Plain. Where the foothills of the Himalayas encounter the plain, small hills known locally as *ghar* (meaning house in Hindi) have been formed by coarse sands and pebbles deposited by mountain streams. Groundwater from these areas flows on the surface where the plains begin and converts large areas along the rivers into swamps. The southern boundary of the plain begins along the edge of the Great Indian Desert in the state of Rajasthan and continues east along the base of the hills of the Central Highlands to the Bay of Bengal. The hills, varying in elevation from 300 to 1,200 meters, lie on a general east-west axis. The Central Highlands are divided into northern and southern parts. The northern part is centered on the Aravalli Range of eastern Rajasthan. In the northern part of the state of Madhya Pradesh, the Malwa Plateau comprises the southern part of the Central Highlands and merges with the Vindhya Range to the south. The main rivers that flow through the southern part of the plain—the Narmada, the Tapti, and the Mahanadi—delineate North India from South India.

Some geographers subdivide the Indo-Gangetic Plain into three parts: the Indus Valley (mostly in Pakistan), the Punjab (divided between India and Pakistan) and Haryana plains, and the middle and lower Ganga. These regional distinctions are based primarily on the availability of water. By another definition, the Indo-Gangetic Plain is divided into two drainage basins by the Delhi Ridge; the western part consists of the Punjab Plain and the Haryana Plain, and the eastern part consists of the Ganga-Brahmaputra drainage systems. This divide is only 300 meters above sea level, contributing to the perception that the Indo-Gangetic Plain appears to be continuous between the two drainage basins. The Punjab Plain is centered in the land between five rivers: the Jhelum, the Chenab, the Ravi, the Beas, and the Sutlej. (The name *Punjab* comes from the Sanskrit *pancha ab*, meaning five waters or rivers.)

Both the Punjab and Haryana plains are irrigated with water from the Ravi, Beas, and Sutlej rivers. The irrigation projects emanating from these rivers have led to a decrease in the flow of water reaching the lower drainage areas in the state of Punjab in India and the Indus Valley in Pakistan. The benefits that increased irrigation has brought to farmers in the state of Haryana are controversial in light of the effects that irrigation has had on agricultural life in the Punjab areas of both India and Pakistan.

The middle Ganga extends from the Yamuna River in the west to the state of West Bengal in the east. The lower Ganga and the Assam Valley are more lush and verdant than the middle Ganga. The lower Ganga is centered in West Bengal from which it flows into Bangladesh and, after joining the Jamuna (as the lower reaches of the Brahmaputra are known in Bangladesh), forms the delta of the Ganga. The Brahmaputra (meaning son of Brahma) rises in Tibet (China's Xizang Autonomous Region) as the Yarlung Zangbo River, flows through Arunachal Pradesh and Assam, and then crosses into Bangladesh. Average annual rainfall increases moving west to east from approximately 600 millimeters in the Punjab Plain to 1,500 millimeters around the lower Ganga and Brahmaputra.

The Himalayas

The Himalayas, the highest mountain range in the world, extend along the northern frontiers of Pakistan, India, Nepal, Bhutan, and Burma. They were formed geologically as a result of the collision of the Indian subcontinent with Asia. This process of plate tectonics is ongoing, and the gradual northward drift of the Indian subcontinent still causes earthquakes. Lesser ranges jut southward from the main body of the Himalayas at both the eastern and western ends.

The Himalayan system, about 2,400 kilometers in length and varying in width from 240 to 330 kilometers, is made up of three parallel ranges—the Greater Himalayas, the Lesser Himalayas, and the Outer Himalayas—sometimes collectively called the Great Himalayan Range. The Greater Himalayas, or northern range, average approximately 6,000 meters in height and contain the three highest mountains on earth: Mount Everest (8,796 meters) on the China-Nepal border; K2 (8,611 meters, also known as Mount Godwin-Austen, and in China as Qogir Feng) in an area claimed by India, Pakistan, and China; and Kanchenjunga (8,598 meters) on the India-Nepal border.

Many major mountains are located entirely within India, such as Nanda Devi (7,817 meters) in the state of Uttar Pradesh. The snow line averages 4,500 to 6,000 meters on the southern side of the Greater Himalayas and 5,500 to 6,000 on the northern side. Because of climatic conditions, the snow line in the eastern

Himalayas averages 4,300 meters, while in the western Himalayas it averages 5,800 meters.

The Lesser Himalayas, located in northwestern India in the states of Himachal Pradesh and Uttar Pradesh, in north-central India in the state of Sikkim, and in northeastern India in the state of Arunachal Pradesh, range from 1,500 to 5,000 meters in height. Located in the Lesser Himalayas are the hill stations of Shimla (Simla) and Darjiling (Darjeeling). During the colonial period, these and other hill stations were used by the British as summer retreats to escape the intense heat of the plains. It is in this transitional vegetation zone that the contrasts between the bare southern slopes and the forested northern slopes become most noticeable.

The Outer or Southern Himalayas, averaging 900 to 1,200 meters in elevation, lie between the Lesser Himalayas and the Indo-Gangetic Plain. In Himachal Pradesh and Uttar Pradesh, this southernmost range is often referred to as the Siwalik Hills. It is possible to identify a fourth, and northernmost range, known as the Trans-Himalaya. This range is located entirely on the Qinghai-Xizang Plateau, north of the great west-to-east trending valley of the Yarlung Zangbo River. Although the Trans-Himalaya Range is divided from the Great Himalayan Range for most of its length, it merges with the Great Himalayan Range in the western section—the Karakoram Range—where India, Pakistan, and China meet.

The southern slopes of each of the Himalayan ranges are too steep to accumulate snow or support much tree life; the northern slopes generally are forested below the snow line. Between the ranges are extensive high plateaus, deep gorges, and fertile valleys, such as the vales of Kashmir and Kulu. The Himalayas serve a very important purpose. They provide a physical screen within which the monsoon system operates and are the source of the great river systems that water the alluvial plains below. As a result of erosion, the rivers coming from the mountains carry vast quantities of silt that enrich the plains.

The area of northeastern India adjacent to Burma and Bangladesh consists of numerous hill tracts, averaging between 1,000 and 2,000 meters in elevation, that are not associated with the eastern part of the Himalayas in Arunachal Pradesh. The Naga Hills, rising to heights of more than 3,000 meters, form the watershed between India and Burma. The Mizo Hills are the southern part of the northeastern ranges in India. The Garo, Khasi, and Jaintia hills are centered in the state of Meghalaya and, isolated from the northeastern ranges, divide the Assam Valley from Bangladesh to the south and west.

The Peninsula

The Peninsula proper is an old, geologically stable region with an average elevation between 300 and 1,800 meters. The Vindhya Range constitutes the main dividing line between the geological regions of the Indo-Gangetic Plain and the Peninsula. This range lies north of the Narmada River, and when viewed from there, it is possible to discern the prominent escarpments that rise between 800 and 1,400 meters. The Vindhya Range defines the north-central and northwestern boundary of the Peninsula, and the Chota Nagpur Plateau of southern Bihar forms the northeastern boundary. The uplifting of the plateau of the central Peninsula and its eastward tilt formed the Western Ghats, a line of hills running from the Tapti River south to the tip of the Peninsula. The Eastern Ghats mark the eastern end of the plateau; they begin in the hills of the Mahanadi River basin and converge with the Western Ghats at the Peninsula's southern tip.

The interior of the Peninsula, south of the Narmada River, often termed the Deccan Plateau or simply the Deccan (from the Sanskrit *daksina*, meaning south), is a series of plateaus topped by rolling hills and intersected by many rivers. The plateau averages roughly 300 to 750 meters in elevation. Its major rivers—the Godavari, the Krishna, and the Kaveri—rise in the Western Ghats and flow eastward into the Bay of Bengal.

The coastal plain borders the plateau. On the northwestern side, it is characterized by tidal marshes, drowned valleys, and estuaries, and in the south by lagoons, marshes, and beach ridges. Coastal plains on the eastern side are wider than those in the west; they are focused on large river deltas that serve as the centres of human settlement.

Offshore Islands

India's offshore islands, constituting roughly one-quarter of 1 percent of the nation's territory, lie in two groups located off the east and west coasts. The northernmost point of the union territory of the Andaman and Nicobar Islands lies 1,100 kilometers southeast of Calcutta. Situated in the Bay of Bengal in a chain stretching some 800 kilometers, the Andaman Islands comprise 204 islands and islets, and their topography is characterized by hills and narrow valleys. Although their location is tropical, the climate of the islands is tempered by sea breezes; rainfall is irregular. The Nicobar Islands, which are south of the Andaman Islands, comprise nineteen islands, some with flat, coral-covered surfaces and others with hills. The islands have a nearly equatorial climate, heavy rainfall, and high temperatures. The union territory of Lakshadweep (the name means 100,000 islands) in the Arabian Sea, comprises—from north to south—the Amindivi, Laccadive, Cannanore, and Minicoy islands. The islands, only ten of which are inhabited, are spread throughout an area of approximately 77,000 square kilometers. The islands are low-lying coral-based formations capable of limited cultivation.

Coasts and Borders

India has 7,000 kilometres of seacoast and shares 14,000 kilometres of land frontier with six nations: Pakistan, China, Nepal, Bhutan, Bangladesh, and Burma. India claims a twelve-nautical-mile territorial sea and an exclusive economic zone of 200 nautical miles. The territorial seas total 314,400 square kilometres.

In the mid-1990s, India had boundary disagreements with Pakistan, China, and Bangladesh; border distances are therefore approximations. The partition of India in 1947 established two India-Pakistan frontiers: one on the west and one on the east.

Disputes over the state of Jammu and Kashmir led to hostilities between India and Pakistan in 1947. The January 1, 1949, cease-fire arranged by the United Nations (UN) divided control of Kashmir. India controls Jammu, the Vale of Kashmir, and the capital, Srinagar, while Pakistan controls the mountainous area to the northwest. Neither side accepts a divided Kashmir as a permanent solution. India regards as illegal the 1963 China-Pakistan border agreement, which ceded to China a portion of Pakistani-controlled Kashmir. The two sides also dispute the Siachen Glacier near the Karakoram Pass. Further India-Pakistan hostilities in the 1965 war were settled through the Soviet-brokered Tashkent Declaration.

In 1968 an international tribunal settled the dispute over the Rann of Kutch, a region of salt flats that is submerged for six months of the year in the state of Gujarat. The following year, a new border was demarcated that recognized Pakistan's claim to about 10 percent of the area.

In 1992 India completed fencing most of the 547-kilometer-long section of the boundary between the Indian state of Punjab and the Pakistani province of Punjab. This measure was undertaken because of the continuing unrest in the region caused by both ethnic and religious disputes among the local Indian population and infiltrators from both sides of the frontier. The more rugged terrain north of Punjab along the entire cease-fire line between India and Pakistan in Jammu and Kashmir continues to be subject to infiltration and local strife.

The 2,000-kilometer-long border with China has eastern, central, and western sections. In the western section, the border regions of Jammu and Kashmir have been the scene of conflicting claims since the nineteenth century. China has not accepted India's definitions of the boundary and has carried out defense and economic activities in parts of eastern Kashmir since the 1950s. In the 1960s, China finished construction of a motor road across Aksai Chin (a region under dispute between India and China), the main transportation route linking China's Xinjiang-Uygur Autonomous Region and Tibet.

In the eastern section, the China-India boundary follows the McMahon Line laid down in 1914 by Sir Arthur Henry McMahon, the British plenipotentiary to a conference of Indian, British, and Chinese representatives at Simla (now known as Shimla, Himachal Pradesh). The Simla Convention, as the agreement is known, set the boundary between India and Tibet. Although the British and Tibetan representatives signed the agreement on July 3, 1914, the Chinese delegate declined to sign. The line agreed to by Britain and Tibet generally follows the crest of the eastern Himalayas from Bhutan to Burma. It serves as a legal boundary, although the Chinese have never formally accepted it. China continued to claim roughly the entire area of Arunachal Pradesh south of the McMahon Line in the early 1990s. In 1962 China and India fought a brief border war in this region, and China occupied certain areas south of the line for several months. India and China took a major step toward resolving their border disputes in 1981 by opening negotiations on the issue. Agreements and talks held in 1993 and 1995 eased tensions along the India-China border. Sikkim, which became an Indian state in 1975, forms the small central section of India's northern border and lies between Nepal and Bhutan.

India's border with Bangladesh is essentially the same as it was before East Pakistan became Bangladesh in 1971. Some minor disputes continued to occur over the size and number of the numerous enclaves each country had on either side of the border. These enclaves were established during the period from 1661 to 1712 during fighting between the Mughal Empire and the principality of Cooch Behar. This complex pattern of enclaves was preserved by the British administration and passed on intact to India and Pakistan.

The 1,300-kilometer frontier with Burma has been delimited but not completely demarcated. On March 10, 1967, the Indian and Burmese governments signed a bilateral treaty delimiting the boundary in detail. India also has a maritime boundary with Burma in the area of the northern Andaman Islands and Burma's Coco Islands in the Bay of Bengal. India's borders with Nepal and Bhutan have remained unchanged since the days of British rule. In 1977 India signed an accord with Indonesia demarcating the entire maritime boundary between the two countries. One year earlier, a similar accord was signed with the Maldives.

Rivers

The country's rivers are classified as Himalayan, peninsular, coastal, and inland-drainage basin rivers. Himalayan rivers are snow fed and maintain a high to medium rate of flow throughout the year. The heavy annual average rainfall levels in the Himalayan catchment areas further add to their rates of flow. During the monsoon months of June to September, the catchment areas are prone to flooding. The volume of the rain-fed peninsular rivers also increases. Coastal streams, especially in the west, are short and episodic. Rivers of the inland system, centered in western Rajasthan state, are few and frequently disappear in years of scant rainfall. The majority of the South Asia's major rivers flow through broad, shallow valleys and drain into the Bay of Bengal.

The Ganga River basin, India's largest, includes approximately 25 percent of the nation's area; it is bounded by the Himalayas in the north and the Vindhya Range to the south. The Ganga has its source in the glaciers of the Greater Himalayas, which form the frontier between India and Tibet in northwestern Uttar Pradesh. Many Indians believe that the legendary source of the Ganga, and several other important Asian rivers, lies in the sacred Mapam Yumco Lake (known to the Indians as Manasarowar Lake) of western Tibet located approximately 75 kilometres northeast of the India-China-Nepal tripoint. In the northern part of the Ganga River basin, practically all of the tributaries of the Ganga are perennial streams. However, in the southern part, located in the states of Rajasthan and Madhya Pradesh, many of the tributaries are not perennial.

The Brahmaputra has the greatest volume of water of all the rivers in India because of heavy annual rainfall levels in its catchment basin. At Dibrugarh the annual rainfall averages 2,800 millimeters, and at Shillong it averages 2,430 millimeters. Rising in Tibet, the Brahmaputra flows south into Arunachal Pradesh after breaking through the Great Himalayan Range and dropping rapidly in elevation. It continues to fall through gorges impassable by man in Arunachal Pradesh until finally entering the Assam Valley where it meanders westward on its way to joining the Ganga in Bangladesh.

The Mahanadi, rising in the state of Madhya Pradesh, is an important river in the state of Orissa. In the upper drainage basin of the Mahanadi, which is centered on the Chhattisgarh Plain, periodic droughts contrast with the situation in the delta region where floods may damage the crops in what is known as the rice bowl of Orissa. Hirakud Dam, constructed in the middle reaches of the Mahanadi, has helped in alleviating these adverse effects by creating a reservoir. The source of the Godavari is northeast of Bombay (Mumbai in the local Marathi language) in the state of Maharashtra, and the river follows a southeasterly course for 1,400 kilometres to its mouth on the Andhra Pradesh coast. The Godavari River basin area is second in size only to the Ganga; its delta on the east coast is also one of the country's main rice-growing areas. It is known as the "Ganga of the South," but its discharge, despite the large catchment area, is moderate because of the medium levels of annual rainfall, for example, about 700 millimeters at Nasik and 1,000 millimeters at Nizamabad.

The Krishna rises in the Western Ghats and flows east into the Bay of Bengal. It has a poor flow because of low levels of rainfall in its catchment area—660 millimetres annually at Pune. Despite its low discharge, the Krishna is the third longest river in India.

The source of the Kaveri is in the state of Karnataka, and the river flows southeastward. The waters of the river have been a source of irrigation since antiquity; in the early 1990s, an estimated 95 percent of the Kaveri was diverted for agricultural use before emptying into the Bay of Bengal. The delta of the Kaveri is so mature that the main river has almost lost its link with the sea, as the Kollidam, the distributary of the Kaveri, bears most of the flow.

The Narmada and the Tapti are the only major rivers that flow into the Arabian Sea. The Narmada rises in Madhya Pradesh and crosses the state, passing swiftly through a narrow valley between the Vindhya Range and spurs of the Satpura Range. It flows into the Gulf of Khambhat (or Cambay). The shorter Tapti follows a generally parallel course, between eighty kilometres and 160 kilometres to the south of the Narmada, flowing through the states of Maharashtra and Gujarat on its way into the Gulf of Khambhat.

Harnessing the waters of the major rivers that flow from the Himalayas is an issue of great concern in Nepal, India, and Bangladesh. Issues of flood control, drought prevention, hydroelectric power generation, job creation, and environmental quality—but also traditional lifestyles and cultural continuities—are at stake as these countries grapple with the political realities, both domestic and international, of altering the flow of the Ganga and Brahmaputra. Although India, Nepal, and Bangladesh seek to alleviate problems through cooperation over Himalayan rivers, irrigation projects altering the flow of Punjab-area rivers are likely to continue to be an irritant between India and Pakistan—countries between which cooperation is less likely to occur—in the second half of the 1990s. Internally, large dam projects, such as one on the Narmada River, are also controversial.

Climate

The Himalayas isolate South Asia from the rest of Asia. South of these mountains, the climate, like the terrain, is highly diverse, but some geographers give it an overall, one-word characterization—violent. What geographers have in mind is the abruptness of change and the intensity of effect when change occurs—the onset of the monsoon rains, sudden flooding, rapid erosion, extremes of temperature, tropical storms, and unpredictable fluctuations in rainfall. Broadly speaking, agriculture in India is constantly challenged by weather uncertainty.

It is possible to identify seasons, although these do not occur uniformly throughout South Asia. The Indian Meteorological Service divides the year into four seasons: the relatively dry, cool winter from December through February; the dry, hot summer from March through May; the southwest monsoon from June through September when the predominating southwest maritime winds bring rains to most of the country; and the northeast, or retreating, monsoon of October and November.

The southwest monsoon blows in from sea to land. The southwest monsoon usually breaks on the west coast early in June and reaches most of South Asia by the first week in July.

Because of the critical importance of monsoon rainfall to agricultural production, predictions of the monsoon's arrival date are eagerly watched by government planners and agronomists who need to determine the optimal dates for plantings.

Theories about why monsoons occur vary. Conventionally, scientists have attributed monsoons to thermal changes in the Asian landmass. Contemporary theory cites other factors—the barrier of the Himalayas and the sun's northward tilt (which shifts the jet stream north). The hot air that rises over South Asia during April and May creates low-pressure areas into which the cooler, moisture-bearing winds from the Indian Ocean flow. These circumstances set off a rush of moisture-rich air from the southern seas over South Asia.

The southwest monsoon occurs in two branches. After breaking on the southern part of the Peninsula in early June, the branch known as the Arabian Sea monsoon reaches Bombay around June 10, and it has settled over most of South Asia by late June, bringing cooler but more humid weather. The other branch, known as the Bay of Bengal monsoon, moves northward in the Bay of Bengal and spreads over most of Assam by the first week of June. On encountering the barrier of the Great Himalayan Range, it is deflected westward along the Indo-Gangetic Plain toward New Delhi. Thereafter the two branches merge as a single current bringing rains to the remaining parts of North India in July.

The withdrawal of the monsoon is a far more gradual process than its onset. It usually withdraws from northwest India by the beginning of October and from the remaining parts of the country by the end of November.

During this period, the northeast winds contribute to the formation of the northeast monsoon over the southern half of the Peninsula in October. It is also known as the retreating monsoon because it follows in the wake of the southwest monsoon. The states of Tamil Nadu, Karnataka, and Kerala receive most of their rainfall from the northeast monsoon during November and December. However, 80 percent of the country receives most of its rainfall from the southwest monsoon from

June to September. South Asia is subject to a wide range of climates—from the subfreezing Himalayan winters to the tropical climate of the Coromandel Coast and from the damp, rainy climate in the states of Assam and West Bengal to the arid Great Indian Desert. Based on precipitation and temperature, experts define seven climatic regions: the Himalayas, Assam and West Bengal, the Indo-Gangetic Plain, the Western Ghats and coast, the Deccan (the interior of the Peninsula south of the Narmada River), and the Eastern Ghats and coast.

In the Himalayan region, climate varies with altitude. At about 2,000 meters, the average summer temperature is near 18°C; at 4,500 meters, it is rarely above 0°C. In the valleys, summer temperatures reach between 32°C and 38°C. The eastern Himalayas receive as much as 1,000 to 2,000 millimetres more precipitation than do the Western Himalayas, and floods are common. Assam and West Bengal are extremely wet and humid. The southeastern part of the state of Meghalaya has the world's highest average annual rainfall, some 10,900 millimetres.

The Indo-Gangetic Plain has a varied climatic pattern. Rainfall and temperature ranges vary significantly between the eastern and western extremes. In the Peninsula region, the Western Ghats and the adjoining coast receive heavy rains during the southwest monsoon. Rainfall in the peninsular interior averages about 650 millimetres a year, although there is considerable variation in different localities and from year to year. The Eastern Ghats receive less rainfall than the western coast. Rainfall there ranges between 900 and 1,300 millimetres annually. The northern Deccan region, bounded by the Western Ghats, the Vindhya Range and the Narmada River to the north, and the Eastern Ghats, receives most of its annual rainfall during the summer monsoon season. The southern Deccan area is in a "rain shadow" and receives only fifty to 1,000 millimetres of rainfall a year. Temperature ranges are wide—from some 15°C to 38°C—making this one of India's most comfortable climatic areas.

Throughout most of non-Himalayan India, the heat can be

oppressive and sometimes, such as was experienced in 1994 and 1995, literally can be a killer. Hot, relatively dry weather is the norm before the southwest monsoons, which, along with heavy rains and high humidity, bring cloud cover that lowers temperatures slightly. Temperatures reach the upper 30s°C and can reach as high as 48°C during the day in the premonsoon months.

Earthquakes

India has experienced some of the world's most devastating earthquakes. Some 19,000 people died in Kangra District, northeastern Himachal Pradesh, in April 1905, and more than 30,000 died in Maharashtra and Andhra Pradesh in September 1993. Although resulting in less extensive loss of life, major earthquakes occurred in Assam in 1950 (more than 1,500 killed) and in Uttarkashi District, Uttar Pradesh, in 1991 (1,600 killed).

10

Politics and Practice of Becoming Geographer

The difference between corporate executives and me, of course, is that their actions in the world are consequential and mine aren't particularly. So one might wonder what the value of this exercise is. I offer it here as a kind of heuristic. I think we should follow Goethe's advice, and am just barely willing to try to do it in public, if only to illustrate the astonishing misperceptions and horrible delusions that may complicate the task. This kind of analysis, being retrospective, is unavoidably neater and more logical than the lived experience, which felt more like a long series of bizarre accidents. It had never, for example, even entered my head to become an academic until years after I was one. So much for clarity.

IDENTITY, COMMITMENTS AND RESEARCH PROJECT

A little bit more in the background, this historical context also produced persistent questions about the misuse of power linked with the misuse of knowledge. That is to say, knowledge about what ought to be done or what is feasible and effective is available and accessible, yet is contravened because those in power are pursuing contradictory goals. So a large and powerful entity (in this case the USA) ends up acting against its own best interests while causing a tremendous amount of damage to others. With the publication of the *Pentagon Papers,* it became abundantly clear that the government had consistently lied to its citizens about nearly everything connected with the origins and prosecution of the war in Vietnam. We also know that the government pursued strategies in that war that it knew in advance would be ineffective because it had to do *something* and couldn't think of anything else to do that would be compatible with its own idea of itself. The costs hardly need enumerating. Vietnam would stand as a monument to a certain kind of human and social folly, were we not actually engaged in repeating the entire process – complete with lies and the misuse of knowledge – in Iraq. Apparently, we cannot yet erect the memorials to this particular pathology.

I want to make two observations about this problem of power and knowledge. The first is that it took a while for it to enter explicitly into my research. For a good ten years I was wholly absorbed in the problem of how and why firms sought to be competitive and to maximize profits through locating in high-cost, highly unionized, and highly regulated places. I wasn't really attuned to the question of how and why they could also make staggering errors of judgement with hideous consequences for many people and places. This lack of attention was perhaps conditioned by my training in both conventional economics and political economy. In the former, individual capitalist rationality leads to rational and good social outcomes. In the latter, individual capitalist rationality leads to irrational and negative social out-comes. Neither theory is looking for irrationality at the firm level. And indeed, the problem is not exactly that the firm *per se* is irrational, but that the people running the firm have conflicting rationalities on behalf of them-selves as social agents and on behalf of the firm as a social agent. I can see this now as analogous to the politically self-serving, identity-preserving yet nationally harmful behaviour of the Vietnam (and Iraq) war strategists. And perhaps this political conditioning allowed me to finally recognize it when I saw it repeatedly in corporations. But it took a while.

The second observation is that use of the phrase 'power and knowledge' seems to cry out for a Foucauldian analysis which I have never engaged in. This is for several reasons, based on a possibly defective reading of Foucault. One is that, for my money, power and society are rather reified concepts in Foucault.

They have their own interests and objectives. These aren't, for me, clearly connected to particular group or class interests. In my ontological universe, it is necessary to understand *whose* power is at issue and why – given whose it is – it wants what it wants. I want the mediation of class and social position, which I find much more clearly and productively articulated in Bourdieu. Further, the reified power of Foucault seeks knowledge in order to discipline people 'in general' and in so doing stabilize the social order. I want also to understand something about how social position and power relate to knowledge of self and the ability to productively use knowledge in general. Or, put another way, I want to understand how social position and power inflect the transformation of information into particular knowledge and how exactly this knowledge will be used.

Back to me. For various reasons connected with my personal and family history, it was both easy and comfortable to choose a corporate and defence focus rather than, say, researching the state directly. My father achieved middle-class status via the military and worked in the defence industry all his life, specializing in international marketing for a number of large, lethal firms. So I am a child of the military–industrial complex and the utterly white-bread suburbs. I suffer a lot from red diaper envy. I also apparently organized my research in part as a way of explaining my father to myself. This I realized so recently it would make a cat laugh.

Beyond that, I worked my way through college and while doing political work for some years afterwards as a secretary, bookkeeper and production analyst, which is how I learned to talk to businessmen (and – key to securing interviews – their secretaries). I also learned something of how they think and what they really spend time thinking about. It turns out if you're a really good secretary (and I was), they don't treat you like a servant. They treat you as an extremely ill-paid junior partner. And along the way I learned how to construct and read financial statements.

I'm not arguing for a perfect isomorphism between historical–geographical moment and research trajectory. But

I think it may help explain why particular issues emerge as the big problems for each of us. We are thinking about them, confronted by them, stumped by them (how do they get *away* with it?!), angered or otherwise impassioned about them all the time. It is what we *need* to do.

PROJECT AND PRACTICE: THE QUESTION AND HOW TO RESEARCH IT

When I was a graduate student, discussions about deindustrialization and the New International Division of Labour were very much in the air. It seemed evident that manufacturing investment was destined to desert the USA and other advanced industrial economies. Indeed, on this subject, there was a curious and troubling convergence between the leftists and mainstream economists.

As I was reading this literature, though, I was also obsessively reading the business press, a habit I acquired working for different left-wing research groups. And in the business press, what I was seeing was a positive flood of announcements of foreign manufacturing investments in the USA. My first reaction was a kind of indignant exasperation: 'What idiots! Don't they know any better?' Then I thought it was probably better not to assume that they didn't know what they were doing. So the question to research seemed plain: what on earth are they up to?

It is childishly easy to show statistically that international manufacturing investment is highly correlated with high wages, unionization and regulation. But the statistical evidence could not produce *explanations* of what I was seeing. The only alternative seemed to be to go talk with the people who were making these decisions. With my background, this seemed both obvious and relatively easy.

We can't, of course, just ask them why and write down their answers. We're not reporters. Neither are we ethnographers, but that model is closer to the point. We don't want to list the practices the natives engage in. We want to understand them in the context of an entire way of life. So you talk with them about the whole way of life, and it is in that story that you find the explanation of the practice. You talk about the history of the firm, the history of the person, etc., and when you've got that in hand, then you ask for their explanations of the specific practices. These explanations are not the answers to your research questions – they are *data* that need to be analysed and interrogated.

For a long while, I resisted any impulse to analyse the *people* who were providing this information. I'm very comfortable with large-scale political economy and the 'logic of capital'; the structure is my natural home. I knew I needed to talk with these guys, and to know enough about them person-ally to interpret the information they provided, but I didn't feel that I needed to *think* about them particularly. But what I had learned in investigating the structure (e.g., how competition works to produce particular social and geographical outcomes) is that firms often make hideous mistakes even though they apparently inhabit the high ground of capitalist rationality. So it wasn't quite enough to get at what the strategy was and the plausible structural explanation behind it. In effect, the failure of strategy forced me to look more closely at the strategists and how they and their strategies are produced.

This meant taking on the capitalists as individuals and as a class simultaneously which was confusing and hard to work out. I turned to culture and identity as a way of managing this inquiry – as a way of thinking through it without going insane. They functioned for me as meso-level categories and conceptual anchors that connected the big structural dynamics (competition, production, investment, accumulation) with how a particular class of agents operated within those dynamics in a particular conjuncture.

So the first version of the work centred on the question 'why do firms work this way?' and answered it by saying 'their behaviour is driven by how competition works in these industries; the competitive strategy forces them to behave in ways that seem to be at odds with purely production-related considerations such as labour costs'. The second version of the work is about the same thing – what firms do and why – but in a different register. It tries to explain where competitive strategy comes from and acknowledges that it does not derive solely from analyzing how markets work in particular industries. What I gained through this shift, I think, is a richer notion of competition among firms, of intra-class competition and the problems and opportunities this creates for firms and workers alike.

But being fixated on the firm as the unit of analysis, competition as the central problem and strategy and culture as the source of movement in the system, also removes many important dynamics from my field of vision. I don't, for example, 'see' gender, labour strategies, or places. These are no small lacunae, and I would feel worse about them were it not for the fact that other people see them extremely well. The question, I suppose, is whether my way of seeing can be brought sufficiently into alignment with theirs that we can achieve real depth of field.

POLITICS AND OBJECTIVITY

Can a confessed leftist be rigorous, honest and fair as a researcher? I believe so. The politics help you identify the important questions, but they can't tell you what the answers are. In my experience, leftist academics are, in general, much more attuned to how their politics shape the questions they are interested in than their mainstream colleagues who cling to the notion that their research is 'value neutral'. So on the whole, I think we're ahead of the game.

Here one might ask: can I seriously believe that politics, questions, theory and methods – hence answers – are not deeply connected? I have to acknowledge that the answers I'm likely to arrive at in my research are not somehow quarantined from the rest of me. My politics inform my theoretical approach, out of which the method really grows. So the kind of results I am able to get are unavoidably shaped by this research *gestalt*. Simple honesty can keep me from fixing the results to accord with my preferences or political commitments. But with the best will in the world, I cannot erase myself from the process. Nor would I want to. However, what I do want is to make sense out of the world and in order to do that, one is bound to be as critical and self-critical as one has the capacity to be. This means, one hopes, wishful thinking is kept to a minimum. Or perhaps I'm entirely wrong about this and should just say, to paraphrase a famous US Secretary of Defence, you work with the self you have, not the self you wish you had.

Do the politics enable me to ask questions that wouldn't otherwise emerge? Certainly a commitment to a political-economic ontology and epistemology which for me is essential to being a leftist, opens up a characteristic set of questions that are not available or particularly interesting to mainstream economists. Rather than an obsession with how scarce resources are allocated by anonymous individual decision-makers, I am obsessed with how resources are produced and distributed in society, who controls them, what they do with them, why they do that, and how it affects everyone else. In a nutshell, I want to know about the creation, distribution and use of wealth and social power and how this is connected with how values concerning, for example, social justice and the environment are constructed and operationalized. There are more ways of getting at those questions than being exactly the kind of leftist/political economist that I am. Within this context, however, they are not only available but unavoidable.

Having said that, a political economic approach generally treats social power as a structural artefact, at least in reference to the ruling classes. It is more interested in the lived experience of power from the point of view of workers, and, plausibly, communities, racial and ethnic groups and women: those who are generally on the weaker end of power-laden relationships and who have to work at countering, resisting, deflecting or otherwise pre-serving themselves from the powerful. In my own work, however, I was focused on what the powerful were doing and why, and, because this wasn't so easy to work out, it led eventually to an interest in how the powerful thought about their world and about themselves – in short, how their actual power was linked to their identities, their interpretation of information, and their strategies. This kind of question doesn't, I think, automatically arise in a classic political-economic analysis, but it does plausibly arise in the context of the kind of political history I've been describing. The *particular* left politics of the USA in the 1970s were in fact quite involved with the question of who these people ('the best and the brightest') were and what they thought they were doing. The policies of the war in Vietnam were located in a social type – Ivy League whiz kids and technocrats – and closely identified with particular people – McNamara, Bundy Colby Kissinger, etc. It seems likely that this helped me find the path from corporate strategy to culture, via questions of power and identity.

INTERLUDE: THE WORK OF MENTORS

There were plenty of reasons to doubt my career potential in academic life, quite apart from the fact that it took me so long to notice that I was having an academic career. Being a leftist, a qualitative researcher and a woman are not the first three indicators of success that leap to mind. In any case, most of us aren't so incredibly brilliant that the system just bows down before us. We're all peculiar in some ways, and we all need help.

This is what makes the work of mentors so important. What, then, do mentors do? They give advice, which is great. Their critical and unsung role, however, is to ensure that the system works fairly and well in your particular case. A lot of the work that the system does in the course of your career happens out of your reach – literally behind closed doors and involving people whose identities are secret. The system may be fair in principle, but it is not working on your behalf. It works for the institution. Mentors are your advocates and watchdogs in the work that the system is doing. I don't mean they fix it so you can't fail. I mean that they watch out for you. They make sure that obvious errors aren't made, that there are answers to questions, that inappropriate criteria or inappropriate people aren't used to judge you, and so on. It's a lot of work.

The other thing a mentor may help you with if you're lucky is to pro-vide some insight into how to live life as a good academic – a good life in the ethical sense. I had two key mentors in my department. These, of course, were David Harvey, who taught me a lot about being a politically committed, rigorous academic, and Reds Wolman, who taught me about openness and the joys of discovery. Neither of them ever urged caution. They were always in favour of taking on new issues that you don't know anything about or taking on the amorphous, probably impossible tasks and just seeing how it goes. That was a big help and is part of how I was able to throw overboard twenty years of accumulated intellectual capital and start over in an entirely new field.

SOCIAL AND ENVIRONMENTAL HISTORY

The new project involves the social and environmental history of gold and gold mining. I'm working on it with a colleague in public health at Hopkins, Ellen Silbergeld. Reds introduced us because he thought we could do something interesting together although, characteristically, I'm sure he had no particular idea what that might be. We worked it out in long walks with our dogs, Sasha and Docker.

The project, in brief, tries to analyse why gold has social value and how that is connected with the distribution and the magnitude of the social and environmental costs of gold mining through the ages. Gold is such a peculiar substance. It has no real material uses – you can't cook or hunt or farm or shelter yourself with it. At the same time, it doesn't corrode, so it never goes away. Most of the gold that has been mined in history is still available. So we do a tremendous amount of damage to get it out of the ground and then mostly what we do is dig another large hole and put it back in the ground for safekeeping. The whole process raises in striking form questions about the relationship between social and environmental values in different social formations and geographical circumstances.

It turns out the project also turns distinctively on questions of power and knowledge, although as usual I didn't anticipate this at the outset. Mining in general and gold mining in particular impose a range of severe social and environmental costs. For gold mining, these include the hyper-exploitation of slave and free wage labour and crushingly arduous physical work. Mining gold has also involved the liberal distribution of mercury in the environment for a thousand years, supplemented, but not entirely replaced, by cyanide over the last century or so. Exposure to environmental toxins spreads far beyond the mining operations and imposes severe health impacts on populations that have nothing to do with mining.

The interesting thing is that these costs have been accurately assessed and commented upon since antiquity. There is no shortage of knowledge about the social and environmental costs of gold mining, but we haven't been able to use this knowledge to curb them to any great degree, despite thousands of years of experience. The reason for this, we believe, is that the one consistent social use of gold over the millennia has been connected with the amassing, display and use of social power. Until fairly recently historically, there has been such a close ruling-class monopoly on the substance that gold and social power have been virtually isomorphic. The users of gold were unaffected and untroubled by the costs which were imposed on populations and places that they had nothing to do with. Even when the information was brought vividly and powerfully to their direct attention, and even when they were Christian enough to worry about the fate of their souls, the rulers' greed for the substance outweighed their moral qualms. So the knowledge was, in effect, cancelled out by the power relations manifested in the metal.

This change in research orientation derived from several sources. One was living in a department with environmental engineers who were never going to see the value of geography if it didn't speak directly (and very slowly and distinctly) to them. This effect was amplified by my growing impression that the engineering *students* as opposed to the faculty were, in fact, very interested in what geography had to offer. So I wanted to reorient my teaching in a way that was more helpful for them. Another factor, of course, was living in a department with Reds Wolman, who is an enthusiastic and inventive interdisciplinarian and who truly is committed to advancing work that explains how we humans are connected to the natural environment and what that means. In sum, I felt a growing need to address environmental questions directly in my teaching and research.

Also, as an economic geographer, I had increasingly the sense that history matters more than we've been able to acknowledge in our work. We tend to use history as background – it provides the context and marks the boundaries of more or less coherent periods. But we're not really growing the history through our work. We are being historicist, in the sense that one thing follows another, but not fundamentally committed to the historical part of historical materialism, even those of us who still take the term seriously (Harvey 2001; Soja 1989).

This is not necessarily a call to the archives. Geographers have a tremendous amount to offer through original synthetic thinking over the *longue durée* and the *grande espace.* In part, the work of historians, like the material gathered from corporate interviews, is our data and not the answer to our questions. We need, of course, to reckon seriously with their interpretations, but we should not simply abstract their conclusions into our own material as a way of foreclosing argument about a question rather than opening it up.

RESEARCH FRONTIERS

Many will be aware of the enormous interest in issues of individual decision-making occasioned by the path-breaking work of economists, decision scientists, and neuropsychologists. Being challenged is the very idea that people are rational in the sense that they act deliberately in accordance with universal rules of logic and reason. In part, research on these issues has focused upon the cognitive skills and capacities of individuals seeking evidence for systematic patterns of so-called 'non-rational' behaviour or at least that behaviour which goes against the precepts of logic and reason. This research agenda is based upon quite specific populations in quite sterile environments. It is remarkable that the base population for much of this research has been undergraduate and MBA students in elite US and European universities, wherein they are required to deal with generic decision-making puzzles in which they have little or no stake. Left out of analysis, more often than not, is the relevance of social identity and cultural location.

Also left out of this research programme is assessment of the role of context in decision-making, and whether it makes a significant difference (or otherwise) to decision-making holding constant cognitive skills and capacities. This is acknowledged to be an important gap in the research programme, but one that related disciplines have found hard to bridge or even conceptualize in terms of the geographical scale of social and economic processes. The theory-first logic of economics and political science, for example, has left those disciplines without sufficient experience to deal with the intersection of cognition and context. But, of course, this is not the case for economic geography; we often argue that context matters although we have done so by intuition and illustration rather than experimental procedure.

Making good on our comparative advantage, in this respect, is very important for the future of economic geography. Our experience with close dialogue, as well as our ability to handle the complex interplay between culture, institutions, and the nature of everyday decision-making through case studies, is rare in the social sciences. If we are able to formalize close dialogue through more rigorous experimental procedures, the discipline may have much to offer in articulating the interplay between context and decision-making. The trick, however, is to translate our experience into a systematic research programme that is theoretical as well as empirical.

At the other end of the spectrum, there is enormous interest in the nature and functioning of global financial markets. For many years, research in finance was dominated by the efficient markets hypothesis so that it ruled out so-called irrational behaviour and the circumstances of different places and different times. All was well for about two decades. However, as the TMT (Technology, Media and Communications) bubble gathered momentum in the late 1990s and came crashing down around 2000/2001, it took with it confidence in the language of finance. Hard questions have been asked about the empirical plausibility of the hitherto unchallenged assumptions underpinning the efficient market hypothesis. Even those with a vested interest in the hypothesis had been forced to concede that market behaviour is different in scope from what was expected (Fama and French 2005).

One consequence has been an enormous flurry of research on three threads of interest. First, there has been a concerted research programme developed around the existence and claimed persistence of behavioural anomalies in financial markets.

It is apparent that heterogeneous expectations and behaviour coexist at any point in time and space. In the absence of a comprehensive winner-take-all reward system, heterogeneity may per-sist within and between markets. Second, it is apparent that many measures of value in the market have proved to be poor predictors of winning and losing stocks. This has brought forth a wide variety of alternative measures of performance, all with their own reliability and tests of relative value.

The market for valuation has exploded; competing ideas, principles, and methods of empirical analysis have enormous implications for issues such as environmental sustainability. Third, there has been renewed interest in the institutions and management of inter-market arbitrage and the fact that markets vary considerably in terms of their social structures and behavioural patterns.

The discipline of geography could be at the very centre of research on global financial markets. But to enter this market of ideas requires research which takes place at two levels: in terms of observed patterns of market trading, market prices, and market arbitrage and in terms of the apparent behavioural imperatives underpinning distinctive geographical patterns of trade and counter-trade (Clark and Wójcik 2007).

Enormous databases require highly sophisticated analytical routines as well as large-scale computing power to process the data. In addition, knowledge is needed of particular places and times, including reference to cultural expectations, social relationships, and economic power reflected, for example, in the relative status of insiders as opposed to outsiders in some countries' financial markets.

By this logic, close dialogue should be an important partner in such research programmes. This is possible by virtue of the fact that the core theoretical precepts of the theory of finance are in a shambles and that heterogeneous market expectations and performance have become the points of reference in analysis.

With the world of finance turned upside-down and a common perception that theory-first is a losing proposition, knowledge of the empirical world is the source of making a profit. Since there is such an intimate relationship between finance academics and finance practitioners, the former cannot afford to ignore the latter. Consequently, knowledge about how and why markets are internally differentiated and knowledge about the nature and persistence of differences between markets are at a premium. To go further, we must find a way of sustaining partnerships with other disciplines so that we are party to building the theoretical logic that will ultimately replace the efficient markets hypothesis.

TRANSPORTATION AND ECONOMIC DEVELOPMENT

Transportation developments that have taken place since the beginning of the industrial revolution have been linked to growing economic opportunities. At each stage of human societal development, a particular transport mode has been developed or adapted. However, it has been observed that throughout history no single mode of transport has been solely responsible for economic growth. Instead, modes have been linked with the direction and the geographical setting in which growth was taking place.

For instance, major flows of international migration that occurred since the eighteenth century were linked with the expansion of international and continental transport systems. Transport has played a catalytic role in these migrations, transforming the economic geography of many nations.

Concomitantly, transportation has been a tool of territorial control and exploitation, particularly during the colonial era where resource-based transport systems supported the extraction of commodities in the developing world.

Each transport mode and technology is linked to a set of economic opportunities, notably in terms of market areas, types of commodities that can be transported (including passengers) and economies of scale. All these issues are related to a scale and level of commercial geography. Prior to the industrial revolution, economic opportunities were limited by the low capacity to move commodities over long distances, as most activities were very localized is scale and scope. The industrial revolution unleashed greater economic opportunities, initially with the development of inland canal systems, steamships and then railway systems. Passenger and freight transportation expanded as well as production and consumption while new markets and resources became available.

In many instances, the development of one transportation mode built on the opportunities developed by another, such as maritime and canal shipping. In other situations, the growth of a new mode of transportation favoured the decline of others, such as the collapse of many inland canal networks in the late nineteenth century because of rail competition.

The development of the mass production system at the beginning of the twentieth century increasingly relied on the commercial opportunities introduced by road transportation, particularly the automobile. Later in the twentieth century, globalization became a possibility with the joint synergy of maritime transportation, roadways, railways, air and telecommunications.

Economic opportunities became global in scale and scope, particularly because of the capacity to maintain an intricate network of trade and transactions through transport systems. More recently, new opportunities arose with the convergence of telecommunications and information technologies, supporting a higher level of management of production, consumption and distribution.

It is expected that such a process, building upon the advantages conferred by other transportation modes, will account for a significant share of economic opportunities in the first half of the twenty-first century.

While some regions benefit from the development of transport systems, others are often marginalized by a set of conditions in which inadequate transportation plays a role. Transport by itself is not a sufficient condition for development, however; the lack of transport infrastructures can be seen as a constraining factor on development.

The relationship between transportation and economic development is thus difficult to formally establish and has been debated for many years. The complexity lies in a variety of possible impacts:

- Timing of the development varies as the impacts of transportation can either precede, occur during or take place after economic development. The lag, concomitant and lead impacts make it difficult to separate the specific contributions of transport to development, therefore. Each case study appears to be specific to a set of timing circumstances that are difficult to replicate elsewhere.
- *Types of impacts vary considerably*. The spectrum of impacts ranges from the positive through the permissive to the negative. In some cases transportation impacts can promote, in others they may hinder, economic development in a region. In many cases, few, if any, direct linkages can be clearly established.

Cycles of economic development provide a revealing conceptual perspective about how transport systems evolve in time and space as they include the timing and the nature of the transport impact on economic development. Transport, as a technology, follows a path of experimentation, introduction, adoption and diffusion and, finally, obsolescence, each of which has an impact on economic development. Succinctly, transport technology can be linked to five major waves of economic development where a specific mode or system emerged:

- *Seaports*. Linked with the early stages of European expansion from the sixteenth to eighteenth centuries. They supported the development of international trade through colonial empires, but were constrained by limited inland access.
- *Rivers and canals*. The first stage of the industrial revolution in the late eighteenth and early nineteenth centuries was linked to the development of canal systems in Western Europe and North America, mainly to transport heavy goods. This permitted the development of rudimentary and constrained inland distribution systems.

- *Railways*. The second stage of the industrial revolution in the nineteenth century was intimately linked to the development and implementation of rail systems enabling a more flexible inland transportation system.
- *Roads*. The twentieth century saw the development of road transportation systems and automobile manufacturing. Individual transportation became a commodity available to the masses, especially after World War II. This process was reinforced by the development of highway systems.
- *Airways and information*. The later part of the twentieth century saw the development of global air and telecommunication networks in conjunction with the globalization of economic activities. New organization, control and maintenance capacities were made possible. Electronic communications have become consistent with transport functions, especially in the rapidly developing realm of logistics and supply chain management.

Technological innovation and economic growth are closely related and can be articulated within the concept of cycles or waves. Each wave represents a diffusion phase of technological innovations, creating entirely new industrial sectors, and thus opportunities for investment and growth. Five waves have been identified so far:

- *1st wave (1785–1845)*. Depended on innovations such as water power, textiles and iron. The beginning of the industrial revolution in England was mainly focused on simple commodities such as clothes and tools. The conventional maritime technology relying on sailships was perfected, supporting the creation of large colonial/trading empires, mainly by the British, the French, the Dutch, and the Spanish. Significant inland waterway systems were also constructed.
- *2nd wave (1845–1900)*. Involved the massive application of coal as a source of energy, mainly through the steam engine. This induced the development of rail transport systems, opening new markets and giving access to a wider array of resources. The steamship had a similar

impact for maritime transportation and permitted further commercial exploitation.

- *3rd wave (1900–50)*. Electrification was a major economic change as it permitted the usage of a variety of machines and appliances. This permitted the development of urban transit systems (subways and tramways). Another significant improvement was the internal combustion engine, around which the whole automotive industry was created.
- *4th wave (1950–90)*. The post-World War II period represented significant industrial changes such as plastics (petrochemicals) and electronics (television). The jet engine expanded the aviation industry towards the mass market.
- *5th wave (1990–2020?)*. The current wave mainly relies on information systems, which have tremendously modified the transactional environment with new methods of communication and more efficient management of production and distribution systems. This has spawned new industries, mainly computer manufacturing and software programming, but more recently e-commerce as information processing converged with telecommunications.

As time progressed, the lapse between each wave got shorter. For instance, the first wave lasted 60 years while the fourth wave lasted 40 years. This reflects a growing capacity for innovation and the capacity of economic systems to derive wealth from it. Innovations are no longer the result of individual efforts, but are organized and concerted actions whose results are rapidly diffused. It is thus expected that the fifth wave will last about 30 years.

Contemporary trends have underlined that economic development has become less dependent on relations with the environment (resources) and more dependent on relations across space. While resources remain the foundation of economic activities, the commodification of the economy has been linked with higher levels of material flows. Concomitantly, resources, capital and even labour have shown increasing levels of mobility.

This is particularly the case for multinational firms that can benefit from transport improvements in two significant markets:

- *Commodity market.* Improvement in the efficiency with which firms have access to raw materials and parts as well as to their respective customers. Thus, transportation expands opportunities to acquire and sell a variety of commodities necessary for industrial and manufacturing systems.
- *Labour market.* Improvement in the access to labour and a reduction in access costs, mainly by improved commuting (local scale) or the use of lower cost labour (global scale).

11

Geography of Population and Family Planning Policy

POPULATION GEOGRAPHY

In size of population, India is the second largest country in the world, after China. She has only 2.4 per cent of the world's land area; but she has about 16.25 per cent of the world's population.

Census and Trends of Population

Census is an official counting of a population:' In India it started in 1881. Since then it has been continued at an interval of 10 years. At the beginning of this century in 1901, the population of the undivided India was 242 millions. After independence the first census was held in 1951 and the population was 361 millions.

The population growth marked a steady increase in the subsequent censuses. It rose to 439 millions in 1961, 548 millions in 1971, 548 millions in 1971, 685 millions in 1981 and 844 millions 1991. The last census was held in 2001 and it recorded a population of 1027 millions. This population explosion poses a serious *socio-economic* problem in the country.

Causes of the population explosion: The main causes of the increase of population are: (i) *better health conditions resulting from effective control of epidemics, (ii) natural increases due to high birth rates, (iii) efficient handling of famine situations and (iv) general improvement in the economic development due to scientific inventions.*

The Distribution of Population

Division According to Density of Population: The distribution of population in India shows the following density pattern according to census 2001. Regions of Shows population Density (density below 100 per sq. km.): In includes *Jammu and Kashmir, Sikkim, Arunachal Pradesh, Mizoram states and Union Territories Andaman and Nicobar*. In the low population density due to ragged is topography and forested land with the severity of climate.

Regions of Medium Population Density (between 101 and 250 per sq. km.): It includes *Himachal Pradesh, Madhya Pradesh, Manipur, Meghalaya, Nagaland, Orissa, Rajasthan, Chhattisgarh and Uttaranchal states*. These regions are hilly, mountainous or forested, and some are deserted. Hence population is medium.

Regions of Considerably High Population Density (between 251 and 500 per sq. km.): This region includes *Andhra Pradesh, Assam, Gujrat, Haryana, Karnataka, Maharashtra, Punjab, Tamil Nadu, Tripura, Goa, Jharkhand states and Union Territories of Darda & Nagar Haveli.* Fairly high population of this region is due to the advancement of agriculture, mining and industry. Economic progress and job opportunities contribute much for this population.

Regions of High Population Density (between 501 and 1000 per sq. km.): *Bihar, Kerala, Uttar Pradesh and West Bengal* are included in this population zone. This high population is due to very fertile soil, advancemant of agriculture, minings, industries, trade and commerce and opportunities for subsistence. Regions of Very High Population Density (above 1001 per sq. km.): It includes the *Union Terrtories of Delhi, Chandigarh, Pandicherry, Lakshadweep and Daman & Diu.* The high density of this region is duc to high cconomic and administrative activites.

The Causes for the Uneven Distribution of Population

The distribution of population in India is not uniform. Some areas have high density of population, while others have medium or low density. The following physical and cultural factors are responsible for the uneven distribution of population in the country. The physical factors are gifts of nature; they influence much for the distribution of population.

Difference in Relief: The relief of the country exerts immense influence in the population distribution of a country. Extremely ragged topography associated with thick forest-cover do not encourage settlement as in the Himalayas and in the northeastern hilly states of India. But the river valleys with alluvial plaints provide easy livings for which the population is high. The population of the Ganga-brahmaputra plain is distinctively high.

Variation in Vlimate: Climate exerts a great influence on human settlement. The *Marausthali of western Rajasthan* is sparsely populated; it is the hottest place in India and it has the extreme type of climate with little rainfall. Due to the adverse climate condition, the *Marusthali* is sparsely populated. On the other hand, the mild and equitable climate of the *Ganga plain* encourages settlements.

Influence of Soil: Agriculture depends on soil condition. The fertility of soil determines the cultivation of crops. Thus the livings and subsistence of the people depend on soil and low on rocky waste or infertile soil. The great northern plains of India have fertile soil and on these plains density of population is remarkably high.

Influence of River: Rivers provide water to agriculture and other indispensable needs (drinking water and others) of the people. They also provide avenues for trade and commerce. That is why it is frequently said; the river valleys are the cradles of civilization. All the river valleys, which have fertile soil and tolerable climate, are thickly populated.

Presence of Minerals: Mineral deposits attract population. The discovery of enormous mineral deposits in the *Chhotanagpur plateau* region has contributed much to the growth of high concentration of population to this region. The cultural factors are also responsible for the uneven distribution of population. These factors are man-made and popularly known as non-physical factors or cultural factors.

Development of Industries: Development of industries also attracts population. A few decades ago, there was very low population in Durgapur region; but with the development of industries in the Durgapur belt, the population has steadily increased.

Historical & Political Factors: After the partition of Bengal, when the Indian indepence was achieved, the population of *West Bengal* grew up rapidly due to the influx of the people from the other side of *Bengal*. Religious Influence: *Varanasi, Mathura, Haridwar, Nabadweep, Puri* are the sacred religious centres of the *Hindus, Agra* of the *Muslims and Amritsar of the Sikhs.* They are densely populated due to religious factors.

SEX RATIO OF INDIA

Sex Ratio is defined as the number of females per 1000 males. Sex Ratio is an important social indicator to measure the extent of prevailing equity between males and females at a given point of time. It is mainly the outcome of the interplay of sex differentials in mortality, sex selective migration, sex ratio at birth and at times the sex differential in population enumeration.

According to the Census of India, 2001, the sex ratio of India stands at 933. This is a marginal improvement from the 1991 Census, which had recorded 927 females for every 1000 males. At the 2001 Census, the sex ratio among the major States ranged from 861 in Haryana to 1058 in Kerala.

State/Union Territory (U.T.)	India Sex Ratio
Jammu & Kashmir	900
Himachal Pradesh	970
Punjab	874
Chandigarh (U.T.)	773
Uttaranchal	964
Haryana	861
Delhi (U.T.)	821
Rajasthan	922
Uttar Pradesh	898
Bihar	921
Sikkim	875
Arunachal Pradesh	901
Nagaland	909

Manipur	978
Mizoram	938
Tripura	950
Meghalaya	975
Assam	932
West Bengal	934
Jharkhand	941
Orissa	972
Chhatisgarh	990
Madhya Pradesh	920
Gujarat	921
Daman & Diu (U.T.)	709
Dadra & Nagar Haveli (U.T.)	811
Maharashtra	922
Andhra Pradesh	978
Karnataka	964
Goa	960
Lakshadweep (U.T.)	947
Kerala	1058
Tamil Nadu	986
Pondicherry (U.T.)	1001
Andaman & Nicobar Islands (U.T.)	846

INDIA'S SEX RATIO CONTINUES TO SLIDE

As many as 35 million girls have been killed before, during or after birth in India over the last 100 years, according to the Indian census commissioner, J.K. Banthia. And the gap between girls and boys is accelerating, especially amongst the wealthier and better educated. A new report, Missing: mapping the adverse child sex ratio in India, issued by the UN Population Fund, shows that the sex ratio, which is calculated as the number of girls per 1000 boys in the 0-6 age bracket, declined from 945 in the 1991 census to 927 in the 2001 census. The normal ratio is about 950 to 1000. The steepest declines took place in the prosperous northern states of Punjab, Haryana, Himachal and Gujarat, which fell below 800 girls per 1000 boys for the first time. The lowest ratio was 754 in Fatehgarh, in Punjab. The top ten districts with healthy sex ratios of more than 1000 girls per 1000 boys are largely in non-Hindu areas like Jammu and

Kashmir and in the northeastern tribal regions. "A stage may soon come where it would become extremely difficult, if not impossible, to make up for the missing girls," says Francois Farah of the UN Population Fund. "Today we are at a stage where many villages are having fewer or no small daughters and... the resulting imbalance can destroy the social and human fabric." At the heart of the decline are numerous doctors offering ultrasound scans to check the sex of the pregnant woman's baby. "Involvement of the medical community in this criminal activity indulged in by parents of the unborn child and the doctors is 100 per cent," says Dr. Puneet Bedi, an independent health activist and gynaecologist.

Sex determination has been banned since 1996, but this has only slowed the spread of the practice, not decreased it, according to the census commissioner. Campaigners against female infanticide complain that doctors are indifferent. Students at India's leading medical school, the All India Institute of Medical Sciences, recently refused to cooperate with an awareness drive. "They are not taught enough about medical ethics," said Dr. M.K. Bhan, a paediatrician at the Institute. "There is a large vacuum in the medical curriculum. The students are young. They are under a lot of pressure. In liberal arts, you are taught about ethics. In medical science, you are not."

SEX RATIO IN INDIA A CONCERN

New Delhi-A disturbing and steady decline has occurred in the ratio between Indian girls to boys born in the past decade, according to a United Nations Population Fund (UNFPA) report published on Tuesday. Several thousand girls and women are "missing", the UNFPA study said, referring to those who should have been part of the population but are not because they were killed for being female.

In both rural and urban India, there is a strong preference for boys. One Indian saying goes: "Nurturing a girl is like watering someone else's garden." Girls are thought to be a burden on their parents, and are usually given less food and little or no education. Parents do not invest in their daughters' health and development, as they will eventually get married and leave home.

'When girls go missing in a society, it shows that compassion is missing' In 1991, there were 945 girls born for every thousand boys in India. By 2001, the national average dropped to 927 girls, the Indian Express newspaper reported.

According to UNFPA, among the main causes for the adverse sex ratio are increasing rates of female foeticide. Indian states with alarmingly low sex ratios are Punjab, Haryana and Himachal Pradesh in the north and Gujarat in the west-all with less than 800 girls on an average for every thousand boys. Development experts and demographers acknowledge that given the same nurturing and opportunities as boys, girls would actually outlive and outnumber them.

The desire for boys transcends caste, social, educational and economic status. "The ratio stands at a mere 770 in Kurukshetra district of Haryana, 814 in Ahmadabad (Gujarat) and 845 in southwest Delhi, which are among the most prosperous regions in the country," the study said.

Federal Minister for Health and Family Welfare Sushma Swaraj said, "When girls go missing in a society, it shows that compassion is missing."

'You will remain unmarried if girl foetuses continue to be destroyed'

Her message to Indian men was: "You will remain unmarried if girl foetuses continue to be destroyed in the womb."-Sapa-dpa

Age structure: *0-14 years:* 31.5% (male 189,238,487/female 172,168,306)

15-64 years: 63.3% (male 374,157,581/female 352,868,003)

65 years and over: 5.2% (male 28,285,796/female 31,277,725) (2008 est.)

Definition: This entry provides the distribution of the population according to age. Information is included by sex and age group (*0-14 years, 15-64 years, 65 years and over*). The age structure of a population affects a nation's key socioeconomic issues. Countries with young populations (high percentage under age 15) need to invest more in schools, while countries with older populations (high percentage ages 65 and over) need to invest more in the health sector. The age structure can also be used to help predict potential political issues. For example, the rapid growth of a young adult population unable to find employment can lead to unrest.

Sex ratio: *at birth:* 1.12 male(s)/female

Under 15 years: 1.1 male(s)/female

15-64 years: 1.06 male(s)/female

65 years and over: 0.9 male(s)/female

Total population: 1.06 male(s)/female (2008 est.)

Definition: This entry includes the number of males for each female in five age groups-*at birth*, *under 15 years*, *15-64 years*, *65 years and over*, and for the *total population*. Sex ratio at birth has recently emerged as an indicator of certain kinds of sex discrimination in some countries. For instance, high sex ratios at birth in some Asian countries are now attributed to sex-selective abortion and infanticide due to a strong preference for sons. This will affect future marriage patterns and fertility patterns. Eventually it could cause unrest among young adult males who are unable to find partners.

POPULATION AND FAMILY PLANNING POLICY

Population growth has long been a concern of the government, and India has a lengthy history of explicit population policy. In the 1950s, the government began, in a modest way, one of the earliest national, government-sponsored family planning efforts in the developing world. The annual population growth rate in the previous decade (1941 to 1951) had been below 1.3 percent, and government planners optimistically believed that the population would continue to grow at roughly the same rate.

Implicitly, the government believed that India could repeat the experience of the developed nations where industrialization and a rise in the standard of living had been accompanied by a drop in the population growth rate. In the 1950s, existing hospitals and health care facilities made birth control information available, but there was no aggressive effort to encourage the use of contraceptives and limitation of family size. By the late 1960s, many policy makers believed that the high rate of population growth was the greatest obstacle to economic development. The government began a massive program to lower the birth rate from forty-one per 1,000 to a target of twenty to twenty-five per 1,000 by the mid-1970s. The National Population Policy adopted in 1976 reflected the growing consensus among policy makers that family planning would enjoy only limited success unless it was part of an integrated program aimed at improving the general welfare of the population. The policy makers assumed that excessive family size was part and parcel of poverty and had to be dealt with as integral to a general development strategy. Education about the population problem became part of school curriculum under the Fifth Five-Year Plan (FY 1974-78). Cases of government-enforced sterilization made many question the propriety of state-sponsored birth control measures, however.

During the 1980s, an increased number of family planning programs were implemented through the state governments with financial assistance from the central government. In rural areas, the programs were further extended through a network of primary health centres and subcenters. By 1991, India had more than 150,000 public health facilities through which family planning programs were offered. Four special family planning projects were implemented under the Seventh Five-Year Plan (FY 1985-89). One was the All-India Hospitals Post-partum Programme at district-and subdistrict-level hospitals. Another program involved the reorganization of primary health care facilities in urban slum areas, while another project reserved a specified number of hospital beds for tubal ligature operations. The final program called for the renovation or remodelling of intrauterine device (IUD) rooms in rural family welfare centres attached to primary health care facilities.

Despite these developments in promoting family planning, the 1991 census results showed that India continued to have one of the most rapidly growing populations in the world. Between 1981 and 1991, the annual rate of population growth was estimated at about 2 percent. The crude birth rate in 1992 was thirty per 1,000, only a small change over the 1981 level of thirty-four per 1,000. However, some demographers credit this slight lowering of the 1981-91 population growth rate to moderate successes of the family planning program. In FY 1986, the number of reproductive-age couples was 132.6 million, of whom only 37.5 percent were estimated to be protected effectively by some form of contraception. A goal of the seventh plan was to achieve an effective couple protection rate of 42 percent, requiring an annual increase of 2 percent in effective use of contraceptives.

The heavy centralization of India's family planning programs often prevents due consideration from being given to regional differences. Centralization is encouraged to a large extent by reliance on central government funding. As a result, many of the goals and assumptions of national population control programs do not correspond exactly with local attitudes toward birth control. At the Jamkhed Project in Maharashtra, which has been in operation since the late 1970s and covers approximately 175 villages, the local project directors noted that it required three to four years of education through direct contact with a couple for the idea of family planning to gain acceptance. Such a timetable was not compatible with targets. However, much was learned about policy and practice from the Jamkhed Project. The successful use of women's clubs as a means of involving women in community-wide family planning activities impressed the state government to the degree that it set about organizing such clubs in every village in the state. The project also serves as a pilot to test ideas that the government wants to incorporate into its programs. Government medical staff members have been sent to Jamkhed for training, and the government has proposed that the project assume the task of selecting and training government health workers for an area of 2.5 million people.

Another important family planning program is the Project for Community Action in Family Planning. Located in Karnataka, the project operates in 154 project villages and 255 control villages. All project villages are of sufficient size to have a health subcenter, although this advantage is offset by the fact that those villages are the most distant from the area's primary health centres. As at Jamkhed, the project is much assisted by local voluntary groups, such as the women's clubs. The local voluntary groups either provide or secure sites suitable as distribution depots for condoms and birth control pills and also make arrangements for the operation of sterilization camps. Data provided by the Project for Community Action in Family Planning show that important achievements have been realized in the field of population control. By the mid-1980s, for example, 43 percent of couples were using family planning, a full 14 percent above the state average. The project has significantly improved the status of women, involving them and empowering them to bring about change in their communities. This contribution is important because of the way in which the deeply entrenched inferior status of women in many communities in India negates official efforts to decrease the fertility rate. Studies have found that most couples in fact regard family planning positively. However, the common fertility pattern in India diverges from the two-child family that policy makers hold as ideal. Women continue to marry young; in the mid-1990s, they average just over eighteen years of age at marriage. When women choose to be sterilized, financial inducements, although helpful, are not the principal incentives. On average, those accepting sterilization already have four living children, of whom two are sons.

The strong preference for sons is a deeply held cultural ideal based on economic roots. Sons not only assist with farm labour as they are growing up (as do daughters) but they provide labour in times of illness and unemployment and serve as their parents' only security in old age. Surveys done by the New Delhi Operations Research Group in 1991 indicated that as many as 72 percent of rural parents continue to have children until at least two sons are born; the preference for more than one son among urban parents was tabulated at 53 percent. Once these goals have been achieved, birth control may be used or, especially in agricultural areas, it may not if additional child labour, later adult labour for the family, is deemed desirable.

A significant result of this eagerness for sons is that the Indian population has a deficiency of females. Slightly higher female infant mortality rates (seventy-nine per 1,000 versus seventy-eight per 1,000 for males) can be attributed to poor health care, abortions of female fetuses, and female infanticide. Human rights activists have estimated that there are at least 10,000 cases of female infanticide annually throughout India. The cost of theoretically illegal dowries and the loss of daughters to their in-laws' families are further disincentives for some parents to have daughters. Sons, of course continue to carry on the family line. The 1991 census revealed that the national sex ratio had declined from 934 females to 1,000 males in 1981 to 927 to 1,000 in 1991. In only one state—Kerala, a state with low fertility and mortality rates and the nation's highest literacy—did females exceed males. The census found, however, that female life expectancy at birth had for the first time exceeded that for males. India's high infant mortality and elevated mortality in early childhood remain significant stumbling blocks to population control. India's fertility rate is decreasing, however, and, at 3.4 in 1994, it is lower than those of its immediate neighbours (Bangladesh had a rate of 4.5 and Pakistan had 6.7). The rate is projected to decrease to 3.0 by 2000, 2.6 by 2010, and 2.3 by 2020. During the 1960s, 1970s, and 1980s, the growth rate had formed a sort of plateau. Some states, such as Kerala, Tamil Nadu, and, to a lesser extent, Punjab, Maharashtra, and Karnataka, had made progress in lowering their growth rates, but most did not. Under such conditions, India's population may not stabilize until 2060.

Life Expectancy and Mortality

The average Indian male born in the 1990s can expect to live 58.5 years; women can expect to live only slightly longer (59.6 years), according to 1995 estimates. Life expectancy has risen dramatically throughout the century from a scant twenty years in the 1911-20 period. Although men enjoyed a slightly longer life expectancy throughout the first part of the twentieth century, by 1990 women had slightly surpassed men. The death rate declined from 48.6 per 1,000 in the 1910-20 period to fifteen per 1,000 in the 1970s, and improved thereafter, reaching ten per 1,000 by 1990, a rate that held steady through the mid-1990s. India's high infant mortality rate was estimated to exceed 76 per 1,000 live births in 1995. Thirty percent of infants had low birth weights, and the death rate for children aged one to four years was around ten per 1,000 of the population.

According to a 1989 National Nutrition Monitoring Bureau report, less than 15 percent of the population was adequately nourished, although 96 percent received an adequate number of calories per day. In 1986 daily average intake was 2,238 calories as compared with 2,630 calories in China. According to UN findings, caloric intake per day in India had fallen slightly to 2,229 in 1989, lending credence to the concerns of some experts who claimed that annual nutritional standards statistics cannot be relied on to show whether poverty is actually being reduced. Instead, such studies may actually pick up short-term amelioration of poverty as the result of a period of good crops rather than a long-term trend.

Official Indian estimates of the poverty level are based on a person's income and corresponding access to minimum nutritional needs. There were 332 million people at or below the poverty level in FY 1991, most of whom lived in rural areas.

Communicable and Noncommunicable Diseases

A number of endemic communicable diseases present a serious public health hazard in India. Over the years, the government has set up a variety of national programs aimed at controlling or eradicating these diseases, including the National Malaria Eradication Programme and the National Filaria Control Programme. Other initiatives seek to limit the incidence of respiratory infections, cholera, diarrheal diseases, trachoma, goiter, and sexually transmitted diseases.

Smallpox, formerly a significant source of mortality, was eradicated as part of the worldwide effort to eliminate that disease. India was declared smallpox-free in 1975. Malaria remains a serious health hazard; although the incidence of the disease declined sharply in the postindependence period, India remains one of the most heavily malarial countries in the world. Only the Himalaya region above 1,500 meters is spared. In 1965 government sources registered only 150,000 cases, a notable drop from the 75 million cases in the early postindependence years. This success was short-lived, however, as the malarial parasites became increasingly resistant to the insecticides and drugs used to combat the disease. By the mid-1970s, there were nearly 6.5 million cases on record. The situation again improved because of more conscientious efforts; by 1982 the number of cases had fallen by roughly two-thirds. This downward trend continued, and in 1987 slightly fewer than 1.7 million cases of malaria were reported. In the early 1990s, about 389 million people were at risk of infection from filaria parasites; 19 million showed symptoms of filariasis, and

25 million were deemed to be hosts to the parasites. Efforts at control, under the National Filaria Control Programme, which was established in 1955, have focused on eliminating the filaria larvae in urban locales, and by the early 1990s there were more than 200 filaria control units in operation.

Leprosy, a major public health and social problem, is endemic, with all the states and union territories reporting cases. However, the prevalence of the disease varies. About 3 million leprosy cases are estimated to exist nationally, of which 15 to 20 percent are infectious. The National Leprosy Control Programme was started in 1955, but it only received high priority after 1980. In FY 1982, it was redesignated as the National Leprosy Eradication Programme. Its goal was to achieve eradication of the disease by 2000. To that end, 758 leprosy control units, 900 urban leprosy centres, 291 temporary hospitalization wards, 285 district leprosy units, and some 6,000 lower-level centres had been established by March 1990. By March 1992, nearly 1.7 million patients were receiving regular multidrug treatment, which is more effective than the standard single drug therapy (Dapsone monotherapy).

India is subject to outbreaks of various diseases. Among them is pneumonic plague, an episode of which spread quickly throughout India in 1994 killing hundreds before being brought under control. Tuberculosis, trachoma, and goiter are endemic. In the early 1980s, there were an estimated 10 million cases of tuberculosis, of which about 25 percent were infectious. During 1991 nearly 1.6 million new tuberculosis cases were detected. The functions of the Trachoma Control Programme, which started in 1968, have been subsumed by the National Programme for the Control of Blindness.

Approximately 45 million Indians are vision-impaired; roughly 12 million are blind. The incidence of goiter is dominant throughout the sub-Himalayan states from Jammu and Kashmir to the northeast. There are some 170 million people who are exposed to iodine deficiency disorders. Starting in the late 1980s, the central government began a salt iodinization program for all edible salt, and by 1991 record production—2.5 million tons—of iodized salt had been achieved. There are as well anemias related to poor nutrition, a variety of diseases caused by vitamin and mineral deficiencies—beriberi, scurvy, osteomalacia, and rickets—and a high incidence of parasitic infection.

Diarrheal diseases, the primary cause of early childhood mortality, are linked to inadequate sewage disposal and lack of safe drinking water. Roughly 50 percent of all illness is attributed to poor sanitation; in rural areas, about 80 percent of all children are infected by parasitic worms. Estimates in the early 1980s suggested that although more than 80 percent of the urban population had access to reasonably safe water, fewer than 5 percent of rural dwellers did. Waterborne sewage systems were woefully overburdened; only around 30 percent of urban populations had adequate sewage disposal, but scarcely any populations outside cities did. In 1990, according to United States sources, only 3 percent of the rural population and 44 percent of the urban population had access to sanitation services, a level relatively low by developing nation standards. There were better findings for access to potable water: 69 percent in the rural areas and 86 percent in urban areas, relatively high percentages by developing nation standards. In the mid-1990s, about 1 million people die each year of diseases associated with diarrhea.

India has an estimated 1.5 million to 2 million cases of cancer, with 500,000 new cases added each year. Annual deaths from cancer total around 300,000. The most common malignancies are cancer of the oral cavity (mostly relating to tobacco use and pan chewing—about 35 percent of all cases), cervix, and breast. Cardiovascular diseases are a major health problem; men and women suffer from them in almost equal numbers (14 million versus 13 million in FY 1990).

Acquired Immune Deficiency Syndrome

The incidence of AIDS cases in India is steadily rising amidst concerns that the nation faces the prospect of an AIDS epidemic. By June 1991, out of a total of more than 900,000 screened, some 5,130 people tested positive for the human immunodeficiency virus (HIV). However, the total number infected with HIV in 1992 was estimated by a New Delhi-based official of the World Health Organization (WHO) at 500,000, and more pessimistic estimates by the World Bank in 1995 suggested a figure of 2 million, the highest in Asia. Confirmed cases of AIDS numbered only 102 by 1991 but had jumped to 885 by 1994, the second highest reported number in Asia after Thailand. Suspected AIDS cases, according to WHO and the Indian government, may be in the area of 80,000 in 1995.

The main factors cited in the spread of the virus are heterosexual transmission, primarily by urban prostitutes and migrant workers, such as long-distance truck drivers; the use of unsterilized needles and syringes by physicians and intravenous drug users; and transfusions of blood from infected donors. Based on the HIV infection rate in 1991, and India's position as the second most populated country in the world, it was projected that by 1995 India would have more HIV and AIDS cases than any other country in the world. This prediction appeared true. By mid-1995 India had been labelled by the media as "ground zero" in the global AIDS epidemic, and new predictions for 2000 were that India would have 1 million AIDS cases and 5 million HIV-positive. In 1987 the newly formed National AIDS Control Programme began limited screening of the blood supply and monitoring of high-risk groups. A national education program aimed at AIDS prevention and control began in 1990. The first AIDS prevention television campaign began in 1991. By the mid-1990s, AIDS awareness signs on public streets, condoms for sale near brothels, and media announcements were more in evidence. There was very negative publicity as well. Posters with the names and photographs of known HIV-positive persons have been seen in New Delhi, and there have been reports of HIV patients chained in medical facilities and deprived of treatment. Fear and ignorance have continued to compound the difficulty of controlling the spread of the virus, and discrimination against AIDS sufferers has surfaced. For example, in 1990 the All-India Institute of Medical Sciences, New Delhi's leading medical facility, reportedly turned away two people infected with HIV because its staff were too scared to treat them.

A new program to control the spread of AIDS was launched in 1991 by the Indian Council of Medical Research. The council looked to ancient scriptures and religious books for traditional messages that preach moderation in sex and describe prostitution as a sin. The council considered that the great extent to which Indian life-styles are shaped by religion rather than by science would cause many people to be confused by foreign-modeled educational campaigns relying on television and printed booklets.

The severity of the growing AIDS crisis in India is clear, according to statistics compiled during the mid-1990s. In Bombay, a city of 12.6 million inhabitants in 1991, the HIV infection rate among the estimated 80,000 prostitutes jumped from 1 percent in 1987 to 30 percent in 1991 to 53 percent in 1993. Migrant workers engaging in promiscuous and unprotected sexual relations in the big city carry the infection to other sexual partners on the road and then to their homes and families.

India's blood supply, despite official blood screening efforts, continues to become infected. In 1991 donated blood was screened for HIV in only four major cities: New Delhi, Calcutta, Madras, and Bombay. One of the leading factors in the contamination of the blood supply is that 30 percent of the blood required comes from private, profit-making banks whose practices are difficult to regulate. Furthermore, professional donors are an integral part of the Indian blood supply network, providing about 30 percent of the annual requirement nationally. These donors are generally poor and tend to engage in high-risk sex and use intravenous drugs more than the general population. Professional donors also tend to donate frequently at different centres and, in many cases, under different names. Reuse of improperly sterilized needles in health care and blood-collection facilities also is a factor. India's minister of health and family welfare reported in 1992 that only 138 out of 608 blood banks were equipped for HIV screening. A 1992 study conducted by the Indian Health Organisation revealed that 86 percent of commercial blood donors surveyed were HIV-positive.

Bibliography

Aaron T.: *Hydropolitics along the Jordan River, Scarce Water and its Impact on the Arab-Israeli Conflict*, NYC, United Nations University Press, 1995.

Anthony D.: *Buildings and Society: Essays on the Social and Human Development of the Built Enviroment*. London: Routledge & Kegan Paul, 1980.

Belden C.: *Geography and Narrative in American Spirituality*, New York: Paulist Press, 1988.

Berry, J.K. : *Beyond Mapping, Concepts, Algorithms and Issues in GIS*, Fort Collins, CO: GIS World Books, 1993.

Bolstad, P. : *GIS Fundamentals, A first text on Geographic Information Systems, Second Edition*, White Bear Lake, MN, Eider Press, 2005.

Cronon, William: *Changes in the Land: Indians, Colonists, and the Ecology of New England*. New York: Hill and Wang, 1983.

Davis, Mike: *Ecology of Fear: Los Angeles and the Imagination of Disaster*. New York: Vintage, 1999.

Duncan, S. : *Discourse, Text, and Metaphor in the Representation of Landscape*. London and New York: Routledge, 1992.

Elangovan K. : *GIS, Fundamentals, Applications and Population Geography*, New India Publishing Agency, New Delhi 2006.

Harvey, David: *Explanation in Geography*. London: Edward Arnold, 1969.

Harvey, Francis : *A Primer of GIS, Fundamental Geographic and Cartographic Concepts*, The Guilford Press, 2008.

Jackson, Peter: *Maps of Meaning: An Introduction to Human Geography*. London and Boston: Unwin Hyman, 1989.

Lewis, Earl. *In Their Own Interests: Race, Class, and Power in Twentieth-Century Norfolk, Virginia*. Berkeley: University of California Press, 1990.

Lewis, Peirce. *New Orleans: The Making of an Urban Landscape*. Cambridge, MA: Ballinger Publishing Co., 1976. Annotation

Liam Kennedy: *Urban Space and Representation*. Sterling, VA: Pluto Press, 2000.

McDonnell, R.A. : *Principles of Geographical Information Systems*, Oxford University Press, Oxford, 1998.

Michael, H.: *City Form and Natural Process: Towards a New Urban Vernacular*. London: Croom Helm, 1984.

Peter, G.: *The Slow Plague: A Human Geography of the AIDS Pandemic*. Oxford and Cambridge, MA: Blackwell Publishers, 1993.

Ritchie, J.: *Landscape and Material Life in Franklin County, Massachusetts, 1770-1860*. Knoxville: University of Tennessee Press, 1991.

Stanton W. Green: *Interpreting Space: GIS and Archaeology*, London and New York: Taylor & Francis, 1990.

Stephen, D.: *Fields of Vision: Landscape Imagery and National Identity in England and the United States*. Cambridge: Polity, 1993.

Victor, A. : *Geography of Art and Culture*, Contributions to Economic Analysis, Elsevier, 2004.

Watkins, Eric: *The Middle Eastern Environment*, London, The British Society for Middle Eastern Studie, 1995.

Index

C

D

E

F

G

H

I

L

M

O

❑❑❑